1001 Tips for Woodworkers

1001 Tips for Woodworkers

Percy W. Blandford

Stobart Davies Ltd

British Library Cataloguing in Publication Data.

A catalogue record of this book is available from the British Library.

ISBN 978-0-85442-145-9

Published 2007 by
Stobart Davies Limited
Stobart House, Pontyclerc,
Penybanc Road, Ammanford,
Carmarthenshire SA18 3HP, UK
www.stobartdavies.com

Printed in the United Kingdom by Cromwell Press Ltd, Trowbridge, Wiltshire

About the Author

Percy Blandford was born in Bristol, England in 1912. He trained as an engineer and was working as a technical teacher in London when World War II started. He then served five years in the Royal Air Force. After the war he moved to his present address near Stratford-upon-Avon, Warwickshire and started full-time writing and designing furniture and boats. He married Ivy before the war and had one son, also an engineer.

He has been a lifelong member of the Scout Association. The Sea Scout Troop he started forty years ago is still thriving as the Sea Scout Troop furthest from the sea.

Although originally an engineer, Percy has always been interested in woodwork, following a family history of woodworking craftsmen. He is interested in equipment and tools for all crafts. From an early age owned woodworking tools and used them. He has tackled all kinds of woodworking projects. He has built over one hundred full-size prototypes of the boats he designed, from canoes to sea-going yachts. He now has a comprehensively equipped workshop, with all kinds of power tools, but he still has a place for hand tools, some dating back to earlier Blandford craftsmen.

Percy and his wife have lived and worked in many parts of the world. Much of Percy's large output was produced with the help of his wife. Both his wife and son are now sadly deceased. Percy is in his mid-nineties and is still working and able to do most things.

Books by the same Author

This is Percy Blandford's 112th book.
Some of his other woodworking books are listed below:

Published in Great Britain
Woodcarving (Foyle)
Woodturning (Foyle)
Boatbuilding (Foyle)
Country Craft Tools (David & Charles, Airlife)
Carpentry (MacDonald)
Canoes & Canoeing (Lutterworth)
Small Boats & Sailing (Lutterworth)
Build Your Own Boat (Stanley Paul)

Published in the United States of America
The Woodworkers Bible (Tab Books)
How to Make Your Own Built-in Furniture (Tab Books)
Wood Turning (Tab Books)
How to Make Colonial Furniture (Tab Books)
How to Make Children's Furniture (Tab Books)
Giant Book of Wooden Toys (Tab Books)
Constructing Outdoor Furniture, with 80 projects (Tab Books)
The Illustrated Handbook of Woodwork Joints (Tab Books)
One Weekend Projects for Woodworkers
Country Furniture
114 Traditional Projects (Tab Books)
The Woodworker's Shop (Tab Books)
49 Easy-to-build Plywood Projects (Tab Books)
Percy Blandford's Favorite Woodwork Projects (Tab Books)
Small Building Handbook (Tab Books)
Playhouses, Gazebos and Sheds (Tab Books)
Country Tools and How to Use Them (Dover)
Build Your Own Boat (Dover)

Contents

Notes

Where sizes on drawings are shown in figures only, they are in millimeters.

Cramps of many sorts are needed in some tips. They are shown in the drawings in many cases, but where a picture of a cramp might obscure or make difficult other details, there are opposing arrows to indicate the location of a cramp.

Epoxy is the only adhesive normally available that will join metal to wood. In Britain, the only readily available epoxy in small quantities is sold under the brand name Araldite.

The seventeen sections of this book are only broad divisions. Many tips are applicable to many sections and some are related when particular work is undertaken. They have been allocated to what seemed the most appropriate section, but readers should consider many sections when looking for particular information. For instance, the three router sections and the three turning sections have information common to each other, or when dealing with joints there may also be something useful in the cramp section.

This book uses English woodworking terms. Fortunately most woodworkers of the world use the same terms, but there is information at the back of the book comparing English and American terms, where they differ. Where sizes are quoted, they are metric. Also at the back of the book, there are approximate conversions.

Introduction

This book is a collection of my tips, all previously contributed to British, American and other magazines over a very long period. The earliest tip in the book was submitted in 1930, while I was still an apprentice, and published in the long defunct magazine, *English Mechanics*.

I have contributed thousands of articles and tips to many magazine, with about 2000 of my tips being published over more than 70 years. The editors of woodworking and other magazines with tips pages have not been able to rely on enough readers contributing tips to fill the pages of every issue, and so many of them have depended on me to keep them supplied with a reserve of tips to fill the gaps. As a result an occasional issue of a magazine has had its tips page written entirely by me. It would not do for every tip to have my name on it, so nearly all of my tips have been under fictitious names.

The majority of tips may appeal to the amateur craftsman in a home workshop, probably limited in size and with limited resources, but many of the ideas should appeal to professionals. We all welcome better ways of doing things, especially if they are economical in terms of time and materials.

Traditional craftsmen over the centuries have done just about everything with hand tools. There is a very large range of power tools available, but most of us do not have all we would wish. Unless you are working against the clock to earn a living regard power tools as aids, if you have them, but not essentials. It was just after WWII that I had my first power tool, and that was a drill. Now I have most power tools available, but I still use all my hand tools. The amateur with limited resources is keeping alive the ideas of traditional craftsmanship.

Enjoy selecting and using some of these tips. I hope they will help you improve your craftsmanship and get as much satisfaction out of working in wood as countless craftsmen have over the centuries. I still do some work in other materials, but none are as satisfying to work and complete as wood.

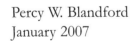

Percy W. Blandford
January 2007

1. Preparation and Layout

The early stages of a project can be as important as the actual fashioning of the wood. Selecting wood and marking out are part of the work. Proper and complete marking out ensures accuracy and economy of time. There is truth in the saying, 'measure twice before cutting once'. Anticipate problems, particularly related to assembly, where doing all you can to parts before assembly avoids what might be difficult or impossible later. Watch squareness; something only slightly out of square may be very obvious in the finished project.

So far as is possible, do all you can to a piece of wood before it is joined to other wood. It may have surfaces needing sanding and taking sharpness off corners.

If it is a project with a carcass that has a top and door, leave final marking out of the top and door parts until the carcass is made and you can match sizes. Put identifying marks on parts and their joints, either directly on the wood or on tape. If any parts are left or right handed make sure you know which is which.

If there are many parts with similar joints, it is best to do the same stage of work on all, rather than make one joint completely at a time. See also the tips on materials and assembly.

When starting a new woodworking project, it is helpful if you can think through all the steps and decide on the sequence of jobs. This will help to avoid problems such as having to do something to a part when it is built in, when it would have been easier to do when it was loose.

Make sure you have all the wood you need and prepare it to width and thickness before doing any other work. For some projects, a few spare pieces may be advisable. If you have to prepare an odd piece later, getting width and thickness exactly right can be a nuisance. Mark face sides and edges.

Grooving for panels and some moulding is best done before other work. Do not cut any wood to its final length until everything else needed has been done to it. If there are fittings to add, such as hinges, handles and catches, get them early, as they might affect sizes.

Make sure that parts that should match do, often by marking them together. Do all you can to a part in the early stage, even to screw holes needed later.

1. Optical Effect

When planning a project, consider the effect of lines. If you want the item or part of it to look wider, have plenty of horizontal lines. If you want it to look taller, have plenty of vertical lines. The identical squares show the visual effect.

2. Proportion

If you are planning a piece of furniture and can choose size and shape, consider the visual effect of proportions. In general, something other than square or cube shaped is more pleasing to the eye. Proportions are debatable, but artists have a formula that is supposed to give the most attractive proportions, which in practical terms works out to having a length slightly less than one and a half times the width. If you are planning something flat, make it longer than it is wide rather than square, or if three-dimensional do this on all faces.

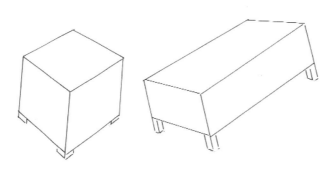

3. Softwood Sizes

When buying PAA (planed all round) softwood, remember the size quoted is as sawn before planing, and it will be much less after going through the mill planers. Expect thicknesses to be about 6mm less and widths about 9mm less.

4. Compress It

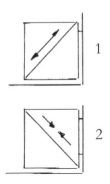

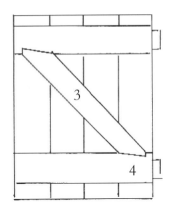

If a door or gate is braced with a diagonal sloping down from the hinged side (1), the diagonal brace will be in tension. If the brace is arranged to slope up from the hinged side (2), the weight of the door or gate puts it in compression.

The problem with having a brace in tension is that it depends on fastenings and there will be inevitable slight movement and the outer edge will drop. It is always better to arrange the brace in compression (3), with its ends pushing against something, so the door cannot go out of shape. Where possible, notch the ends of the brace into another part (4).

5. Symmetry

If you want to layout a shape, such as a shield, symmetrical about a center line, a quick and accurate way is to use carbon paper.

Draw half the design full-size on paper. Draw a centre line on the wood. Put two pieces of carbon paper under the drawing, with the upper piece face up and other face down. Put this over the centre line on the wood and go over the design fairly heavily with a pencil. This will draw the design onto the wood and repeat it reversed on the underside of the top paper. Turn that over with one piece of carbon paper and go over the design on that side to complete the drawing on the wood.

6. Pattern Transfer

If you wish to transfer a pattern from paper to wood, you can get the shape, in reverse, by using a photocopying machine. Make a print and put it face down on the wood. Use a domestic iron on the back. It works with print from many machines.

7. Chalked Wood

It is a good idea to always have a few sticks of school chalk in the tool box. Its marks will show on sawn or planed wood and are easily removed. It is helpful for temporary marks when sorting wood.

8. Triangulate

A four-sided figure can be pushed out of shape. A three-sided one cannot. If you want rigidity in any structure, include some triangles. Look at an electricity pylon - it is entirely made of triangles.

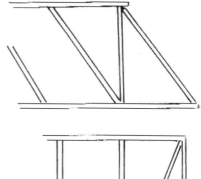

If a four-sided frame is covered with plywood or other rigid sheet, it will not go out of shape, but if the covering is in strips, it could. An open fence should have at least one diagonal strut to triangulate a section, especially if there will be an opening - as for a gate.

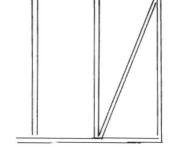

If you build a garden shed and cover it with weather-boarding, which will not prevent movement, include a diagonal in one or both ends to create triangles. Do the same with wind-bracing in the roof. Your shed will not develop a lean.

9. Check Twist

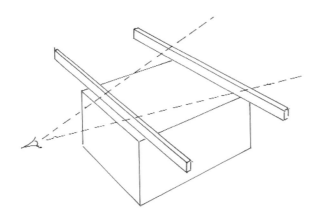

You can assemble a cabinet, box or any squared assembly, and check that all angles are square, yet still have a twist. If it is wide enough you can just sight across it, but it is helpful to put two long straight strips across to exaggerate any twist, then stand back and sight over them.

10. Step Up

When laying out stairs, steps or fixed ladders, it is important for safety reasons that all the risers are the same, including from where you step on to the surface to where you step off, i.e. the vertical height from the top of the treads or the top of the ladder rungs to the floor or landing. If there is a landing partway, risers up and down from this should be the same. In some places this is a legal requirement.

11. Keep Wood Flat

If wood is stored on crossbars, make sure they are close enough to prevent wood sagging between and developing warps. Narrow and thin strips of wood are particularly affected. Store them over or on top of thicker wood. This can apply to wood stood on end. Lean strips against boards so they do not bend and ensure everything is as near to upright as possible.

12. Mixed Sizes

Do not mix metric and imperial sizes together when working on a project. A conversion table gives close equivalents, but they are not exact and there could be errors in your work.

13. Accurate Assembly

If you are making parts that will be assembled it is easier, and ensures accuracy, if you check with a similar or matching part instead of with a rule.

14. No Wobble

If you correct four legs of a table or chair for wobble on a flat surface and then fit the top, you may have to do it again, due to slight distortion. In most cases, a better way of checking that the table or chair will stand level, is to invert it and put two straight pieces of wood on the legs, then stand back and sight over them.

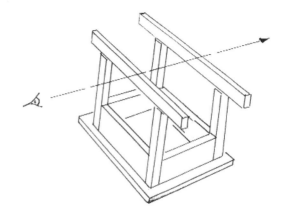

15. Twist?

When you assemble a frame, you need to check that it is free from twist before the glue sets. This is not always easy by sighting across the frame itself. If you use the method shown, any twist is exaggerated and more easily seen.

Put two flat pieces across the frame near its ends and stand try squares on them. The squares need not be the same size. Sight along the edges of the squares, which should be parallel if the frame is free of twist.

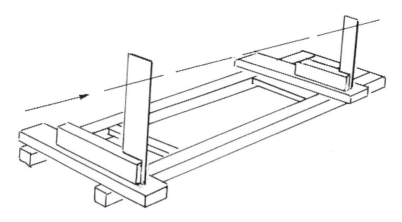

16. Try Square Height Gauge

When you need to compare heights, as when cutting stool legs parallel with the top, the gauge based on a try square, as illustrated, will be useful. It is shown able to extend a short distance above the blade of the square, but it could be made taller.

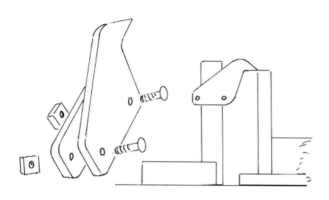

Plywood is a suitable material. Make the arm piece and a straight piece to go behind it, so two bolts can go through, just far enough apart to clear the width of the square blade. They can be adjusted to slide, then tightened when you have the height you want.

17. Level-Less

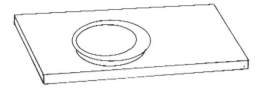

If there is no spirit level available, you can still check a level with a small bowl or saucer of water. The surface of the water when placed on a flat surface will be level. If you put the container on the job and the water goes to one side, that side is lower and you can adjust until the water becomes level.

18. Square Squares

If you test two squares by fitting them together and find they match, you should be able to assume that both are accurate, as it is extremely unlikely that both would have the same error.

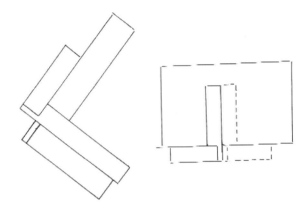

If you are still doubtful, you can also try the standard test by putting a square against the straight edge of a piece of wood, drawing a line, then turn the square over to see if it matches the line.

19. Chalk Line

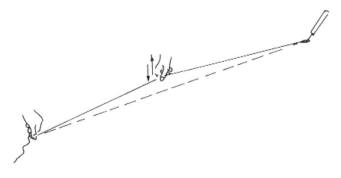

A stretched string is a straight line, whatever its length. If you want to draw a line longer than any straightedge you have, use a chalk line. You could use any available piece of cord. Builder's chalk line is fairly coarse. If you want to buy a line, get crochet cotton. It deposits a fine line and is very strong. Loop the end on an awl or get a helper to hold it, then walk backwards stretching the line and rubbing it with blackboard chalk.

Pull it tight and hold it down. If it is a very long line, get a helper to lift near the middle of the line and release it to snap down and deposit a line of chalk. If it is not too long, you might reach yourself and snap the line.

20. Both Ways

A pencil point lasts longer when marking wood if it has a chisel point, which is the reason for special carpenters' pencils. There are occasions when you need a round point. To allow for both circumstances you can sharpen opposite ends of one pencil, leaving one end round, but rubbing opposite sides of the other end on abrasive paper to make a chisel point.

21. Strengthened Pattern

If you wish to cut wood shapes from a paper pattern, strengthen it first by putting masking tape, preferably wide, underneath the shaped drawing.

22. Plastic Notes

Most plastic laminate has a surface that will take pencil marks, which can be rubbed out with a cloth or your finger. If you need to note down a measurement or some other information, it helps to have an off cut of plastic laminate on the bench on which to use the pencil you probably have in your hand. Drill a hole in it to hang it on a nail.

23. Pleasing Chamfers

When you chamfer edges there are proportions that give you the best visual effect. A single chamfer should not be more than one-third the total thickness (1). If both edges are chamfered, leave at least half the total thickness flat at the centre (2).

24. Always Matching

It is important that sets of parts, such as the four legs of a framed assembly, match exactly. To ensure this it is advisable to establish a routine. True the end of all pieces and fully mark out one piece. Put the parts together with the face

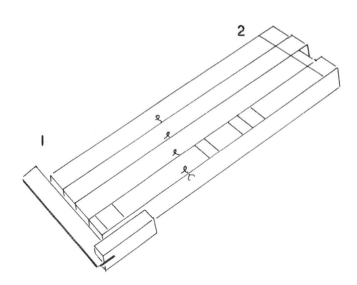

mark all one way, then use a try square to get the trued ends level (1). Go to the furthest mark and square that across (2). This gives you two reference points if you need to relocate after a slip. Square across all other marks and you can then be certain these parts will match and the final assembly should be accurate.

25. Matching Mitres

It is important that matching mitered parts are identical. They should be squared first before the mitres are marked, as shown.

26. Accurate Rails

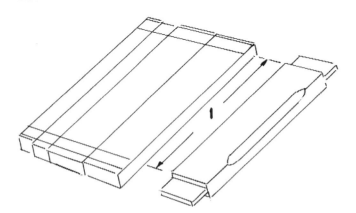

In a mortise and tenoned assembly, the important dimension on the rails is between the shoulders. This must be exactly the same on all in one direction, so they should be marked out together. Other sizes might also be marked, but it is the length between shoulders (1) that is important. Slight differences in tenon lengths are not important.

27. Shop Set Square

Angles used in the workshop are mostly 30°, 45°and 60°, so if you wish to lay these out or set an adjustable bevel to them, you need two set squares. An alternative is a single square as shown.

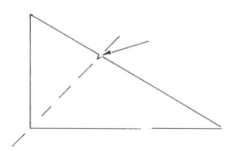

It could be made of thin plywood as a 30°/60° set square with a length of 300 mm, or whatever would suit your needs. Bisect the 90° corner and at the opposite edge cut a deep nick with its point on this 45° line. You can use this instead of a 45° square to layout 45° or set a bevel to it.

28. Bigger Bevel

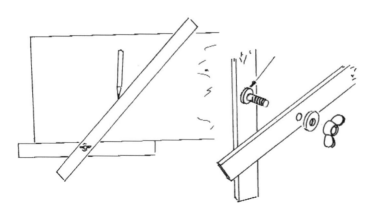

There is often a need to mark out or check bigger angles than can be reached with the usual adjustable bevel. The tool shown can be made to any size and used for long angular lines.

The wood need not be very thick, but should be straight-grained and free from warping. Use a bolt with a washer and wing nut. Include a rubber washer (arrowed in illustration) to provide friction in the joint. A water tap washer is suitable.

29. Mini Mitre

Try and mitre squares are made large enough to accommodate various jobs. If you are dealing with small work they are bigger than necessary and seem clumsy. A shop-made square, maybe with just a 50mm extension, is easier and more accurate to use.

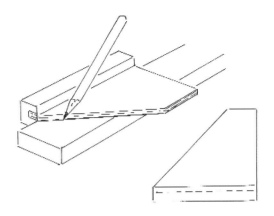

Use thin plywood and groove a stock to suit it. Cut the ends at 45° and 90°. Give the angles a final check after assembly and make sure no oozed-out glue is left along the joint that could interfere with any work to be undertaken.

30. Precisely Square

In the days when most wood was cut to size with hand tools, it was important to know which were the most accurate surfaces, and these were squared and used to measure from. With machined accuracy these considerations are not quite as important, but it is still good practice to settle on the face side and edge to work from, and match up during assembly. Traditional marks are shown below. For the

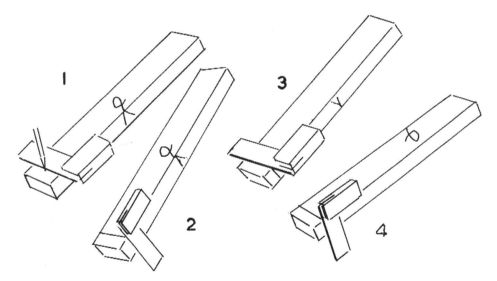

utmost accuracy in marking out, the first line squared across the grain should have the stock of the square against the edge where the marked surfaces meet (1). The next line should be squared down the face edge (2). Turn the wood over and take the line over the opposite side, with the stock against the face edge (3). Finally link these marks with a line down the opposite edge and the square being guided by the face side (4).

31. Accurate Marks

If you use a combination square and a pencil instead of a marking gauge to draw a line parallel with an edge, you avoid making a scratch that would be difficult to remove later. It is difficult to keep the pencil on the end of the rule part of the square. To keep it there when drawing a line, without affecting the square for its other uses, make a small

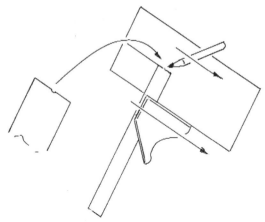

hollow in the rule. The edge of a half-round file will do it.

32. Clearest Lines

The most accurate way of marking lines across the grain is with a knife (1), but the cut line is not easily seen in some woods.

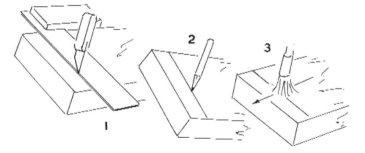

Running a pencil along the line (2) will help, but this leaves graphite dust on the surface. Instead of wiping and smudging this, it is better to use a soft brush (3) to lightly remove the dust and leave a clearly visible accurate line.

33. The Middle Always

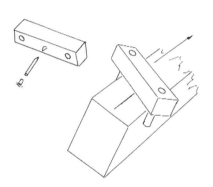

There are many occasions when you need to mark a centre line on the edge of a strip of wood. You can avoid the need to measure with the illustrated gauge. It will scratch a centre line on any width of wood less than the space between the pegs, by twisting it so that it rubs along the wood. Even if the wood tapers, the mark will always be central.

Estimate the widest wood you can expect to mark. Use a piece of wood thick enough to comfortably handle, and space holes drilled squarely for pieces of dowel rod. A piece of wood 25mm square and 6mm or 8mm dowel rods should be suitable.

34. Squaring Bigger

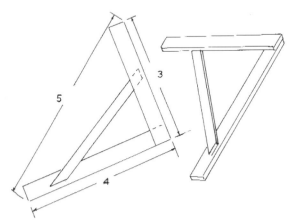

If you have to layout something square, that is much bigger than any normal try or set square, it is unsatisfactory to try and extend the line of either of them. It is better to use the geometric method, where in the three sides of a triangle in the proportions 3:4:5 there is a right angle between the two shorter sides.

You can choose suitable measurements and set them out with pegs and string, but for moderate sizes it is worthwhile having a temporary try square, made with straight pieces of wood nailed together. Any size is possible, if you select measurements to suit the job.

35. Many Squarings

If you want to set out many right-angles on the floor or ground and wish to use the 3:4:5 method of producing a triangle with a square corner, you can save time by using a marked cord. Modern synthetic cord, except nylon, does not stretch and can be relied on to keep its accuracy for this work.

Choose units of measurement that will give you lines as long as you need. Put a small loop in one end of the cord. Measure 3 units from the first loop and make another small loop. Do the same at 4 units from the second loop and then 5 units. Peg out the 4 units side and bring together the 3 and 5 units sides, then you have your right-angle.

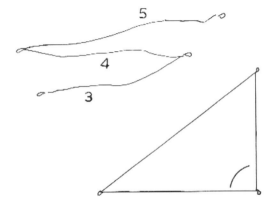

36. Big Square

If you need to set out a right-angle of almost any size, you have to use the fact that in a triangle with the sides in the proportion 3:4:5 (A) the corner between the 3 and 4 sides will be 90°. Choose units of measurement that will produce sides longer than you need. It is never wise to mark an angle and then extend it.

Layout a line with two points 4 units apart (B). From the point on it where you need to extend the right-angle, draw an arc that will obviously pass through the square point (C). Move to the other mark and measure 5 units to a point on the

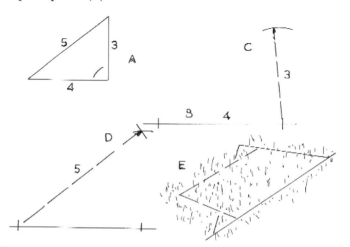

arc (D). This crossing will be square to the mark on the base line. Join these marks. If it is the outline of the foundations for a hut, or something similar, you can mark other lines parallel to the first lines (E).

37. Corner Angle Square

If you make built-in furniture, in many houses you will have to match angles, which look square, but are not. This tool can be fitted to a corner and locked at the angle to then reproduce on to wood.

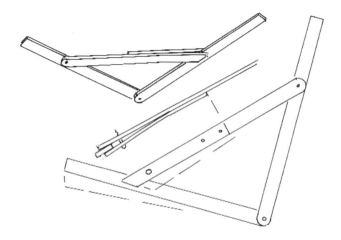

Use straight laths or battens of approximately the same length as the furniture you expect to make. Round the meeting parts at the corner and hinge them with a screw. Arrange the diagonal part with two pieces at one end, as shown. They spring on a sidepiece and a screw through controls the amount of friction, which will prevent movement when you have set the tool to an angle.

38. Simple Mitering

We have tools to mark and cut mitres for 90° corners, but mitres for corners of other angles can be found accurately with very little marking out, whether very acute or very obtuse.

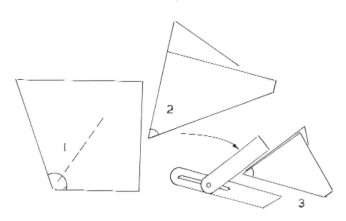

Mark and cut the angle on a piece of stiff paper (1). Fold the two edges of the mitre together (2). This is your mitre angle (3).

39. Set/Try Squares

Set squares used for drawing have their uses in the workshop, but they can be improved to use in a try square mode if you put a stock on one edge. The stock could be glued on permanently or made a push fit, so the square can still be used in its original form. If you have several squares of the same thickness, one stock might suit them all.

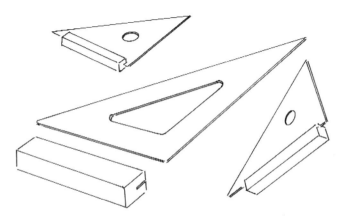

If you do much technical drawing you probably have a large 60° and 30° square and another 45° one. All of these will also mark 90°, so they will mark the angles you are most likely to need.

40. Large Square

If you do much marking out of sheet material, you will find it useful to have the large square shown. Make it from thin plywood to a size that suits your needs. Groove a piece of wood to glue on to the short edge. It is also helpful to have a hand hole of some sort near the middle. After the strip is glued on, check squareness in the usual way by marking a line and turning the square over to see that it matches.

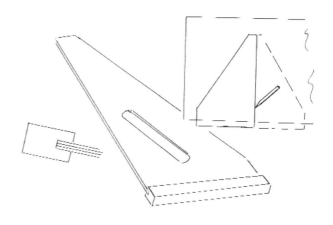

41. Other Mitres

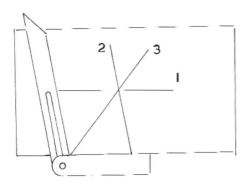

A 45° mitre is usual, but you have a problem if the corner is other than square. Sometimes corners that should be square are several degrees more or less. This often happens with room corners, and you must take this into account if you are planning to make a corner fitting or have to fit skirting boards.

You could mark out the angle on a board with an adjustable bevel set to the angle, and use a compass to bisect the angle in the classic way. It is simpler and probably more accurate to use the method shown. Draw a line parallel to the edge of the board (1) and another one the same distance from the line marked with the adjustable bevel (2). Draw a line from the corner through their crossing and this is the new mitre angle (3).

42. Mitered with a Try Square

You can mark out mitres with a plain try square on wood up to the length of the stock in width. Mark on the inner edge of the blade the exact length of the end of the stock from the blade. If you put a rule or anything straight against this

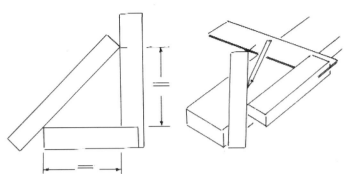

mark and the end of the stock, it will be at 45° to blade and stock. If you file a shallow nick at this point on the blade, a rule end can be easily located at the correct spot.

43. Maximum Hexagon (1)

The usual way of laying out a hexagon, by joining points stepping off the radius around the circumference of a circle, is satisfactory. However, it does not work if you want to use the maximum width of a board for a table top, or something similar.

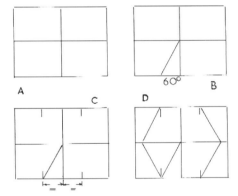

If you want the maximum size, so the sides of the board are also the sides of the hexagon, start by drawing centre lines both ways (A). Set an adjustable bevel to 60° and draw a line from where these lines cross to the edge (B). Mark the same distance along the edge the other way and project the marks to the opposite edge (C). Draw lines at 60° to the edges from these points to form a maximum size hexagon (D).

44. Maximum Hexagon (2)

The following is an alternative method of completion when getting the maximum size hexagon out of a board.

Draw the centre lines and use an adjustable bevel to mark the first 60° (E). Turn the bevel over to mark 60° the other way (F). Project these points on the edge to the opposite edge (G). These are four corners of the hexagon. The length of one of the diagonals is the radius of a circle that would contain the point of a maximum hexagon, so measure this length both ways along the horizontal line (H) to get the last two points in the hexagon (J).

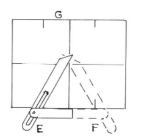

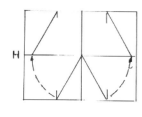

45. Exact Angles

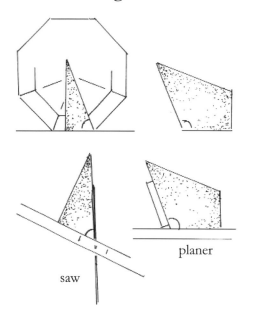

saw

planer

If you have to mark out and cut mitres with corners not 90°, you can calculate the angle and set an adjustable bevel with a protractor. However, this can easily involve part-degrees, and it is safer to set out the shape, not necessarily full-size, and work from that. If it is a regular shape, extend the mitre lines to the centre.

Make one or two templates, as needed. An acute one will set a circular saw, while an obtuse one is needed for a planer fence.

46. Divide It

We are sometimes faced with the need to mark equal divisions in an area that does not easily divide. Instead of using approximations or awkward calculations, this can be done exactly without difficulty, as shown.

Square down a line from one end of the area to be divided and tilt a rule from the starting end, until you see a length that is easily divided in the way you want.

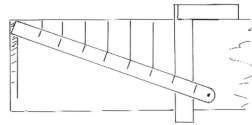

Mark these points and project them with the try square to the edge or line that is to be divided. That will then be marked in equal divisions.

47. Spacing Dovetails

When marking out dovetails to be cut by hand it may not be easy to arrange satisfactory spacing to suit the wood. Instead of trying to work out spacing straight across, it is simpler to use a strip of wood or paper, longer than the width of the wood, and layout the tails and spaces to convenient measurements. Tilt the piece of paper on the wood until the limits of the marking

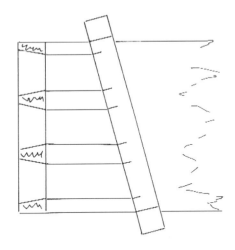

match the edges of the wood, and then project along it. The same idea can be used if you need equal spacing, or some other divisions that will not divide easily.

48. Better Knives

The most accurate line to work from across the grain is cut with a knife. Today, most of this is done with a knife sharpened on both sides in the normal way. This may be satisfactory for most purposes, but for the greatest precision, the knife should be kept close to the try square or other tool by holding it flat on its side. A problem then is that you need another knife to cut the other way. At one time it was possible to buy a 'striking knife', sharpened both ways

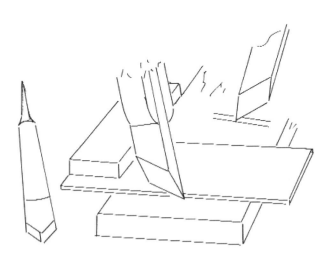

against a flat side. It had wood cheek handles and usually a point, which probably had a cover. You might alter another knife to make this type of blade.

49. Better Laminates

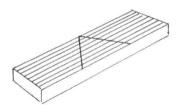

Strips for a laminated form are usually cut from one wide piece of wood. Even if there are only three or four, they will fit together better if they are assembled in the order they were cut. Mark prominently across the wood before sawing it into pieces to identify the strips later.

50. Exactly

An expanding tape measure is a convenient tool as its graduations are easy to see, although rather thick. Its hooked end does not allow for extreme precision if it is included in a short measurement. It is better to measure from a point further along the measuring tape, such as 100mm, providing this is allowed for. A steel rule is a much more precise tool for accurate marking out of wood parts, but it could lead to errors if you work from the end. Again, it is better to measure from another point, such as 100mm.

51. See It

The graduations on some steel rules are not very easy to see, especially if the rule is old or the light is poor. They become less clear when the steel gets dull or dirty, so it will help to rub the rule with fine emery cloth or another abrasive. Follow this with black shoe polish. Leave it a short time, then wipe most off. What is left should fill the graduations and make them more prominent.

52. Divide Not Add

It is a rule of designing to divide an overall measurement and not try to add the parts together. For instance if you want ten spaces to be 100mm and you measure each individually, the total distance will probably be a little more or less than 1000mm. The same applies to spaces of different size. As with parts of a piece of furniture, settle the overall size, if that is a key measurement, and arrange spacing of other shelves, cupboards etc. as part of it, rather than adding them one at a time.

53. Plumb Level

If you want to draw a horizontal line on a wall or check that something you are fixing is level, you can do this without a spirit level.

Draw a line square to the straight edge of a piece of plywood or other sheet material. Drive a nail in the line near the edge and hang something heavy from it with cord. If you hold this up, when the cord matches the line, the top edge will be horizontal.

54. Diagonals

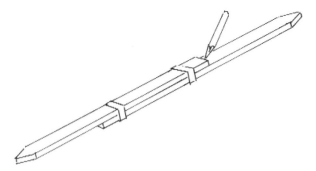

It is good practice to check squareness of a large assembly by comparing diagonal measurements. A simple tool for doing this is shown. Use two light laths long enough to have a good overlap. Point their ends and hold them together with rubber bands. Set to one diagonal and mark the overlap, then do it the other way and see how the marks compare.

55. Diagonal Testing

When squareness is tested, by comparing diagonal measurements, it is usual to have some sort of fastening at the overlap of the strips used. For furniture sizes, the pieces can be held by hand if a supporting piece is put under one. You can then hold them and mark the test distance on the adjoining tops.

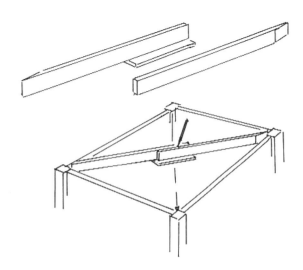

56. Ready Width

If you have to join two pieces of wood to make up a width and need to know the width of the second piece, there is no need for calculations. Put a rule or tape measure across the first piece, with the total width you need at its edge. The width of the piece you need to make up the width is at the other edge.

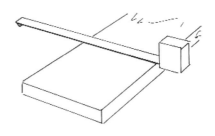

57. Note There

When marking out and needing to remember more than one measurement, such as the length and width of a piece of sheet material, we often jot it down on a scrap of wood or paper. It is better to take it with you where it cannot be lost. Put a piece of masking tape on the side of your measuring tape and write the sizes on that. Peel it off when the job is done.

58. Another Rule

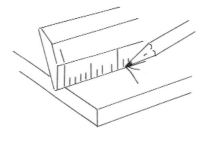

The calibrations on a steel rule may be accurate, but even with good eyesight and a clear light, they are not always easy to see. If you have difficulty, an alternative is a plastic office rule. Most are transparent or tinted translucent, but the markings are very clear. Remember there is an unmarked section at the end and a thickness at the edge. Use the end marking and tilt the rule on its edge for the greatest accuracy and to avoid errors of parallax.

59. Error Free

When marking out sheet material by measuring from an edge, there is a risk of a mistake if you only measure in two places. Measure in three, then if they line up when you draw a line through them, you know the line is where you want it.

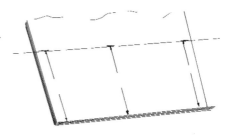

60. Peck It

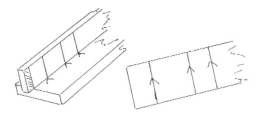

If you want to transfer measurements from one piece of wood to another a short pencil mark is not very obvious or accurate. The expert uses 'peck marks'. These are freehand Vs, with the point of the V on the mark. They are easy to see, cannot be mistaken and a line through the point of the V is as accurate as can be.

61. Even Overhang

If the top of a table or other piece of furniture has to overhang evenly, any error will be obvious. Measuring will guide, but there could be movement in fixing. It helps to have a block cut to the amount of overhang, to test in many places as you locate and fit the top.

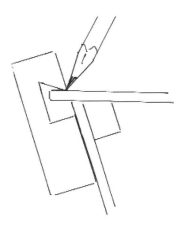

62. Centre Lines (1)

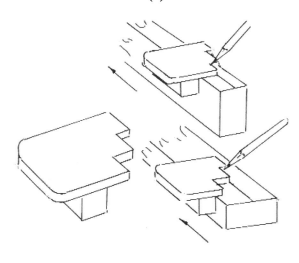

If you regularly use prepared strips such as 50mm by 25mm you will find yourself frequently setting a marking gauge to mark centre lines. A thumb gauge to use with a pencil will avoid this chore and ensure the same setting every time.

Mark the distance for the two centre lines from a guide block position in a piece of thin plywood and cut two notches, with a little extra at the end. The gauge is easier to handle if it has a projecting rounded end.

63. Centre Lines (2)

Most of us use a few standard thicknesses of wood, bought 'planed all round' and often have to set a gauge to mark its centre line. You can avoid that and always have the same setting by making this little gauge with the common settings.

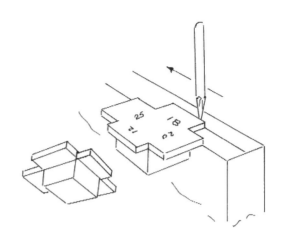

The central block could be 50mm square and the top thin plywood. Make some trial marks to check the settings.

64. Middle?

If you need to find the centre of a strip of wood and do not have a rule or tape measure available, put a mark where you estimate the middle to be. Use a piece of scrap wood, card or paper and put one end on the end of the strip you are measuring and mark on its edge the position you have guessed. Do the same from the other end. The actual centre will be midway between these marks. If it is rectangular sheet material you can do the same the other way to find two lines that will cross at its centre.

65. Tapered Octagon

A regular octagon can be drawn on a square by projecting half diagonals to the sides and joining them. This can be done on the end of a square piece of wood (A). Use this measurement to mark lines along the wood in readiness for planing off the corners. There is a complication if the wood is a long taper, such as a table leg.

The device shown is a gauge for marking long tapers, based on one used by boat builders when making long wood masts.

At the large end of the wood mark the positions of the corners of an octagon and transfer this to a square strip of wood (B). Square over these marks and draw the lines shown (C). Cut down to half thickness in the centre area and cut Vs in

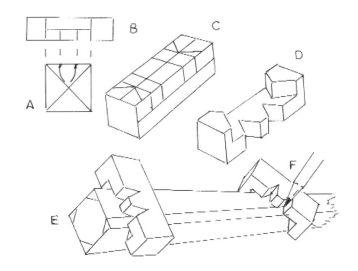

at the line positions, with the points of the Vs in line with the outer points. This will fit over the large end of the wood, with the V cuts on the line positions (E). If you draw the block along the wood with a pencil in a notch and twist the block to keep the outer points always against the wood (F), the line drawn will progressively allow for the narrowing of the wood and always be in the proportional right position for planing the corners off for the correct taper.

66. Another Centre Marker

This tool will scratch a centre line on wood of any width or thickness up to larger sizes than most other markers, but it will not go as close to an end. It depends on accurate marking out.

The size depends on your needs, but a reasonable size would be about 25mm by 12mm section, 200mm long, with 12mm dowels. Mark and drill the two pieces to match exactly. Drill the central hole to suit a stout nail, which should be filed to a round point for marking. The dowels in one piece are longer than the other, to allow for the overlap Experiment with the amount the nail projects for satisfactory marking.

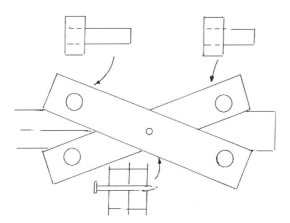

To mark a line, use both hands and close the dowels on the wood as you draw the tool along.

67. Round the Corner

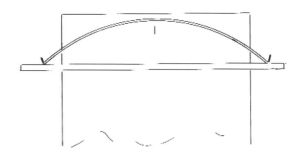

Curved corners are needed on all sorts of wood constructions. Instead of using a compass, it is easier to mark round something solid. It is worthwhile keeping an assortment of suitable things for this purpose, ranging from many sizes of washers, to bottle tops and jars to jar and can lids. These will enable you to draw a corner curve from the smallest curve up to anything you are likely to need.

68. Biggest Circle

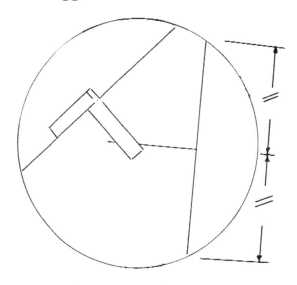

Centre squares are useful for jobs of lathe work size, but how do you find the centre of something large, like an oil drum or a barrel, or even a round garden plot?

Draw a line across as near the estimated centre as your biggest try square is likely to reach. Find the centre of this line and put the try square on it, then draw a line. This will pass through the centre. Do this in another place. The second line does not have to be the same length as the first. The lines will cross at the centre. As a check, you can do it a third time.

69. Circle with Square

If you are without a compass, or wish to draw a circle larger than the reach of your compass, you can draw a circle with a steel square, up to the diameter of the reach of its shorter arm.

Mark the diameter (d) and drive two pins or nails (1). Put the square against these points. Keep it bearing tightly against the pins and pull it round with a pencil in its corner from one point to the other (2). This will draw a semicircle. Do the same at the other side of the pins for a full circle (3).

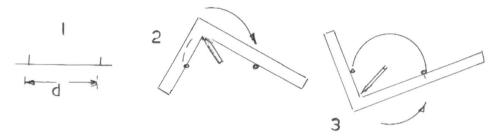

70. Centering with a Square

You can find the centre of any circle within the range of the arms of a steel square. Put the square on the circle, so its inner corner is on the circumference and the arms overlap the circumference (1) , Mark these points (A). A line between them passes through the centre, so if you do this in another position, the centre will be where the lines cross. If you wish to check this, mark halfway on a line drawn inside an arm of the square and move the square along the line to that point. The edge of the other arm will also pass through the centre (2). If you move to another position and repeat the process, you will get another line crossing at the centre (3).

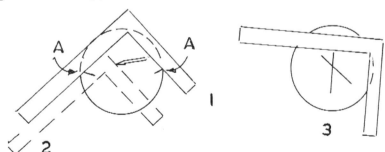

71. String Ellipse

There are several ways of drawing an ellipse, but a simple practical method uses a piece of string and two nails. If it is to be a table top, or similar part, draw centre lines both ways (A). These are the axes of the ellipse. Measure half of the length of the long axis (1) and measure the same distance from the top of the short axis to mark a point on the long axis (2). Mark the same distance the other way and drive in upright nails a short distance at these points (B). Put string around and make a loop that reaches from one nail, past the other, and touches the end of the long axis (C). Put a pencil point in the loop and go round, keeping the string tensioned and the pencil upright (D). This will produce an ellipse of the correct size (E).

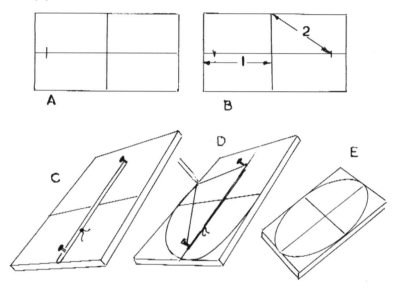

2. Bench

The bench is usually the central point for your work. It should not move and should have a thick top, at least at the front, and there should also be at least one good vice. Some extras may seem desirable, but maintain a clear top.

Folding benches are useful, in and away from the workshop, but do not expect too much from them. One or two bench hooks (sawing boards) are almost essential bench accessories. Treat them as consumables. Let them take blows and cuts that might otherwise damage the bench.

72. Better Well

If you have a bench with a central lower well to retain tools, it will probably be open-ended to facilitate sweeping out. You can improve it by fitting a block, as shown, at one or both ends. The flat top is level with the sidepieces and will support any job that extends across. The sloping part allows shavings and other debris to be swept out.

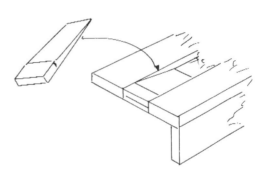

73. Take-down Joint

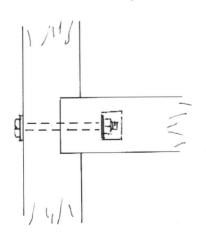

If you want to make a take-down bench or similar framed assembly, you can use a joint borrowed from wooden bed frame makers. You can buy bed bolts, but ordinary long bolts will do.

Let the rail into the leg. There is no need to cut a tenon. Measure the projection of the bolt, which should be long enough to give it a good pull in solid wood. Drill for the bolt in both parts. Cut through a square hole, and insert a washer and the nut so the bolt end can go right through the nut. You can hold something against the nut while you tighten from outside.

74. Bench Out

In a compact workshop, the bench may not be as big as you wish or you cannot permanently mount all the power tools. This is a removable side extension that can be added at the end of a bench when you need a little extra area or want to use a light machine tool. Make a shelf of the size you need. Put a crosspiece at its inner end to make the depth the same as the bench top. Put a support on the bench that this will drop into. Put another crosspiece at the outer end and hinge a support to this to fit into a piece on the bench leg. The whole thing can be lifted off and folded.

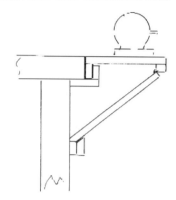

75. Abrasive Paper Tearing

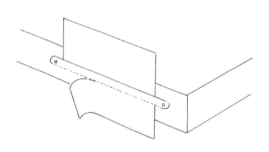

The teeth of a fine hacksaw blade provide a good edge for tearing sheets of abrasive paper. You can keep one ready to use if you fix it on the end of your bench. Attach it with its teeth downwards, with screws that leave it loose enough to slide an abrasive sheet behind. Hold the sheet in place and pull an end towards you.

76. Edgewise Across

If you need to hold a piece of wood on edge across the bench, you can support it by holding a cramp in the vice and gripping it with that.

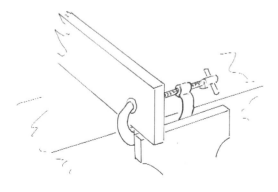

77. Rolling Bench

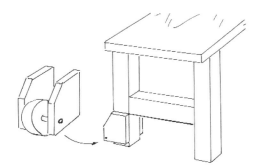

If the workshop is part of the garage, the bench may have to be moved to make room for the car. The arrangement shown has wheels on the back legs, so the front can be lifted slightly and bench moved back easily.

Castor wheels might be used, but a larger diameter with a rod axle would be better. Support the wheels and axles so a wheel is only just clear of the floor when the bench is standing normally, then only a slight lift will be needed at the front to lower it on to the floor.

78. Adjustable Bench Stop

This bench stop can be lowered flush into the bench or raised to provide something to plane wood against. Cut the stop from hardwood. Slope its ends, as shown. Cut the recess in the bench top to match and drill through it for a countersunk bolt engaging with a

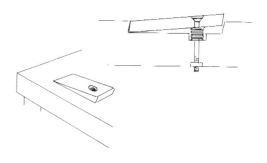

nut let in under the bench, or held to it with epoxy adhesive. Enlarge the top of the hole in the bench to take a small coil spring that will lift the stop, as the bolt is unscrewed.

79. On Edge

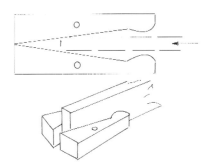

This is a way of holding thin wood on edge on the top of the bench for planing or other work. When wood is pushed into the jaws, they pivot and grip the wood; planing pressure keeps them tight. Use thick hardwood. Arrange the jaws so they close tightly before the wood pushes through the end. The jaws could pivot on stout screws.

If they are to be removable, use dowels, glued into the jaws and pushed into holes in the bench.

80. Thin Hold

If you want to plane thin wood of much length, it is better supported on a bench top than in a vice, however there is the problem of holding it on edge.

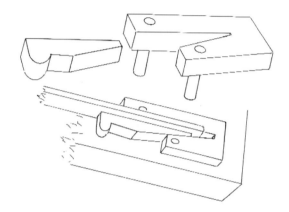

This jig is adaptable to wood of many sizes. Use fairly thick hardwood, with hardwood dowels to fit into holes in the bench and lift away. Use the jig as a template for drilling the holes in the bench top before gluing in its dowels. Keep the wedge long. A slope of about 1 in 7 should suit.

81. Support Edgewise

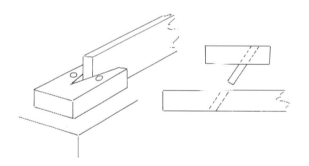

Some wood to be planed by hand and on edge is better supported on a bench top than in a vice, but something is needed to hold it steady. This removable V-block can hold wood of any normal thickness. Make it of thick hardwood and use hardwood dowel rods. Drill the block and bench at an angle, as shown, so that the action of planing or other work tightens the fit.

82. Wider Stop

Ordinary bench stops are not very wide and there are occasions when a wider stop would be preferable to push wood against for planing or other work.

The stop shown is held in the vice and does not involve alterations to the bench. The parts should be glued and screwed squarely together. One thickness of stop should hold many thicknesses of boards being worked on, but you could make another to deal with other thicknesses.

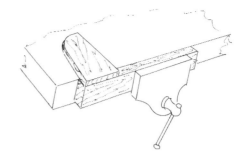

83. On/Off Stops

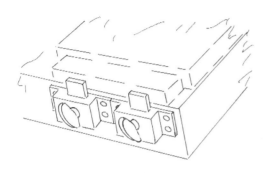

For many jobs on the bench a wide stop at the end is useful, and it is convenient if the stop can be lowered out of the way. This dual arrangement is made with two cupboard catches screwed to the end of the bench. One alone could be used for narrow work, but two will take wide boards for planing, as shown.

84. Undistorted Vice

Most of us use one side of the vice more than the other when holding narrow wood. Long use can distort the vice so the jaws will be out of parallel, making the grip poor when holding something full width.

To keep the jaws under even strain, it is worthwhile having one or more packings, to put in the opposite side, as shown. Thickness should match your commonly used wood. This also provides a better grip on the job. A packing can be kept in place with a bit of dowel rod and kept from loss with a cord to an eye screw in a bench leg.

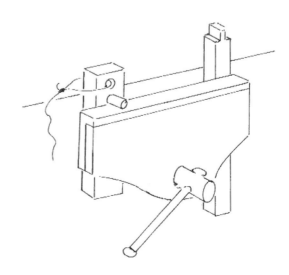

85. Sideways Hold

If you are planing or doing other work on a large board against a stop, it is helpful if it can be prevented from moving sideways. One way of doing this is with two holdfasts in holes in the bench. 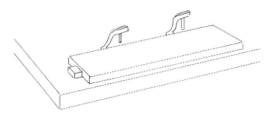 Close them on the bench, so that there is nothing below them. Their ends should be below the thickness of most boards.

86. Vice Pads

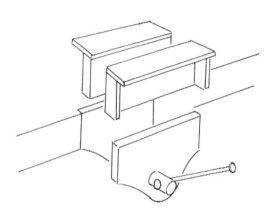

If you prefer to have a steel parallel-action vice installed without permanent pads, there will be occasions when you need wood facings against the work piece.

Make two pads the width of the jaws and almost deep enough to reach the guide rods. Put thin plywood tops on them and sidepieces to hold the front one in place.

87. Grip Vice

If you need an additional vice on your bench or elsewhere, this wedge-action vice can be made to do the job, at minimum cost.

Make it from close-grained hardwood, as deep as the top of the bench. A wedge slope of 1 in 6 should provide a good grip. Fix the main block to the bench tightly to resist strain. A cord from the wedge to a screw eye in it will keep the wedge within reach.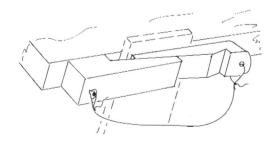

88. Bench Measure

In a draper's store you will always find a measuring piece, usually brass, along the edge of the counter. It is used for measuring cloth and other materials. A similar reference, not necessarily on the front edge, could be useful on a woodworker's bench. A self-adhesive plastic measuring length could be stuck on.

89. Protect Planes

Planes are often hung so that a rail gives support under the cap irons. This means a plane is placed on the rack in a planing action against the back of the rack. If the cutter projects very much it can cut the wood or be damaged. This can be avoided and the plane soles padded if the back of the rack is lined with carpet, as arrowed in the illustration.

90. Bar Cramp Grip

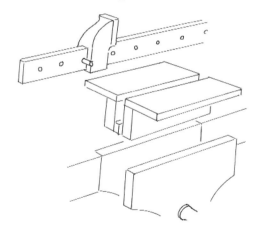

It is sometimes helpful to hold a bar cramp in the bench vice. It needs packing for clearance at the sides, and to be held at a height that allows the cramp jaws to be used. Instead of using scrap pieces of wood, the pair of packings shown will hold the bar so everything fits automatically in position.

Make the side pieces thick enough to give clearance to the jaws and allow the screw to be used. Put a strip slightly thinner than the bar at the bottom of one piece to hold the cramp with its jaws above the bench top.

91. Grip Thin Sheet

If you have to grip thin sheet material edgewise in the vice for planing or other edge work, it has to be kept flat and supported. Put stiff strips each side of the sheet and grip them and the sheet at one end in the vice. Use a cramp at the

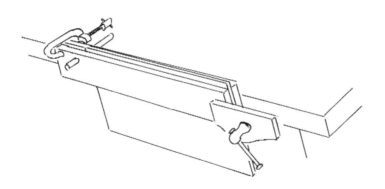

other end. The cramp resting on the bench may be sufficient support, but it is better to put a piece of dowel rod through the strips and bear on that.

92. Vice Clamps

If you need to hold anything round upright in the vice without support, it may wobble or become damaged by over tightening. The vice clamps shown will hold anything round from small dowel rods up to a paint can, and keep them steady.

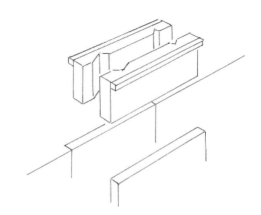

Make the pair of clamps fairly thick and nearly as deep as the capacity of the bench vice. Cut the notches fairly near the ends, then if you need to hold any long round thing you can slide the clamps along so that it will go clear through. The small notch can be cut with an internal angle of about 90°, but cut the larger one to a wider angle, which will be better for oversized round objects.

93. Dowel Grip

If pieces of dowel rod have to be held on end for work to be done on them, gripping directly in the vice may allow movement and make flats on the dowel.

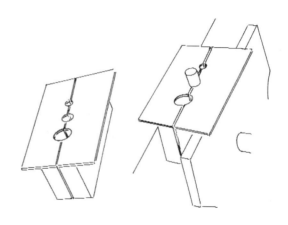

The jig shown can be made for any number of usual diameters. The top is made from thin plywood or hard plastic and the bottom could be made from 50mm square wood. Drill holes to suit the dowels, then cut the assembly in half. The saw kerf removes enough wood to make the jig grip a dowel when squeezed by the vice.

94. Thin Hold

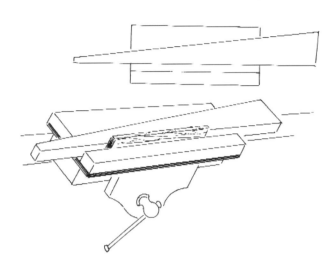

When making models or other small things it is often necessary to hold thin, and often narrow, wood to plane on the edge and this may be difficult or awkward to hold in the normal bench vice. The jig shown can hold the smallest piece of wood securely with its edge ready for planing or other work.

It could be any size to suit your needs, but the main part could be about 250mm long. A wedge about twice as long and with a slope of 1 in 10, would allow you to grip anything in thickness from 0.1 to 8mm. The working parts are 15mm thick mounted on plywood with a block below to grip in the bench vice. The wedge should enter as shown, then the action of planing tends to tighten it.

95. Bench Dog Wedges

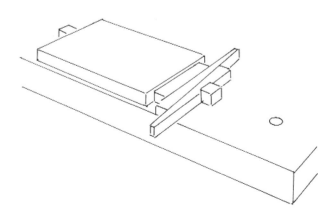

If your bench has holes to take bench dogs, there are many occasions when you would like to hold wood between them, but the distance is wrong. Keep a pair of fairly long matching wedges to use as folding wedges to use with scrap wood to hold the wood between dogs.

96. Dog It

You may have dogs to fit in your bench, but they are widely spaced and intended for larger symmetrical pieces of wood. If you have to work on smaller pieces of awkward shapes, they will not hold them. Instead, you could make the board shown, to grip in the vice. You could drill holes to suit the dogs at random

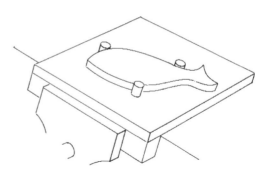

spacing or drill as required for a particular work piece. In any case, the board can be used many times. If you do not already have dogs, you can substitute pieces of dowel rod.

97. Better Pegs

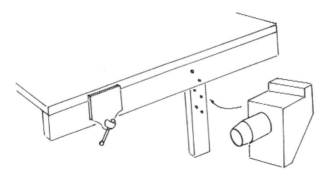

To support long wood extending from the vice many craftsmen have holes in the apron of the bench, or a post extending to the floor, and push in a peg for the wood to rest on. A simple peg will wear and sag and it does not stop a board falling off. The support block shown is an improvement. The block has a ledge to retain the work. To resist tilting it extends below the peg at a slight downward tilt.

98. Stronger Dogs

If you have holes in the bench for dogs, these are usually just round pegs. If you make dogs as shown. they will be better able to take thrust and pressure. The extending piece on the bench top shares the pressure and reduces wear on the hole.

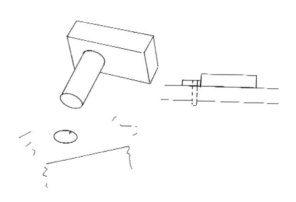

99. Tight Dogs

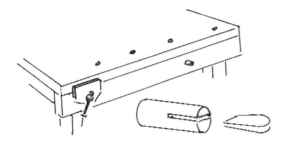

If you use pieces of dowel rod as dogs on top of the bench or pegs to support wood extending from the vice, they probably are not always as firmly held as you wish. You can tighten a dowel with a fairly long saw cut and a wedge to push in by hand.

100. Cam Dog

With plain bench dogs there is no arrangement for tightening a work piece between dogs. The dog shown has a round top. The peg goes through a slightly off-centre hole, so the top can be turned as a cam by a metal or wood rod in holes to adjust it, through a limited amount, to alter its hold.

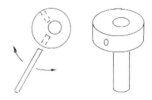

101. Dog Thrust

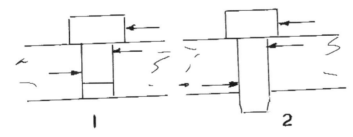

If you make dogs to use in holes in the bench, the thrust on the top in use has the effect of pushing the top of the peg forward in the hole and the reaction of the bottom of the peg trying to push back. Make any dog long enough to go through the hole. A short peg (1) does not offer as much resistance, so strength is less and wear is greater. A longer peg (2) has maximum strength and wear in the hole is less.

102. No Slide Off

If you fit a shelf under a bench or table, put a small stop at the back, even if occasionally you will put things on from that side. This will mark the limit and keep things in place.

103. Jaws

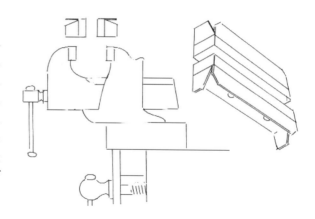

You probably have a metalworking vice mounted on a block to grip in the bench vice. Besides the odd metalworking job, it is also at a suitable height for some fine and small woodworking, but the jaws will mark the wood if not covered.

You can make a pair of wood-faced vice clamps to provide a smooth secure grip on wood. Cut thin sheet pieces to wrap round the jaws, as shown. Fit two wood faces to them with screws through holes. Countersink well for the screws and ensure the jaws finish parallel.

104. Squared Fastening

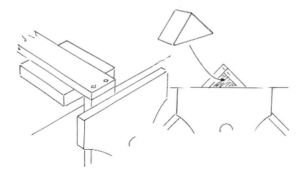

If you need to nail or screw strips together at 90°, the simplest way is to have one piece upright in the vice and support the other piece squarely over it on the bench top. If the parts are unsuitable for doing this and have to be held together diagonally in the vice, it is helpful to have a triangular block, as shown. So long as the corner is square, it need not be at 45°. Have this thick enough to partially rest on the bench top or vice.

105. Better Long Support

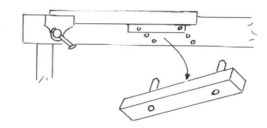

A peg driven into a hole in the apron of a bench is a common way of supporting a board extending from the vice, but there are times when a longer support would be preferable. If two sets of matching holes are drilled, it is still possible to use a single peg, but when more support is needed, a piece with two pegs can be used, as shown.

106. Paired Bench Hooks

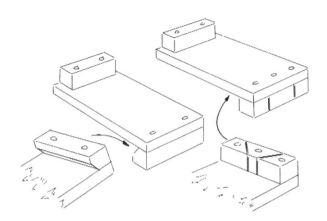

A bench hook, or sawing board, can have many uses besides simply sawing wood across. For even greater use, it is a good idea to make a pair, with the same overall sizes, but some different details. They can be used wide apart to support long work or individually for other work.

For straightforward sawing across, you can avoid the saw dropping on and damaging the bench top, by cutting the end pieces short. To stop round rods or thin wood lifting, cut it chamfered before you fix it. You may be glad of mitre slots in one end. Attach the end before cutting the slits. Use the same saw you expect to use for mitered work. Assemble with glue and dowels, so there will be no metal for tools to touch.

107. Truly Square

The sawing board or bench hook can be used for planing edges and ends of smaller pieces, as well as sawing. If you need to plane an end after sawing, planing in the vice may finish out of square. If you use a plane on its side, as shown, you can see any marking out on the surface and the wood will finish square across.

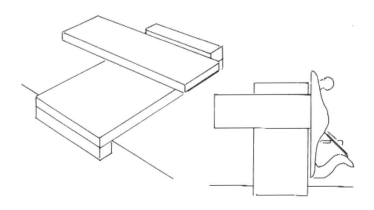

108. Two-part Hook

The usual bench hook performs many jobs and will hold shorter pieces being worked on. If you have a longer job, some extra support is needed. This double bench hook can be used with the parts together for normal jobs, but when support is needed for something long, the parts can be moved to any distance.

The sections could be made separately, but to ensure matching, it is better to make as one, then saw apart. A hole through the meeting edges will show you which way to put them together.

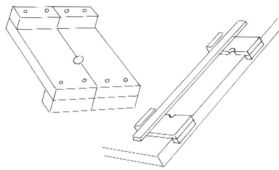

109. Secured Bench Hook

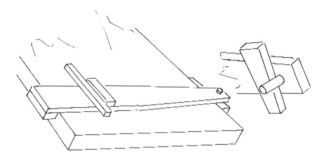

The common bench hook or sawing board hooked on to the bench edge has nothing to hold it in place. The extended board shown can be locked in place as required.

Make the working part the normal size, but lengthen it to the other side of the bench, where a piece of dowel rod through it can take the thrust of a wedge against the bench.

110. Mitre Bench Hook

Small mitred work, such as photograph frames, are usually better prepared by hand sawing and planing. The bench hook shown has one end like a normal bench sawing board, but at the other end there are two pieces square to each other and at 45° to the sides. Marked

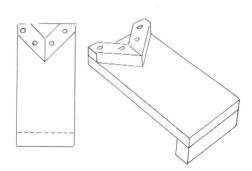

wood can be sawn, then the mitre shot with a plane sliding on the bench top on its side.

Make this hook a little longer than a sawing board, but otherwise very similar. Use dowels to avoid any metal in the construction.

111. More Accurate Mitres

It is sometimes suggested that mitre cuts could be made in a bench hook. In a normal hook this does not give much lengthwise support to the piece being cut. The board shown has longer arms for more support and the end piece could be thicker and wider to give more support to the saw being used.

Make the end piece in one length, at least twice as long as the width of the board.

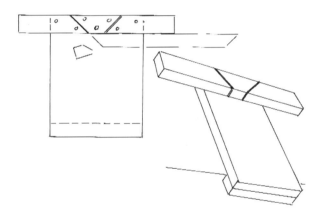

Mark it out and glue it squarely across the baseboard, then drill for dowels and make the mitre cut with the same saw that will be used cutting work pieces. If the other end is made in the usual way, this board can be turned over and used for other purposes.

112. Sawing Grip

It is not always easy to hold a piece of wood across a bench hook. This lever grip will help to free your hand for other things. It consists of a solid wood disc on an offset dowel rod with a lever, so when it is turned it has a cam action

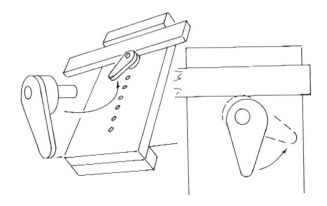

For the usual bench hook a disc 32mm diameter on a

9mm dowel should be suitable. Offset the dowel hole about 3mm from the centre. If you drill holes along the centre of the bench hook, this should allow gripping almost any width, but you could drill two rows at staggered spacing for fine adjustment.

113. Better Small Mitres

It is convenient to have one end of a bench hook cut to serve as a mitre block for small work, but the crosspiece has to be secured properly if its part are not to move.

Cut a rabbet for the end, so it fits in with some solid wood below the cuts. Glue it in with dowels arranged within the three sections.

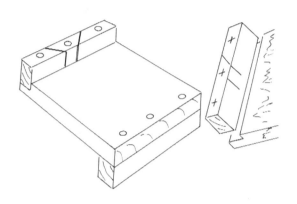

114. Multi Cut Gauge

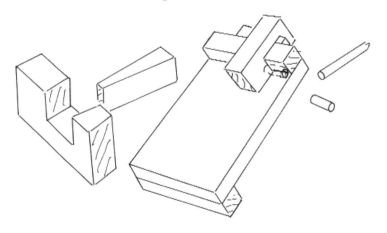

If you want to cut dowels to the same length from a long piece of rod, this clip-on gauge to fit your bench hook will set the size for hand sawing. Make it to notch over one end of the bench hook and lock with a wedge. A fairly long wedge with a slope about 1 in 6 could be tightened or loosened by hand.

115. More Rigid Hook

If your bench hook moves more readily than you want, make one as shown. The

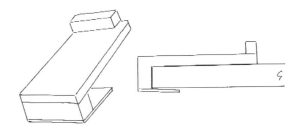

hook part is as deep as the thickness of the bench and has a slight angle on the bottom. A piece of plywood on this slips easily on the bench edge, but is tight when pushed close.

116. Undercut Hook

There is no reason why the pieces across a bench hook need to have square sections. Next time you make a new one, slope the ends, as shown. This will stop thin and round wood riding up and the end against the bench will resist lifting.

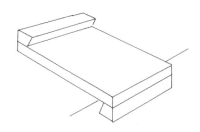

117. Longer Life for a Bench Hook

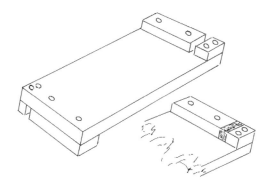

A bench hook needs replacing occasionally. Usually the edge of the board gets badly damaged where the saw breaks though at the edge, interfering with accurate cutting.

A bench hook with the sawing position away from the edge will last longer. Even if the saw grooves the bench hook, the wood being sawn will be held accurately. To ensure accuracy at each end, make a cross piece in one length and glue and dowel it in position, then make the cut-out. Make both ends the same or have one left handed if you wish.

118. Sheet Support

If you have no space to keep a permanent support for sheet material overhanging the bench, this take-down support can be made from two pieces of thick plywood. The long piece is bench height and the other part supports it. For extra steadiness, put strips each side of the slots.

119. Better Trestle Top

Trestles for use in the workshop may fold for storage. A pair with plain tops are useful for assembly work, but have limited use singly. A flat top increases the usefulness of a trestle considerably.

A trestle is made in the usual way, with halving joints. The tops of both parts are bevelled so they are paralleled with the floor when the trestle is in the open position. Locate the hinges so they are as high as possible without projecting. Make a top board of the size you want and attach it to one side only, so it overlaps evenly all round when the trestle is open.

120. Stool/Bench

A workshop stool, made as shown, can have many uses. It should be made just above knee height. It is an assembly bench, a sawing trestle and a seat. The slots along the centre are wide enough to pass cramp heads, and have many uses, such as holding wood being worked on with a jigsaw or router. This is a more convenient height for these jobs than the normal bench.

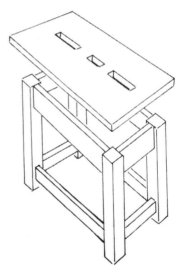

121. Trestle Stop

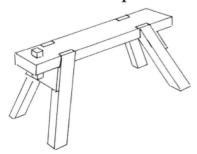

If you need to plane wood away from the bench, it is a help to have a stop on the sawing trestle. It would interfere with normal use of the trestle if it projected permanently, so use a square stop held by friction in its hole, and it can be knocked up or down.

122. Steadier Trestle

If you use a pair of sawing trestles, with the tops of the legs projecting, you can improve them by adding the stops shown. One or more of these on each trestle will provide something to push against when sawing or doing other work. Pivot the piece low down on a stout screw

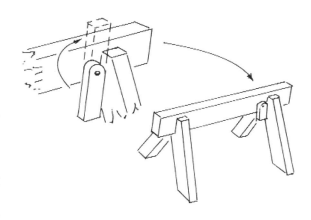

and make it long enough to swing up and extend a worthwhile amount.

123. Three-leg Trestle

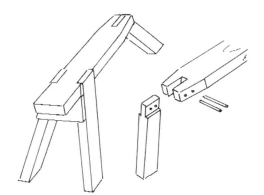

If you expect to use a trestle outdoors as well as in the workshop, make it with three legs, as shown. It uses the tripod principle and will stand without wobbling on the most uneven ground.

Make the two-leg end in the usual way, with a good spread for stability. Notch the single leg in tightly. Use waterproof glue and put two hardwood dowels through for extra strength.

124. Unipod

If you have to handle a standard 2440mm x 1220mm (8ft x 4ft) piece of plywood or other sheet material alone and need to get it horizontal extending from a bench or machine table, you will usually need support at the extreme end. This single support, or unipod, attaches to the sheet, so it will not fall over at the wrong moment.

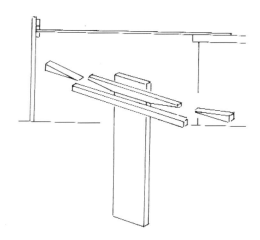

Use a wide board extending a little higher than the bench. Put a strip across it at bench height. Put another piece above it with a gap enough for the thickest material you expect to handle. Bevel under its ends to take wedges. For most sheet material the wedges should tighten fully, but for very thin sheets you may need packings. If you want to deal with a second set of heights, you could put another set of supports on the other side.

125. Traditional Sawing Horse

This sawing horse has been the common method of holding logs to be sawn for firewood, but it can be used for holding other sections of wood for sawing and other purposes. It is worth having in any workshop.

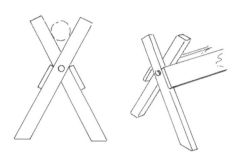

Use stout wood (75mm by 50mm would be suitable) and bolt the crossing pieces at a comfortable working height. Use two wide boards between the ends. They stop the horse opening too wide and provide rigidity.

126. Workmate Cramping

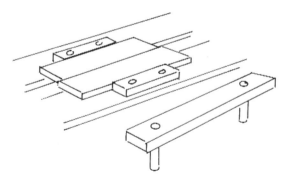

There is a limit to the amount of pressure that can be transferred by single dogs. If you want to use the screws of a Workmate to cramp a glued joint, the cramping will be spread better and therefore more thorough, if you make pieces, as shown, to spread over pairs of holes.

127. Tighter Workmate

The screws on a Workmate are wide apart and anything put near the middle does not get a maximum grip. To get the greatest pressure, as when cramping, put the wood in the jaws near one end. Close the jaws on it. Tighten the screw at the near end, then go to the other screw and tighten that. The leverage due to the length of the jaws will close them even tighter. A check on the first screw, and you have all the pressure possible.

128. Endwise Grip

The screws on a Workmate can exert considerable pressure, but the rather thin top boards do not transfer much of a grip. This pair of pads will hold upright wood with a better and tighter spread of pressure. A width of 100mm should suit most jobs. The wood held could be short or reach to the floor.

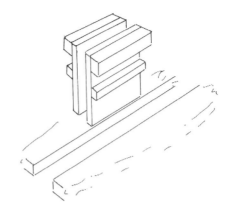

129. Workmate Trough

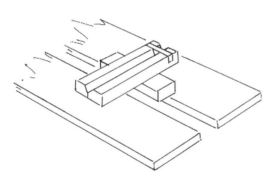

If you use a trough to hold square wood while you plane off the corners or dowels while sawing glue grooves, and you use a Workmate or similar folding bench, it is worthwhile making a trough to mount as shown.

Make it long enough to bridge the gap and have the fixing block long, so the trough cannot wobble in use.

130. Workmate Widened

The Workmate folding bench, and others of the type, are supplied with dogs or pegs to fit into a series of holes in the top halves. These allow wood to be gripped by using the screw action, within the limits of the bench and its adjustment. A set of four extension pieces will allow much wider pieces to be held.

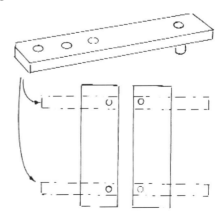

Size and the number of holes should be arranged to suit your needs. At the inner end of each piece, glue in a dowel that will press into one of the existing holes. The other holes take the standard dogs.

131. Tougher Top

The top of a folding bench is thin compared with a standard shop bench, but it may be expected to stand up to heavier and larger work than it is designed for. One way of helping it is to make an auxiliary top. The one shown can double the thickness and could be made up to double the area.

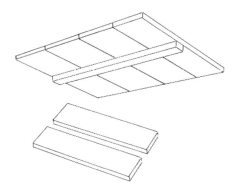

Use a strong central spine and glue 18mm boards together across the direction of the grain of the bench top. There could be strips under the board ends. Level the top surface. In use, restrict heavy hitting to the double thickness at the centre, while assembly and lighter work can be done anywhere.

132. Workmate Vice

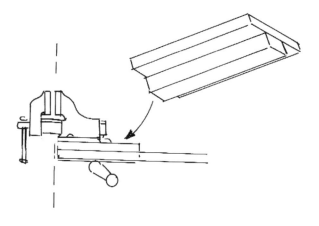

A metalworking vice on a removable pad to clamp in the end of a Workmate or similar portable bench can be used for small wood parts as well as metal or plastic.

Make the pad long enough to provide a good clamping area between the sides of the bench - 300mm at least, even if the vice base is much shorter. Use wood at least 18mm thick and with a good spread, to absorb the shock of hammering in the vice. Bolt the vice to the pad so the face of the inner jaw is forward of the edge of the pad, then when fitting the pad to the Workmate, keep its end level with the bench top, so anything upright in the vice can extend to the floor, if required.

133. Workmate Pegs

Workmate and many similar folding benches are supplied with pegs to fit holes in their tops, to use with a screw action to cramp jobs on the surface of the bench. You may not wish to cut or alter these pegs, but there are occasions when a different shape would match a job, or it would be better to have a peg lower than standard. It is a good idea to turn some softwood pegs to fit the holes, but with unfinished tops. Then, when you need a square edge or a lower plug or some other adaptation, you can easily change plug to suit the job.

134. Workmate Mitre Board

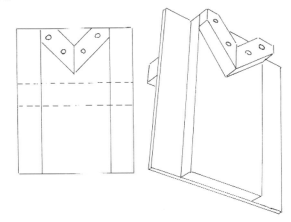

When making smaller mitred parts, such as those for photograph frames, the mitres can be cut and finished by hand. The board shown is intended to be used with a tenon saw and plane and is designed to mount on a Workmate or similar folding bench.

There are two pieces fixed to the base with dowels and at 45° to the sides. Using two pieces instead of a solid block leaves an opening for fingers gripping the wood being cut.

The base is extended each side with plywood wide enough to allow a plane to slide on it on its side to shoot the mitres after sawing. A block underneath is for gripping between the two parts of the top of the Workmate.

135. Workmate Tool Box

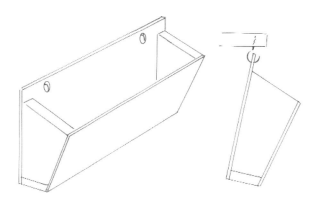

If you make much use of a Workmate or similar folding bench, you soon discover there is limited space for tools and they drop on the floor. This box hangs from two hooks under the top, so it can be removed and the hooks should not interfere with folding.

Check the length between legs. You should be able to fit in a box about 350mm long. Make the ends and bottom from solid wood, and the other parts in thin plywood. Measure your tools. If you need considerable capacity, there could be another box at the other side. Use screw hooks large enough to go into the holes easily and strong enough to take the weight.

136. Better Grip

The two adjustable sides of a Workmate or similar folding bench are not very

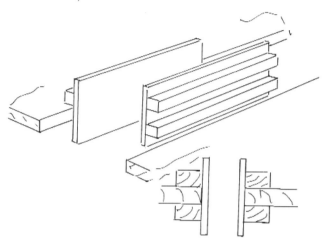

thick, and therefore do not have the grip of a bench vice. They are not steady enough for holding things like wide boards on edge.

The pair of auxiliary jaws shown will give a broader support to the work. They press into place when needed.

137 Work Safely

A Workmate folding bench is a convenient stand for a power tool, such as a circular saw, which should be held safely, as lifting or other movement whist it is in use could be dangerous. The method of mounting is usually a block to grip between the bench sides and this could be improved to hold better.

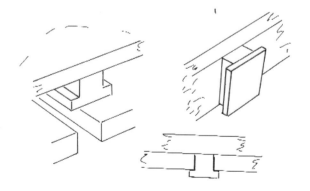

Extend the block so it has lips below the bench top. You could rout rabbets in the block and attach an extended piece of plywood below the block. Even stronger would be a piece of solid wood with the grain across.

138. Clean Bench

When putting a jointed assembly together it is impossible to avoid drips of glue. If you are working directly on the bench top, it may be impossible to remove these drips until they have hardened, and this may damage the surface. If using newspaper, it may get stuck to the bench or job. Plastic sheeting gives better protection. Keep and open old plastic bags, rubbish bags, and old plastic tablecloths, all of which can be used more than once.

139. Another Bench Hook

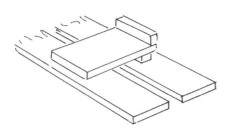

If you use a Workmate, or similar folding bench, as your second or only bench, you will want to saw across it as you would on the main bench, but the ordinary bench hook is not best to use. The bench hook shown allows you to do all the usual jobs and has the advantage of being secured. Make the base long enough to bridge the gap, so working pressure comes on the far side. Dowel the parts together so there are no screws for saws or edge tools to touch.

140. Best Hanging

If all you need to hang a tool on the wall is a screw, there is no need for anything more elaborate. A round head screw looks better than a countersunk head. One with a plain neck is better than one with its thread to the head. Enter it at an angle. If you cut a rabbet above a row of screws, you will have more space for your fingers to remove the tool.

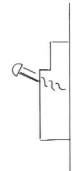

141. Re-cycle Pots

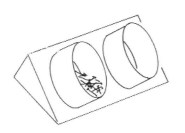

Discarded plastic food containers and pots, such as those for yogurt, are strong enough for workshop use, such as nails and screws needed for the job in hand. The contents are easier to scoop out if they are tilted. A row of containers could be mounted on a triangular-section piece of wood at the back of the bench or it could be taken to the job.

142. Keep Square

Try squares should be stored carefully. A damaged square means inaccurate work. The rack shown takes a large flat square and two sizes of try square, but the idea could be developed to suit what you have. This 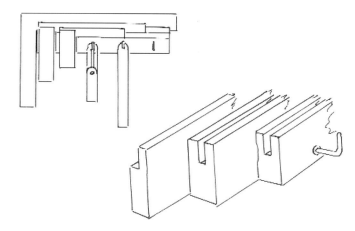 rack is in three depths for squares with space for hooks on the front. For a flat square you can cut a rabbet at the back. Make grooves, with plenty of spare width for the try squares. Overall length is decided by the largest square. Screw and glue the strips together. Graduate their widths so bottoms are level.

143. How Many Millimetres?

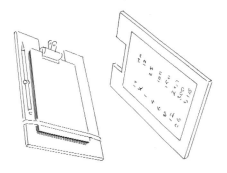

If most of your woodworking has been done in imperial measure, it is difficult to visualise sizes in metric measure. It is worthwhile having a note of some approximate equivalents available for reference.

A notepad is worth having. If you do not already have one, a suitable design is shown. Decide on a size of paper – A5 is half the usual typing paper and magazine size. Cut a piece of thin plywood a little bigger and recess the top for a clip. A clip for a pencil at one side is also a good idea.

Glue a piece of paper to the other side and put on this a list of approximate equivalents that you can refer to when necessary.

144. Clip It

When you have a project in hand, there could be a complete drawing, or odd notes or calculations on bits of paper, that get lost or damaged in the clutter on the bench. It is a good idea to fix clips of the Bulldog type at a few points, such as tool racks around your working areas, so papers can be hung safely out of the way and readily visible for use. Where clips have large holes put washers under the screw heads.

145. Workshop Drawing File

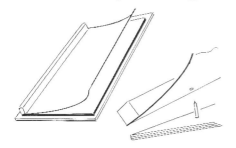

Drawings or notes will soon get damaged or lost in a workshop. If you expect to draw or write on the paper as well, it needs a firm backing. This file will keep a thick pile of papers together, keep them clean and easily accessible or removable.

Use a piece of thin plywood, a little larger than the paper you expect to use. Use a piece of flexible card, almost as big as a cover, and glue and nail a strip of wood along one edge. Put two or more nails through the plywood to push into holes drilled through the card into the wood. Papers can be pressed on to the nails and the cover pressed on to them.

146. Hammer Racks

Hammers are sometimes hung from notches in the edge of a shelf, but are liable to fall out. The rack shown keeps them safe and, with two rows of staggered supports, takes up minimum space. For normal hammers use

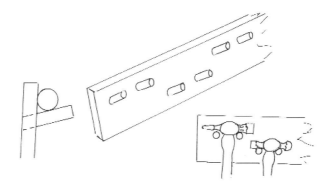

12mm dowel rod and drill the holes to give about a 15° slope.

147. Tidy?

Keep your workshop floor swept and cleaned frequently. Walking amongst rubbish could harm your footwear and take dirt where it should not be. If you drop something small, you may not find it. A clean floor encourages you to do better work.

148. Compact Drill Storage

The inside of a small door is a suitable place to store drills. The arrangement shown will suit restricted height and allow drills to be tilted for easy handling. The drills fit into holes in a strip pivoted on two screws or dowels at the ends. Bevel the back of the strip to allow enough tilt when it is stopped.

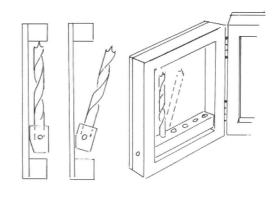

149. Safe Chisel Pack

Chisels are often stored through slots in a shelf, where the sharp edges are dangerously exposed.

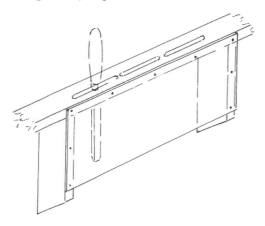

This rack has a row of several slots. A slot can hold about four chisels. Do not make any slot too long or chisels left after others are withdrawn may tilt too much. The shelf could extend to take other tools. Arrange supports deeper than the chisel blades and fix transparent Perspex in front, so the blades are visible but protected.

150. Stroke It Out

Most of us put things like panel pins and screws needed for the job on the bench into anything available, such as a jar lid or box top and then find it difficult to pick up just the one needed immediately, possibly when one hand is holding the parts to be

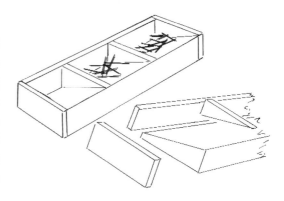

fastened. The box shown will allow you to stroke out a single nail or screw with just one finger. The main part is a wedge of the length you need. A suitable section can start as 100mm x 25mm. Box this around with thin strips, to the height of the front edge.

151. Safer Tools

Most of us put tools such as chisels, screwdrivers and files on the wall in narrow slotted shelves, but there is a risk that they may fall out. This can be prevented by 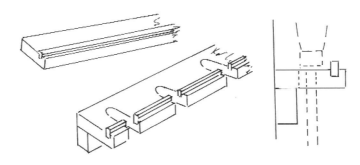 making shelves with a spline into the front to provide a stop.

Rout a groove to take a small strip of wood with a rounded top that projects enough to restrain the tools without making it difficult to remove or replace them. Cut the slots, but glue the spline in one piece and cut it to match the slots after the glue has set.

152. Cramp Rack

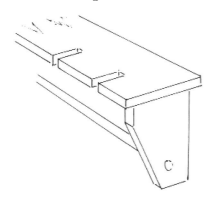 If you discard a metal towel rail from the bathroom, recycle it in the workshop as a rack for all kinds of small cramps. The plated metal rail will stand up to use much better than dowel rod. If you think it looks too much like the bathroom for your workshop, cut the ends off and use the rail with wood ends, which could be extended above, with a notched shelf to take bar cramps of various types and sizes.

153. Wipe Cleanly

Old car windscreen wipers can be given a further use in the workshop after they have served their original purpose. One will wipe dust off newly sanded wood or any other dusty surface.

154. High Rack

If a rack for punches and other tools that can be stored in holes is to be located above eye level, it will be easier to see and access if the holes are arranged at a slight angle.

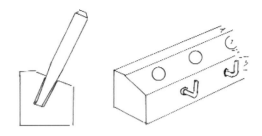

155. Blow It

If you use any type of power sander, a dust extractor will not remove all the dust and tools in the vicinity will acquire a coating of dust. After brushing, there will still be dust in corners and crannies, particularly around screws, which ought to be clean. A piece of plastic tube is useful for blowing dust out of these spaces.

156. Cord Guide

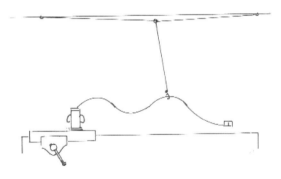

Cordless power tools have reduced the number of electric cables trailing about the bench, but some corded tools are still needed. A way to keep cable safely out of the way is shown. Fix a length of expanding curtain wire to the ceiling above the bench. Have a curtain or other hook running on it and hang from it a length of elastic shock cord. Have a hook or clip on on the end of the cord, through which the cable can slide easily. This should travel the length of the bench and keep the cable above things on the bench.

157. Mitre Jig

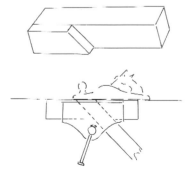

Glue holds better on a planed surface than a sawn one, so even if a mitre is accurately sawn it ought to be skimmed with a plane. If this is done freehand, there is a risk of causing inaccuracy. The jig shown, controls the wood and the plane so that accuracy is maintained.

The main block should be accurately squared and be wide enough to keep the plane from wobbling in use. The guide piece should be cut to 45° and be thinner than the thinnest wood expected to be held, to ensure the vice closes on the job and not the guide piece.

158. Thinner Planing

It is difficult to plane narrow and thin piece of wood, such as an edging, since it cannot stand on a bench, and is not stiff enough for holding in a vice. It is best supported by a grooved piece of wood.

Use a router to make a groove that it will fit in. Drive a nail through to act as a stop and either rest this on the bench or hold it in the vice.

159. Grooving Aid

When you drive a dowel into a hole, there should be a groove to let air and surplus glue escape. Cutting a groove with a saw can be awkward. In order to make each groove easier to cut, it is helpful to make a small V-block to use with a bench hook, by bevelling a length of wood at 45°, cutting it and joining the halves. There could be a thin plywood base, for strength.

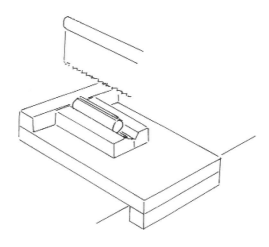

160. Hard Hitting

If you need to do hard hitting, locate the work piece over a bench leg. Part of the success of what you are doing depends on the reaction of the support. If you are working away from the support of a leg, the flexing of the bench top reduces this. It is even more of a problem if working on an improvised support, such as a table or chair.

161. Big Support

If you are making a drawer or box
and need to plane the sides after
assembly, the whole thing may not
be suitable for holding in the vice.
You can hold it as shown, with two
strips of wood, fitting closely inside
and cramped to the bench. If a
bottom is already fitted, the strips
can go inside.

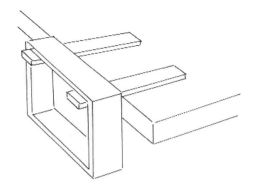

162. Wood Hold Fast

A metal holdfast was the traditional woodworker's method of holding wood to
the bench surface. There are modern screw-action versions, but you can make a
wooden holdfast
that acts in the
old way.

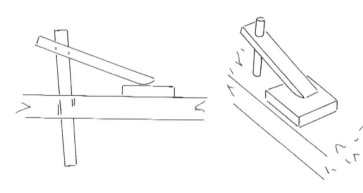

Use a strip of
hardwood and
round its working
end. Near the
other end drill at
an angle for a
stout hardwood
dowel rod, which can be glued in. Drill a hole in the bench that will make an easy
fit on the dowel rod. In use, rest the rounded end on the wood to be held and
drive the dowel rod in. It will tilt slightly in the hole and friction will hold the
pressure on the job. To release the holdfast, knock the back of the top upwards
and towards the job.

163. Safe Bench

Nails are often driven into parts of an
assembly before meeting the other part. If
driven too far, they could mark the bench. To
prevent this, use your cabinet scraper as a
barrier.

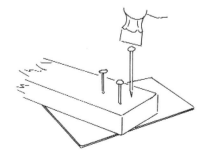

3. Hand Tools

Hand tools are essential even if you have many power tools. Not everything can be done with powered equipment. Acquire and master the basic hand tools. Some hand tools can be made. Edge tools must be kept sharp. Have adequate sharpening equipment and know how to use it.

164. Multi-File

When you need a quick rub with abrasive paper, it is useful to have some already mounted on a wood backing. This is a strip of wood with two grades of paper on each side to use for removing rough corners or edges, and correcting curves and similar small jobs. The 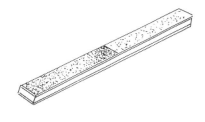 paper could be glued directly to the wood or to a cork backing, which will cushion the work and extend the life of the abrasive. Wood about 25mm wide and 300mm long would be suitable.

165. Flat Filing

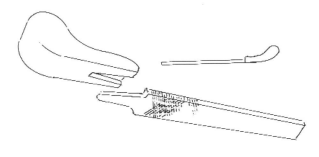

For most work done by a metalworker the usual round file handle is adequate. A woodworker often needs to reach metal, such as a screw end projecting through the wood a distance from an edge, but a round handle prevents holding the file flat on the surface. A one-sided handle can provide a grip for normal filing, as well as allowing the file to remain flat anywhere on a surface. A suitable shape is shown. Fix the file tang in the recess with epoxy adhesive.

166. Really Clean Files

Files and rasps only work well if they are clean, and when used on wood they soon clog. Wire brushing is not always successful, particularly after use on resinous wood. Soaking in washing-up water before it is thrown away will usually release clogging, so it can be brushed out. Dry with heat, if possible.

167. Hard Files

Files are made of hard steel, and have sharp teeth. If they come into contact with other cutting tools, the other tools will be the ones to suffer damage. Store files separately from other tools and each other, or hang them up.

168. Homemade Files

If abrasive paper has a good backing it will be effective for a long time. At one time cork hand sanding blocks could be bought. I have borrowed the idea by using cork floor tiles, which are about 5mm thick, glued to wood with abrasive paper glued to them.

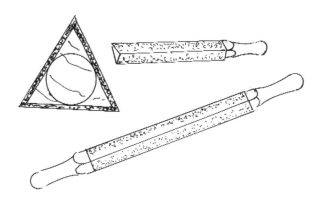

Flat-handled abrasive files, made in this way, are useful, but I make most use of those with turned handles and the abrasive part triangular.

A small file sharpens pencils and a longer file serves for general work, while a two-handled file, with coarse paper glued on, shapes wood quickly.

169. Saw To Knife

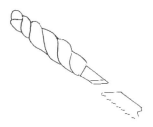

It seems a pity to throw-away a blunt hacksaw blade and waste this piece of good quality tool steel. Marking and other knives can be made from an old blade, but you cannot drill or cut it.

Grind across with the edge of a grinding wheel, preferably on both sides of the line you want, then snap it off, and grind the cutting edge and then grind the teeth off for a short distance above the cutting edge. Make a handle by binding with electrician's tape.

170. Flat Filing

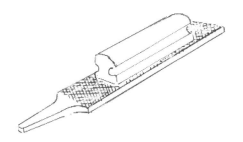

For most purposes a file is satisfactory to use with its handle, but if you need to file some distance from an edge, the handle prevents the tool being kept flat. A common woodworking use is removing the ends of projecting nails and screws. You can adapt an old file for this purpose by removing the normal handle and giving it one on top. The handle could be just a block of wood, but it is better to give it some shaping. Attach it to the file with epoxy adhesive.

171. Careful Planing

If you want to get a surface straight and flat, make sure the whole of the length of the plane is on the wood. This is important on edges (1). It also applies to surfaces, but if you have a knot or awkward piece of grain to make smooth and level, a slicing cut may be the answer (2).

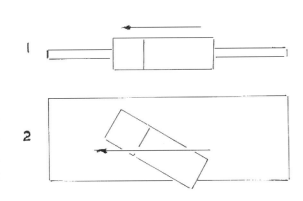

172. Good Planing

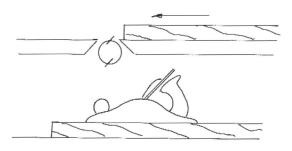

Wood is a natural product with many variations, including grain direction in a cut piece. It is rare for grain to be absolutely parallel to the surface in a board. You get a better surface if you plane with the grain instead of against it. That can be very obvious sometimes in hand planing, but power planing can have the effect of being comparable either way, until you examine it. It helps to imagine the plane cutter is stroking out sloping fibres when it is in the right direction.

173. Shuting

In the days when most woodwork was done by hand, most workshops had a shooting board (usually spelt 'shuting'). If you depend on hand tools or like to hand plane an edge after power planing it, a shuting board is an aid for getting square edges. The board to be planed is held against the stop and a plane used on its side to true it.

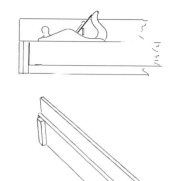

Make the top board thick enough to bring the centre of your plane at about the centre of the edge of an average board. The lower board extends enough to support the plane. The shuting board could be used flat on the bench against a stop, or you could put a block under it to grip in the vice.

174. Easier Planing

When hand planing some woods, especially resinous ones, particles of wood dust may build up on the blade between its edge and the cap iron. This interferes with the smooth flow of shavings, making it harder to push the plane. This problem can be reduced if you spray the blade and cap iron with WD40 or similar oil before assembling them after sharpening. Although this evaporates, it leaves a lubricated surface that resists wood dust sticking to it.

175. Hand Square

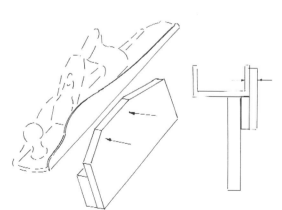

When you wish to join boards edge-to-edge, you may get the meeting edges straight and square on a planer, but the rotating cutter blades tend to pound the surface and leave it so it does not readily absorb glue thoroughly. You can put this right by hand planing with your longest plane, but it has to be held squarely.

To help you keep the edge square, you can add the guide shown. The plane sides are at 90° to the sole, so if this is held tight to a side with small cramps and allowed to bear on the board, the cut will be square. Make the bottom part thick enough to hold the wood away from the cutter edge.

176. Better Grip

A plane handle is good-looking and has a fitness-for-purpose feel, but if you have to lift and control a large plane, such as a jack or bigger, with one hand you may want a better grip. You can improve the grip by making the shallow hollows shown. Three should be enough and you can make them with a half-round or round file, then varnish over.

177. Safe Edging

It is usual to glue edging strips slightly wider than the wood, to allow adjustment, and then plane level after the glue has set. When doing this, care is needed to avoid planing the main

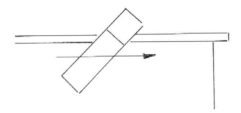

part, which if plywood, it is very easy to plane through the outer veneer. It helps to use a slicing cut with most of the sole of the plane on the work piece, as shown.

178. Planing end grain

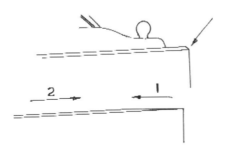

When planing across end grain, a common practice is to make a small chamfer at the far side of the cut. This prevents breakout, but has to be just right or in a place where the remains of a chamfer will not matter. Another way is to plane back at a slight angle, to the depth you want, from the far side (1), then finish the right way (2).

179. No Roll

Wood carvers use a large number of chisel-type tools, usually fairly narrow with the common barrel-shaped handles, which tend to roll. This tendency is reduced by making a flat on the underside of each handle, as shown.

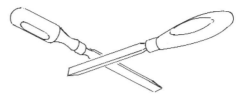

There is the same problem with ordinary narrow bench chisels. The blades of wide chisels usually stop them rolling. Plane a flat in line with the underside of the blade. Besides stopping rolling, the flat shows you which way up the chisel is when you pick it up, without having to look.

180. Chisel Sheath

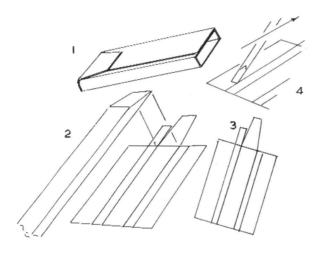

If you need to carry a chisel amongst other tools, you should protect its edge in some way. A cardboard sheath (1) is suitable and does not increase bulk.

Mark it out from the chisel (2). Allow a good overlap and it helps to include a flap (3) at the end to give a double thickness over the sharp end. To get sharp folds exactly where you want them, score along the lines with a screwdriver for slot-head screws (4), or something similar. Fold on the chisel and glue the overlaps. You can further strengthen the sheath and make it easier to see if you wrap it with coloured electrician's tape.

181. Square Paring

If you make an internal cut with straight or curved edges using a jigsaw the edges are unlikely to be square to the surface if the wood is very thick. You have to pare with a chisel or gouge. To make sure you are paring upright, it is helpful to have a thick guide block with a square edge cramped over the edge (arrowed).

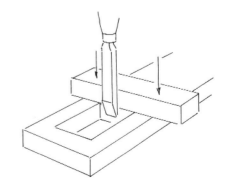

182. Really Bevel Edged

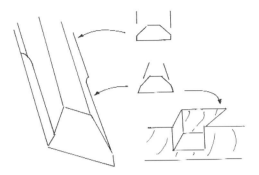

Most chisels are described as bevel-edged, but the bevels do not go to the edge, and have square edges a millimetre or so high. For most purposes this does not matter. These chisels should be useful for cleaning out the corners of dovetails, but the square edge stops the chisel going just where you want it.

You can alter the end of a chisel for dovetail work as shown. Grind the edges to less than a dovetail angle, far enough back to be more than the thickest wood you expect to use. This will not affect the chisel for other uses.

183. Umbrella Gouge

The ribs and frames of an umbrella are hardened steel. Most have a deep U-shaped section and spring to the shape of the umbrella when it is opened. An old umbrella rib can be cut to make small gouges for model work or carving.

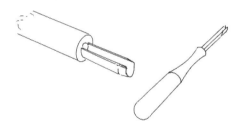

To cut off a piece, grind it partly through on the edge of a grinding wheel and snap it. For sharpening mount the piece in a handle and grind and hone a cutting edge. Remove the burr inside with a folded piece of abrasive paper. If there is any varnish or other finish inside, this should also be rubbed off.

184. Safe Hit

The correct technique may be to hit something wooden with a mallet and something metal with a hammer, but we tend to reach for a hammer, whatever we want to hit. This can damage the end of a wooden chisel handle. A good way to protect this is to drill it and drive in a large-headed nail.

185. Triangular Chisel

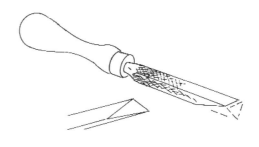

If a triangular file has come to the end of its life as a file, it can be converted to a chisel. Grind the file teeth off one side near the end. Grind across the other two faces to make a sharpening bevel. Smooth the flat surface by honing and sharpen in the usual way. Do not use the chisel with a hammer or mallet. A file is tempered much harder than the usual chisel, so it is more brittle and could break if hit.

186. Little Chisels

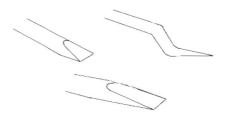

If you need a narrow chisel for model work or carving, you can make a temporary narrow tool from a masonry nail, which is hardened steel. It is not tempered as hard as a normal chisel, but it will take an edge that will stand up to brief use by grinding and honing. Cut off the head of a nail and drive the other end into a hole in a piece of dowel rod as a handle. Keep the grinding angle fairly short for strength in the cut when hammering. Have longer bevels for paring. A nail can be cranked for getting into a recess or background.

187. Blade to Blade

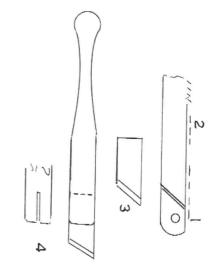

Most hacksaw blades are made of good quality high-speed steel, tempered for cutting. Rather than throw away a worn-out blade, you can convert a piece to a marking knife blade. The temper suits this,. but the steel is too brittle for a long knife blade.

Use the edge of a grinding wheel to make a groove across the blade (1), so that you can snap it off. Grind off the teeth a little further along than you expect to use (2). Sharpen the cutting edge while you still have the rest of the blade to hold (3). Grind to break the blade at the length you need. Turn a suitable handle, or you could just use a piece of dowel rod. Make a saw cut in it (4), and fix the blade in with epoxy adhesive.

188. Pencil Gauge (1)

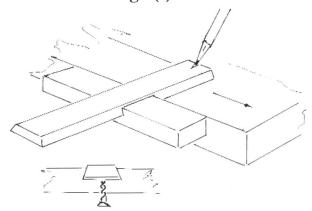

This gauge has less risk of wobbling than an ordinary marking gauge and will draw a pencil line parallel to an edge up to the length you make the blade. The blade should be parallel and bevelled on its edges. Make a notch for the pencil point. Cut a groove squarely across the

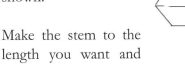

stock to match the blade and allow it to slide easily. Put a screw with a flattened point centrally under the groove, to lock the blade in position.

189. Pencil Gauge (2)

Putting a pencil through the opposite end of a marking gauge is a compromise for occasional use, but for frequent use it is better to have the pencil in a cutback in a broader stem, as shown.

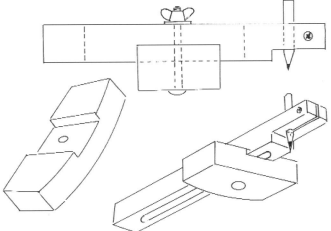

Make the stem to the length you want and cut it back so the pencil point does not project too far. The stock is shown with one side rounded. This is useful if you want to gauge against a curved edge. Make the slot so the bolt slides easily and long enough for the stock to move close to the pencil.

190. Rule Gauge

A steel rule is often used to measure from an edge by holding the measurement at the edge of the wood and marking across its end. This can be developed into a gauge, as shown. Cut a groove across a straight block, with its sides sloping so as to retain the rule fairly tightly.

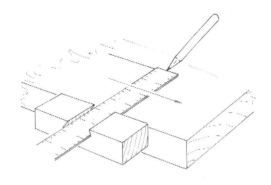

The rule can be pushed through and held in place by one hand while the other holds the pencil.

191. Closer Gauge

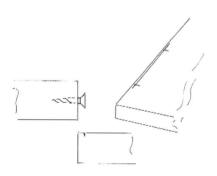

It is difficult to set a marking gauge for a line close to an edge, as when marking the thickness to be cut when fitting a hinge. An alternative is to use a screw in a block of wood.

Leave it projecting the amount needed to mark a line and let its head make a line on the wood. If it is a slot-head screw, have the end of the slot downwards so it will cut.

192. Mini Mortise Gauge

If you find you use similar width mortise and tenon joints frequently, setting a mortise gauge each time can be a nuisance and you may not always get it right. A shop made fixed mortise gauge is the answer.

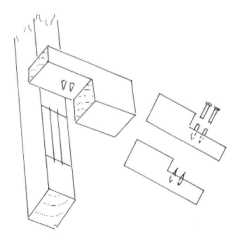

Notch a piece of wood large enough to grip and use with two hands when necessary. Make the permanent marking points from two nails, driven in, cut off and filed to points. If a trial gauging is not quite right, you can correct it by filing more off one side of a point.

193. Permanent Marking Gauge

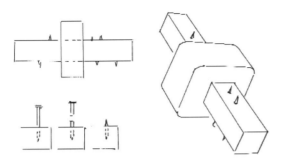

Most woodworkers set their marking or mortise gauge to the same size many times in the course of their work on various projects. Some of these standard settings could be included in a permanently set gauge, as shown. With a square stem, there could be up to eight sets of marking points. A suitable size would be close-grained hardwood about 15mm square, as long as needed, and a stock about three times this square.

Make the points with nails. The common 25mm wire nail should be suitable. Drive a nail, cut it off at a suitable height and file a point. Try each setting and file the sides to correct the point, if necessary. Mark the settings beside the points.

194. Multiple Marking

This marking gauge for eight settings uses two stems through a tall stock. Using close-grained hardwood, if possible, make the square holes close or touching. Drive in nails or panel pins as accurately as possible, but after you have cut them off and filed the points, you can try and correct them, if necessary, by filing more off one side.

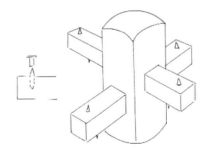

195. Height Marker

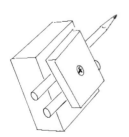

If you need to check or mark a height on legs or an uneven surface, there is no need for anything elaborate, unless you expect to have many uses for such a tool.

To improvise, have a block with a level bottom and cramp a pencil to it with a screwed piece and packing about the same thickness as the pencil. You can tilt the pencil over a large range to get the height you want.

196. Centre It

Many of us use wood of a standard thickness for many jobs, e.g. 20mm thick softwood from a builders' supplier. In many constructions we need to mark centre-lines.

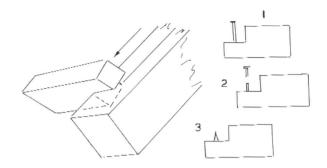

Instead of having to check and set a marking gauge, the fixed gauge shown can be used. Make the block long enough for comfortable handling. Drive in a nail, cut it off and file a point. You can make small corrections if you file more off one side than the other.

197. Recycled Needle

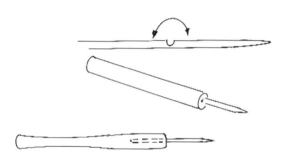

There are still discarded steel knitting needles about, made of good steel, tempered quite hard. They are too hard to saw, but a piece can be cut off by making a groove across on a grinding wheel, then snapping it.

A scriber or plain awl can be made by grinding an end to a point and mounting the piece in a handle, either just a tight fit in a hole or securing it in the hole with epoxy adhesive. Dowel rod might do, but a better tool is made by turning a handle. If you want a bradawl for starting screws or nails, grind the end to a chisel shape and make a pushing-type handle.

198. Marking Gauge Repair

If you break or lose the screw from a marking gauge, it is unlikely you will be able to get or make a replacement. One way of putting the gauge back into use is shown. Use a bolt

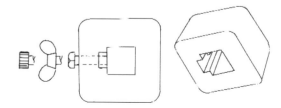

with a square nut. It could have a square or hexagonal head, but would be better with a knurled or wing head, for easier hand tightening.

Cut a groove through one side of the opening in the stock for the nut to slide in. If necessary, drill out the old screw hole. If the end of the bolt is rounded, file the end flat.

199. Pencil Multi-Gauge

Using a notched piece of wood with a pencil as a marking gauge can be extended, as shown, to provide notches for measurements frequently needed. The blade could be solid wood, but plywood is suitable. In the simplest form, there could be notches for the number of sizes you want to one side of a block forming the stock, but if you carry the blade across the stock you can have another set of notches on the other side. Four each way are shown. As a further step, if more sizes are needed, you can cross two blades, so one acts as the stock for the other.

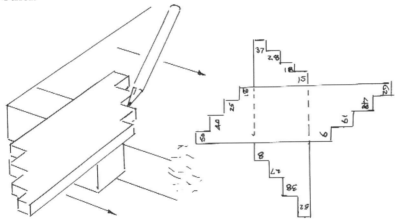

200. Mini Square

When you have to square across or around fairly narrow wood, even a small try square feels rather clumsy. For this work you can make a mini square, as shown. A suitable size could have a projection of 60mm and a width about 30mm. Bevel the edges of the blade. If you put a small chamfer on the edge of the block under the blade, it will be certain to fit closely.

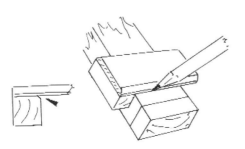

201. Finer Sawing

If you need to saw wood so the cut is fine and as smooth as possible, you can get metalworking hacksaw blades with finer teeth than the finest dovetail saw. Use one of these blades tightly tensioned in a normal hacksaw frame. It will cut wood as well as a woodworking saw.

202. Escape Grooves

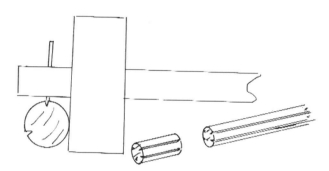

A dowel fits better if it is grooved to let air and excess glue escape when it is driven. An easy way to make grooves is with a marking gauge. You can cut them in a long length of dowel rod before cutting off the dowels you need.

203. Pencil Gauge

If you alter a marking gauge, or make a new one, for use with a pencil, just making a hole for the pencil results in too much projection. It is better to cut back the stem, so the pencil point is then at about the same level as a steel point would be. To lock the pencil, do not stop the cut at the hole. There will be more spring in the wood if you cut through it.

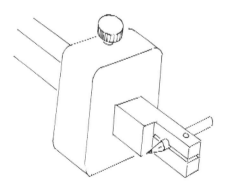

204. Saw Teeth Protection

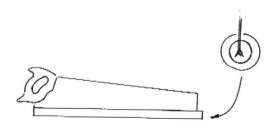

A good cover for saw teeth can be made from garden hose. Cut it longer than the saw edge and cut through it lengthwise. It will slide on and have enough spring to stay there.

205. Improved Hacksaw Handle

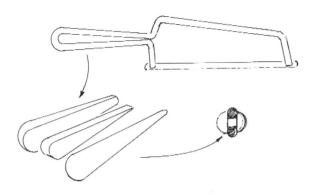

The common junior hacksaw is rather basic. The bent steel rod handle is uncomfortable and does not give good control. If can be improved by enlarging it with wood.

Make a piece the same thickness as the rod to fit inside the metal handle. Turn a piece with an outline almost to the size of the outline of the metal. Cut it down the middle and glue the pieces each side of the middle filler piece.

206. Protect Your Saw

Traditionally, saws of all types have had their teeth protected with a strip of wood with a saw cut. This is still a good idea, but there are some points to watch. Make the strip as close a fit to the handle as possible. If the blade is clear of the

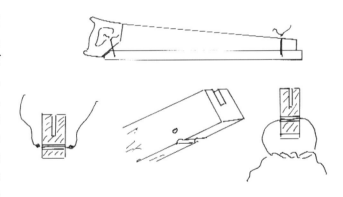

handle, extend the wood under it. At the other end, allow a little excess length.

Modern cordage is synthetic, slippery and liable to unravel. To stop an end coming apart, heat it briefly in a match flame and use moistened finger and thumb to roll it. To keep the cord in the hole, you can tie a knot each side, but it is better to have a groove below the hole and twist the cord several times round itself tightly in it, before taking the ends around the saw.

207. Finger Power

You have five fingers on each hand. What do you do with them when holding a saw? The old time craftsman, who did just about all sawing by hand, always kept his first finger pointing along the side of the handle. He claimed better control that way. Try it. It could also apply to holding an electric drill.

208. Stationery Protection

The cost of re-sharpening and setting a saw is considerable, so keeping a saw in condition for as long as possible is advisable. Tenon and dovetail saws are traditionally protected with a slotted piece of wood, but there is a neater way using something available from stationery suppliers.

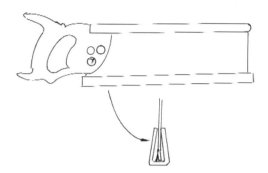

These are coloured plastic spring strips intended to hold sheets of paper together. The standard size is over 300mm long to suit A4 size paper, which is about right for the common 300mm (12 inch) tenon saw. A strip will slide on the saw over the teeth. It can be cut to suit shorter saws and a bright colour helps you find it amongst all that accumulates on a bench.

209. No Break Out

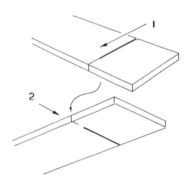

When hand sawing across a board, particularly softwood, there is a tendency for the final strokes to cause splintering along the edge as the saw breaks through. This can be avoided if you make the last cuts the other way. To do this accurately, square over a pencil mark a short distance on the second side. You can then cut most of the way on the first side (1) and cut back from the second side (2), knowing it will be accurate.

210. Cleaner Sawing

When sawing wood, some raggedness on the far side cannot be avoided. This is inevitable and is more pronounced with some softwoods and plywoods. Finer saw teeth cause less raggedness, but may not cut as quickly as you wish. Smoother sawing results from having as many teeth in action as possible.

This can be achieved on thicker wood without worrying too much about the angle of cut. On thinner wood, particularly plywood, you get a smoother edge and less raggedness if you use the saw at a flatter angle, in order to get more teeth in contact with the wood.

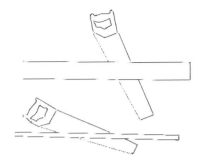

211 Sprayed Saws

If a hand saw sticks in use, particularly in resinous wood, it can be eased by spraying on wax furniture polish. This can be used as a clean lubricant on saw benches and similar surfaces.

212. Close Sawing

A hacksaw blade should be tensioned in a frame whenever possible, but there are places where the bulk of the frame will not go, as when working in a confined space or cutting the ends of nails or screws level with a surface.

You can make a temporary saw for this purpose by wrapping insulating tape around a blade in a thick enough lump to make a handle. Arrange for the cut to be on the pull stroke. The blade need not be full-length, so you could use a broken piece that still has life in it.

213. Handy Saw Jig

You will make most internal cuts with a jigsaw, but there is sometimes a need to finish off a corner or other part, where a hand saw would be helpful. At one time you could buy a keyhole saw for this work, but you can make a modern alternative by mounting a jigsaw blade in a handle.

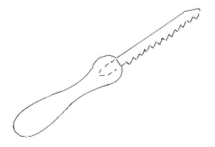

You could use a bought file handle, turn one or just use a piece of dowel rod. Secure the blade in the hole with epoxy adhesive. Like the power jig saw or a keyhole saw, it cuts on the pull stroke.

214. Holding Help

It is difficult to hold small nails and panel pins without risking hitting your fingers. Screwdrivers for slot-head screws are needed less today and a spare small magnetic one can be adapted for holding steel nails and pins, as shown. A small V in the end is all that is needed.

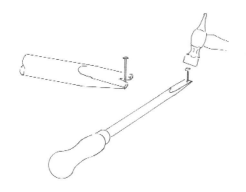

215. Smaller Nailing

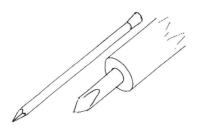

Small nails and panel pins are difficult to hold and press into the wood ready for hammering. Points are round or square and often not sharp. It would be helpful to drill shallow holes to suit, but most ordinary drills are not fine enough. You can make a suitable drill for starting nails with a nail.

Flatten the end of a nail by hammering it on an iron block or a vice jaw. File to a width where it has spread and file a point centrally. The angle is not critical. Cut off the head. This could be used in a hand or power drill, but mounting it in a piece of dowel rod for use as a bradawl may be all you need to steady a nail ready to be hit.

216. Tiny Nails

It is difficult to hold small nails and panel pins to press into the wood ready for hitting. A prepared hollow or shallow hole would help. You are unlikely to have an ordinary drill bit small enough, but fretwork drill bits, intended for making holes to thread fretsaw blades through, are small enough. For fretwork they are used in an Archimedean drill, but they can be used in a hand or power drill.

217. Nail Holding

A plastic hair comb is useful when driving short or fine nails. Instead of risking hitting your fingers, a nail can be held temporarily between two comb teeth. Most combs give you a choice of size.

218. Handled Punch

Cheaper hand screwdrivers for crosshead screws soon get worn and do not turn screws successfully. They are very securely bonded to plastic handles and trying to remove a handle to release the steel for other purposes is frustrating. One use you can make of the whole thing is to convert it to a nail punch, more comfortable to use than the usual small steel type. Grind off the end. Grind it tapered all round to the size you want and grind the end flat. Quench frequently to avoid overheating and drawing the temper.

219. Where are the Bradawls?

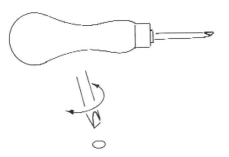

Before the days of electric drills every craftsman had several bradawls of different sizes. A bradawl is still useful. With its crosswise sharp end started across the grain and a few quarter rotations each way, it will make a hole. Unlike a drill, there is no wood removed, so a screw should get a tighter grip. Smaller screws can be driven all the way. Larger screws can be put in the shallow hole and given a tap with a hammer, before power driving. Use a bradawl to mark the location of all screws to be driven.

220. Safer Grip

Your hold on a wooden-handled hammer may become slippery in use. It will be easier to hold firmly if you cut finger grooves on the lower side.

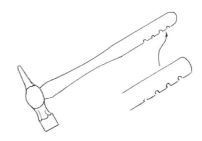

221. Claw Grip

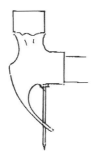

If you have to work one-handed, as when holding on to a ladder, and need to drive a nail, you can hold a nail with a claw hammer, as shown. You can make the first blow as it is, then release the nail and drive it the rest of the way with the normal hammer face.

222. Pin Hold

An alternative to hitting your fingers when driving panel pins is to adapt an ordinary wooden clothes peg. It will also pick up individual nails, pins and screws.

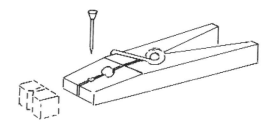

Cut off the extreme notched end. Drill through near the cut end with a drill as small as the smallest pin. You could use the whole thickness of the peg with most pins, but tapering, as shown, gives you more hammering space.

223. Lever Wedge

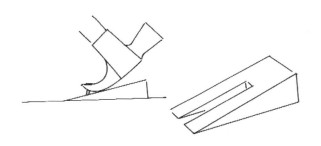

If you use a claw hammer to withdraw a nail, there is a limit to how much you can pull out before the end of the hammerhead goes flat on the bench. If it is a long nail, you can get more leverage by using the slotted wedge shown.

224. Safe Fingers

You can avoid hitting your fingers when driving panel pins and short nails using thin cardboard, possibly from a cereal packet, which is the right thickness. Cut a few strips and make acute slots in the ends. You can use an end to hold pins many times, before having to cut off the end and make a new slot.

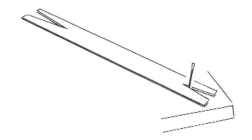

225. Cord Hammer Grip

Wrapped cord makes a good non-slip gripping surface on the handle of a hammer. A method of holding the cord tight without knots is similar to the traditional way of whipping a rope with fine line.

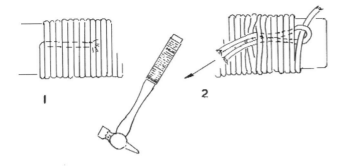

At one end of the grip, lay the end of the cord along the handle and start binding tightly over it (1). Continue until you are approaching the other end of the grip. Lay in a short loop of cord and bind over this.

Cut off the cord so there is just a short piece to tuck under the last turns. Put this through the loop and pull the protruding ends (2), until the working end is released inside and you can pull out the loop.

226. Little Fastenings

Small screws and panel pins are difficult to hold while driving. One of the simplest ways of holding is to push the screw or pin through a strip of paper, then tear the paper away when it has been partly driven. One strip of paper can be used several times.

227. Dual Centre Square

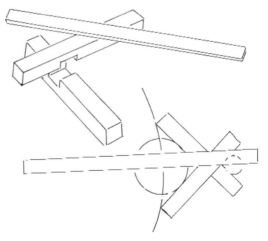

This centre square will deal with small round objects within its capacity. Round objects can fit between the crossed pieces forming the stock or a large curved edge can rest against the points on the large side.

Accuracy in construction is important. Use wood to suit your needs. Make the crossed pieces exactly square at the halving joint. The legs each way could be cut to length after the joint has been assembled. Make sure the edge of the blade exactly bisects the angle both ways.

228. True Scraper

To refurbish a scraper edge after frequent use, it has to be worked exactly square again, before turning over new cutting edges.

If you file the edge by hand, it may not be truly square or straight. It is safer to use a filing jig, as shown. Knock off the file handle. Rout a groove in a straight piece of wood, into which the file fits easily. Drill for two widely spaced screws. Drive them to cut threads, then withdraw them and file their ends flat for a good bearing on the file.

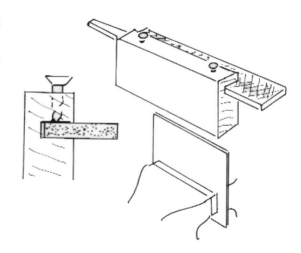

229. Chisel Scrape

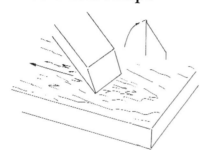

If you have a piece of wood with an awkward bit of grain, which would benefit from work with a cabinet scraper, but you do not have one, try using a wide chisel instead. Make a sharp edge, then turn it over like a scraper. You can do this with the body or another chisel or gouge, drawn across with plenty of pressure. It will work as well as a proper scraper, but it will need sharpening for its normal use afterwards.

230. Square Scraper Edge

When a cabinet scraper is sharpened and its edge is to be turned over to cut (ticketing), this should start truly square. This can be done by rubbing on an oil or waterstone, but it is unwise to trust hand-holding. One way of holding squareness is to grip the scraper against a piece of

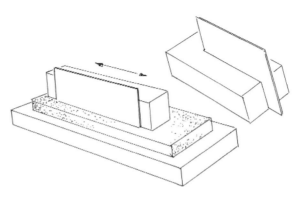

wood as it is rubbed, but this depends on your grip. A better way is to make a saw cut in the wood block and push the scraper into that.

231. Scrape with Glass

When glass is cut, the edge is sharp and can be used like a cabinet scraper to finish the surface of wood. Holding the glass directly in your hands is risky. Exposed edges might cut your hands or the glass might break.

Make a holder, as shown, with two piece of plywood separated with the packing the same thickness as the glass. Allow a good overlap. With thin plywood, finger pressure lets you squeeze and hold the glass.

232. Scraping Comfort

The edges of a cabinet scraper are sharp, even on the parts not prepared for scraping, so they can be rough on your hands when you spring the steel to the slight curve needed for scraping. You can spring the scraper to a good shape and have a more comfortable grip if you use a pair of handles, as shown. They are blocks with slots to fit over the ends of the scraper and well rounded for comfort. For most scrapers a saw slot is adequate.

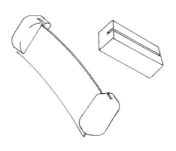

233. Scraper Curve

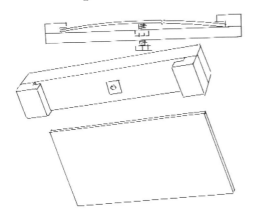

A cabinet scraper has to be held at a slight curve, often by hand. If you do much scraping, it can be a strain maintaining the curve correctly. This holder holds the blade to the curve and gives more than thin steel to hold.

Using hardwood, make the handle about half the depth of the scraper. Cut the notched pieces to an easy fit on the scraper and join them securely to the main part. In the middle and below the centre, drill for a small bolt and nut. Hold it there with epoxy adhesive. Round the outside corners to provide a comfortable grip.

234. Sharper Scraper

Traditionally a cabinet scraper is sharpened square across, so a scraping burr can be made on both sides. There is something to be said for a more acute angle, although this only allows one side to be used. A few degrees less than 90°, say about 75° could be used.

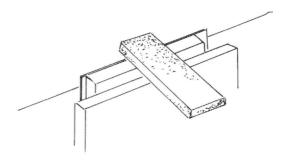

If you wish to do this, plane the edge of a guide piece of wood, which can be used when cramping the scraper in the vice for filing and honing. If you wish to round its corners, the wood should be a little shorter than the width of the scraper. File the angle, then hone it and the face surface. Put it back in the vice and turn over the cutting edge with a hard steel burnisher, or if you do not have one the back of a chisel or gouge.

235. Safe Scraper

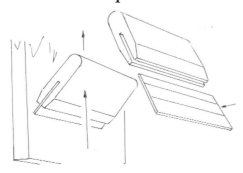

Window glass makes a good wood scraper. To avoid the risk of cutting your hand the glass can be put in a slot in a piece of wood. To avoid it moving put masking tape (arrowed) on one or both sides of the glass, to give a grip in the slot.

236. All-in-one Dovetails

This dovetail gauge will mark 1 in 6 dovetails for softwood and 1 in 8 dovetails for hardwood as well, as squaring down over the edges. It is long enough to not wobble in use and it can be turned over for use either way.

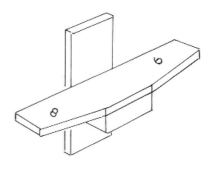

The block forming the stock could be 25mm thick and 50mm square and the blades could be 6mm thick and extend 50mm either way.

237. Smaller Mitres

Nearly all marking out involves 90° and less often 45°. Ordinary try and mitre

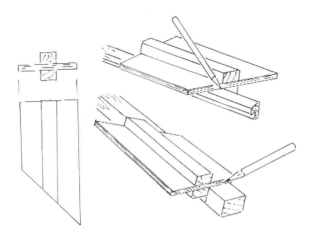

squares are large enough to accommodate many sizes of job and can be rather clumsy to use on small jobs. A simple double-ended tool, as shown, is easier to use when the work is small or narrow.

A suitable tool is made from thin plywood about 125mm wide and 250mm long, with 20mm square strips each side.

238. Little Angles

The standard adjustable bevel is made to suit most sizes of job, but could be too big and clumsy for small work because of the length of the blade. For these situations and many others, such as marking on edges, the tool shown is more useful. It could be single-ended, but having two blades allows two settings at the same time.

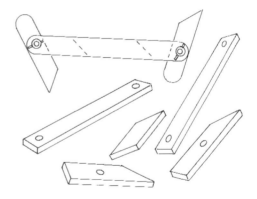

You can make it to suit your needs, but using 6mm wood with the stock 30mm wide and 220mm long is a good general-purpose size. The rounded ends of the blade provide a grip when setting. The pivots can be 6mm screws with washers and wing or knurled nuts.

239. Big Bevel

Very big adjustable bevels are not normally available, yet large angular shapes often have to be marked out and tested. Boat builders usually made for themselves quite large bevels. For most of us, a tool that will reach 400mm or so will be adequate.

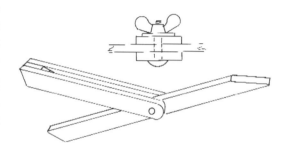

Using straight-grained hardwood, 40mm by 7mm section could be used for all parts, although the sides of the stock could be thinner than the blade. Make the packing very slightly thicker than the blade, for ease of action. The square neck of a coach bolt will hold it in the wood. Lock the tool with a wing nut over a large washer.

240. Improved Square

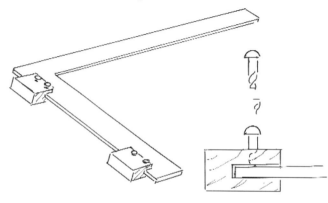

A large flat square gives you a right-angle much larger than a try square. This is useful for marking out sheet material and testing large assemblies, but you have to locate two edges every time. It would be improved for many jobs if it could be held against an edge like a try square. The guide blocks shown allow you to do this.

Rout a groove in a piece of wood long enough to make two blocks. It should be wide enough for the square edge to slide in easily and fairly deep. Drive in two screws to cut threads, then withdraw them. Cut off the points and file them level, so they have a good bearing on the square.

241 Steady Stock

When using a try square to mark across a board, the stock may drop, so the square tilts. To stop this, drill a hole centrally in the stock, as shown, into which you can push a panel pin, and withdraw it when the square is needed for other purposes.

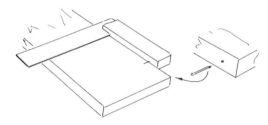

242. Hook Driver

Screw hooks, whether straight or curved, are not always easy to drive, particularly the final turn. If you use pliers, they may mark the hook and could be awkward. This driver is simple to make. Cut a slot that will clear most hooks you expect to use. Drive a nail through close to one side, to stop a hook slipping through. A piece of dowel rod at the other end gives you leverage when turning.

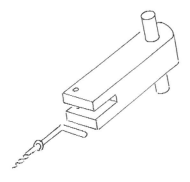

243. Improved Squaring

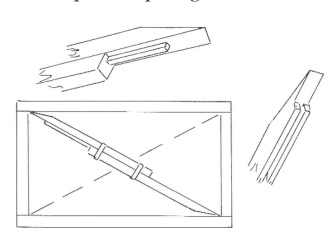

The common way of checking the squareness of a frame is to use overlapping strips to compare diagonal measurements, but two loose splines or battens are difficult to handle and hold together. The pair of battens shown have matching tongues and grooves, so they do not slip away from each other and they can be held together with rubber bands or cramps.

Make the tongue and groove a sliding fit. Taper the battens at the ends and cut back the joints to give plenty of clearance there.

244. Big Curves

An improvised compass for large circles may be made with a piece of scrap wood with a nail through it and a pencil against the end. If you are likely to need to use this frequently, it is worthwhile making a large compass that will be more efficient. This has the pencil through a hole locked by a screw and the pivot piece slides along a slot and takes an awl to act as centre.

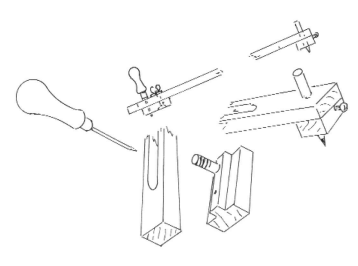

The beam should be as long as you expect to need, with a groove along most of its length. At one end thicken it with a block below and drill through for a pencil, which can be locked with a wood screw. Make the adjustable block long enough not to wobble in the slot and drill it for the awl and a screw of the coach bolt type, projecting far enough to lock in any position with a wing nut and large washer. The awl should push fit into it's hole.

245. More Hand Power

Large screws can be very hard to turn when driving or extracting, particularly in hardwood. If you have to do this by hand, it is usually possible to provide extra torque with your other hand. Most large screwdrivers have a flat section somewhere in their length and this can be used to slide on a temporary second handle, as shown. Use hardwood. The slot can be a loose fit. If you want a better-looking handle, it could be turned.

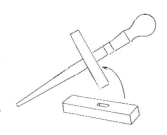

246. Secure V-block

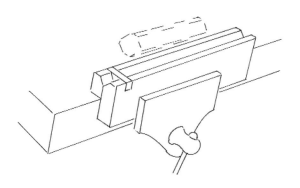

If you regularly use a V-block to hold wood while gripping it in the vice, there is an advantage in making the V-block with one side deeper to go in the vice while the other side rests on the bench. The bench top takes the pressure and the block will not tilt in the vice if that is not tight enough.

247. Quicker Pockets

The traditional way of making pockets, when screwing upwards to secure a table top to its rails, involved careful work with chisel and gouge, which was slow and tedious. It is simpler and just as satisfactory to use a 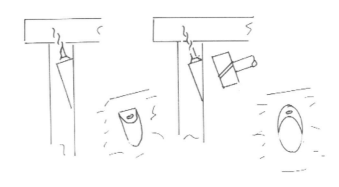 Forstner bit at an angle. As there is no point, you can drill as deep as necessary without risk of breaking through the outside.

248. Close-fit Pincers

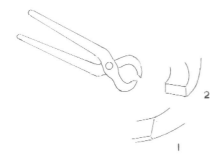

Many pairs of pincers are supplied with rounded ends or a slight bevel the wrong way at the tip (1). This stops you getting close under the head of a stubborn nail. The ends of the jaws should have the inside slope taken to the outside edge (2). You can improve a pair of pincers by using a file or abrasive slip to correct this. Keep the same inner angle. Do not sharpen to a cutting edge.

249. Pincer Grip

Most pincers do not have comfortable handles. They can be improved by pushing on pieces of rubber tubing. Most tubing is soft enough to push on, but can be softened in hot water.

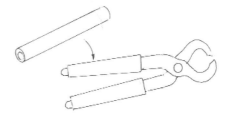

250. Brace

The place of the traditional carpenter's brace has been mostly taken by the electric drill, but a brace, preferably ratchet, is still worth having. Power countersinking often goes too far. A rose bit in a brace gives you more control. Power screw driving is fine for smaller screws, but a socket head often does not stand up to driving a large screw in hardwood. A screwdriver bit in a brace can get a large slot-head screw much tighter without trouble. There is nothing like a brace for getting screws out of old work.

251. Hold a Chalk Line

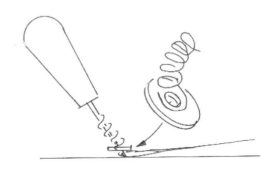

When setting out with a chalk line, both ends have to be held down close to the floor. If you are single-handed, you will need to hold the looped end with an awl. The line tends to ride up the awl, so the line does not strike a clear line on the floor. This problem can be solved by using a loosely fitting washer, and a small compression coil spring. Solder one end of the spring to the washer and the other end to the awl in a position where the washer is just above the point of the awl when it is not compressed. When the awl is pushed into the floor the washer will hold the chalk line down.

252. Rust Away

Steel wire wool will remove surface rust from tools and leave the tool clean, but there can be tiny particles from the wire wool left behind, which may encourage more rust; wipe a cleaned surface with an oily cloth.

253. Cam Pressure

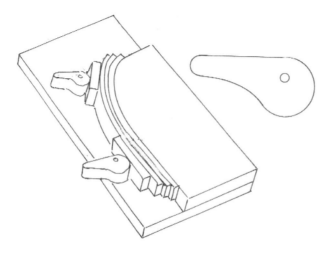

Cams can apply pressure over a limited range. Each cam has a circular end and an extending piece to act as a lever. An offset screw hole acts as a pivot. The amount of movement depends on how much this is offset, but the greater the pressure the smaller the offset.

254. Drawknife Safety

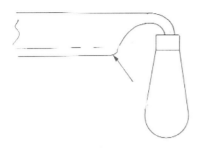

A drawknife is a useful tool for quickly removing wood, but its long sharp blade can be hazardous. The corners of the blade are not far from your hands, and could slip on to them. You can reduce this danger by grinding the corners round. The extreme ends of the cutting edge are not used for cutting, so this does not affect the tool.

255. Make a Marking Knife

If a table knife comes to the end of its life as a piece of cutlery, you can take advantage of its good steel and knife temper and make a marking knife that will work as well as anything you can buy. The blade is too hard to cut with a tool. Make a groove across it in the position you want the new edge (A) with the edge of a grinding wheel and snap it off. Grind away the original cutting edge

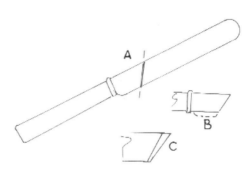

in line with the handle (B). Sharpen the end on both sides. This will taper a little, as the back of the table knife is thicker (C) giving strength to the new cutting edge where it is needed.

If the plastic handle is damaged, break it off the steel tang and make a wooden handle, with the tang held in the hole with epoxy adhesive.

256. Safer Cutting

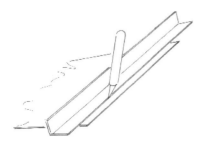

Cutting along the edge of a steel rule may be satisfactory, but there is always the risk of the knife slipping and cutting the holding hand. A better idea, especially when making several heavy deep cuts, is a length of angled metal, preferably aluminium. You can cut against the flat part, and hold the upright part.

257. Veneer Cuts

When cutting through wood that has been veneered, it is important that the veneer should not be broken or chipped. It is advisable to make a deep knife cut before using a fine-toothed saw. A steel straight-edge should be held firmly with a strip of wood (cramped where possible). Draw the knife along several times, to penetrate deeply (1). Without moving the straight edge, scrape along with the point of the knife (2) to make a slight hollow on the waste side of the line.

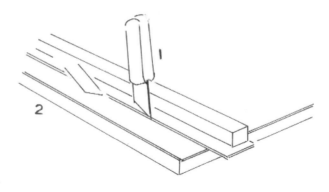

258. Masonry Help

Masonry nails are made of hardened steel. This may not be tool quality, but there are possibilities for improvisation. A nail in a handle or piece of dowel rod can be ground to a point for use as an awl. The end could be ground to a sharp crossed end for use as a bradawl for starting screws. If you need a narrow chisel, a nail in a handle can have it's end ground and honed to a chisel for temporary use. In all grinding, cool frequently to avoid drawing the temper.

259. Fine Spread

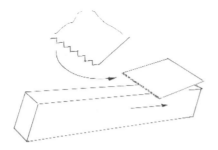

Serrated edge spreaders will produce an even layer of glue on an edge or a large area. Pinking shears with serrated edges, which are designed to cut out fabric, can be used to cut pieces of postcard to make good disposable glue spreaders.

260. Carving Vice

A carver's screw mounting is essential for some work, but expensive if you rarely need it. This improvisation will do the same job. The vital part is a screw bolt, with a wood screw at one end and a metal thread at the other.

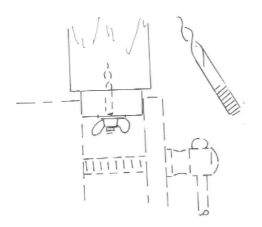

To use it, jam two nuts together on the metal thread, and using the nuts and a spanner, drive the wood screw end into a hole in the wood to be carved. Release the nuts and put the bolt end through a block of wood, to take a washer and wing nut, and fit into your vice.

261. Handy Punch

You can always have a nail punch available if you stow one in the handle of a hammer. Drill far enough into the handle to take the punch loosely, then enlarge the hole far enough to take a bottle cork.

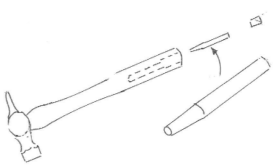

262 Wedge Angles

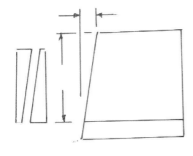

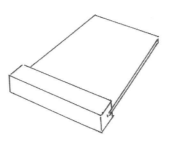

When you need wedges, you usually want several all at the same slope. This shop made square can be used on a cross grain strip of wood to mark a set of wedges of uniform angles. One side is square, while the other side is at the chosen angle. For many purposes this could be 1 in 6.

Cut a piece of thin plywood to shape, large enough to deal with any wedges you expect to need. Glue this into a groove in a strip of wood or, if you do not have facilities for cutting a suitable groove, put strips each side of the plywood. Check squareness and the wedge angle, and plane true if necessary.

263. Pick-up Grip

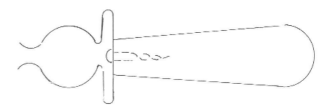

A spring tool clip has enough grip to hold many things and can even hold thin glued parts together. If one is fixed to a handle, it will hold small parts while you work on them. It will pick up many things and will surprise you with its uses, once you have made it.

264. Release The Bits

A horseshoe magnet is useful for picking up nails, filings and any steel scrap from the floor or bench, but you then have the problem of releasing them from the magnet, which is easy with large items, but a nuisance with anything like filings.

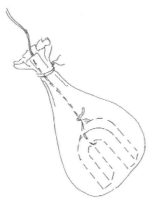

The arrangement shown will help. The magnet is on a string inside a clear plastic bag. It picks up just as well through the plastic. You can take off anything large, then hold the bag over the waste bin and pull the plastic away from the magnet, so all that you do not want will fall off.

265. Extended Level

A short spirit level used to check a long surface, may not give a correct reading as it could be affected by an uneven surface. Putting the level on a straight batten is better, but errors might still creep in.

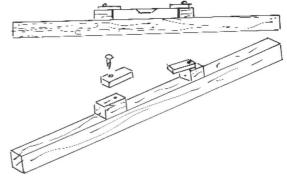

For better results the level should be held down on the batten with turn buttons, as shown. This scheme also holds the two together when checking a vertical surface.

4. Workshop Techniques

Most of what we do in a workshop may be considered technique, but this section contains tips on techniques that do not fit into other sections, including many of a general type. We are dealing with wood, tools, adhesives and fastenings, as well as other materials and there are often ways of working that can improve results.

266. System

When preparing and sorting wood for a project, in a particular section, pick the long parts first. You cannot make up long pieces from the off cuts by cutting short pieces first. If there is difference in grain patterns, knots or blemishes, you may be able to include them in less-prominent parts and keep the better material for where it shows. You may have off cuts from the narrower strips that can be glued for wider parts. With careful planning there should not be much waste wood.

267. Chalk Sort

If you are sorting sawn wood and wish to mark its size or purpose, blackboard chalk marks are easy to see on the rough surface and easy to remove later.

268. Warpless

Wood warps when it loses moisture from one side more than the other. If wood has warped to a curve, moisten the hollow side and leave it for a few hours. If it dries, add more water. If it is part of an assembly, build it in as soon as possible, to prevent it warping again.

269. Seasoned Logs

If you have wood from a recently felled fruit or other tree, that seems suitable for turning a bowl or other object, it is unwise to just leave a section of log to season and let the sap dry out, as cracks are likely to develop. It is better to roughly turn it oversize and leave it for a few months, before doing the final turning. This releases some internal stress during drying and cracking is less likely, as there is less thickness to season.

270. Figuring

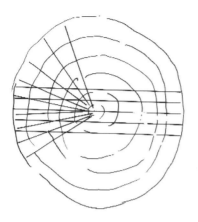

The grain markings on all woods are made by the annual rings formed as the tree grows. There are other lines, called medullary rays, which radiate from the centre of the tree fairly straight to the outside, crossing the grain lines. In nearly all woods used for furniture and constructional work they are invisible to the naked eye. Oak is an exception; figured oak shows the medullary rays. Not every oak board has these markings. As can be seen, it is only boards cut across near the middle of the tree that will have the rays nearly flat on the surface. Those cut further out may show only slight marking or have no rays visible. The most prized oak may have had as many boards as possible cut radially, usually by cutting the log into quarters first. This is wasteful and if you specify figured oak, expect it to be expensive.

271. How Long?

Spare wood is often stacked against the wall. When selecting a piece for a job, the first thing you need to know is if it is long enough. If you mark heights from the floor on the wall, you can quickly judge the approximate length of a piece of wood.

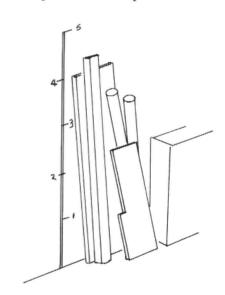

272. Re-cycle

Good wood is becoming increasingly expensive and it seems wasteful to throw away off cuts. With most modern glues claiming to be stronger than the wood, it is reasonable to glue pieces to make up useable sizes. If they are unsuitable for important face parts, they can be used for interiors. An example is a drawer side. Any number of narrow pieces can be glued to make up a width. Squares can be built up for turning. The action of turning helps to obscure a joint. Length can be made with a diagonal splice. This has long been used in boat building, where a slope of 1 in 7 is considered satisfactory.

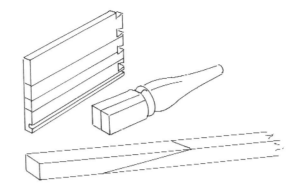

273. Hold Up Sheets

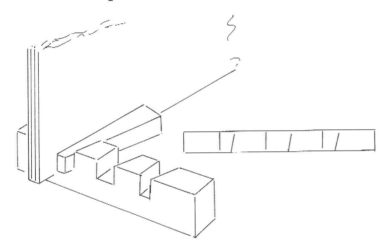

If you need to hold plywood or other sheet material on edge, a pair of wedged feet will steady it. Use wedges with a slope about 1 in 6. Cut notches of differing thickness. Allow for the wedges to project on both sides, so you can hit them in or out.

274. Sheet Carrying

The standard size of 2440mm x 1220mm (8ft by 4ft) for sheet material is supposed to be the largest size that a man can conveniently

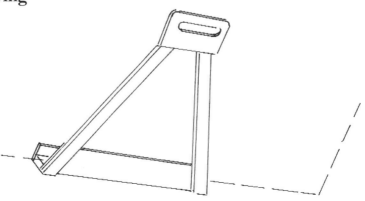

carry. However, this involves spreading the arms across the width, which can be awkward to carry over any distance, especially in a wind.

This carrier allows one or more sheets to be carried under an arm. Experiment with your arm length, but for most men the handgrip should be at, or a little above, the centre of the sheet. Make the trough long enough to withstand wobble – probably 600mm (2ft). It can be much wider than the thickness of a single sheet. Have the arms outside the plywood side of the trough and the handgrip outside them, in order to keep your knuckles clear of the sheet.

275. Big Carrying

Large pieces of sheet material, such as 2440mm x 1220mm (8ft by 4ft) sheets of plywood, are difficult to carry unaided, especially in a wind. This sling shown allows you to lift a sheet under your arm and clear of the ground. An adjustment allows for different sizes of sheet and reach.

Use rope thick enough to be comfortable in your hand. Tie a loop in one end that will fit over the corner of a sheet, as shown. Use a short piece of the rope to make a matching loop for the opposite corner. Adjust the length of the other piece so it can double through it and back to a slider. Make the slider with three holes that will easily pass the rope and cut out the middle hole to make a notch. Thread the rope through (1) so you can adjust it to allow the middle of the rope to be grasped. Lock at this position by taking the rope through the notch and behind the knot (2).

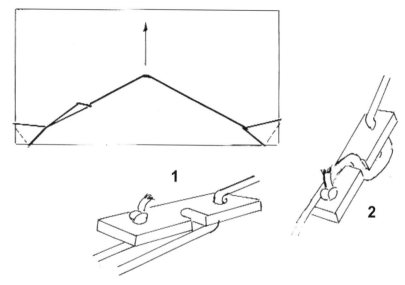

276. Hairline Cracks

If you have to deal with a hairline crack along the grain, you probably cannot press stopping into it. Instead, try glue and dust. Wipe glue over and into the crack. Let the glue start to set, then sand the wood, across the grain at first, then along it. The dust from sanding will mix with the glue. The mixture should dry to almost the same appearance as the surrounding wood.

277. Glue Mix

Some resin glues have to be mixed before use and this must not be done in a metal container. Aerosol, and similar plastic tops make suitable containers for mixing small quantities of glue. Surplus Cascamite glue hardens in a plastic container, but does not stick to it and can be pulled out, leaving the container ready for further use.

278. Biscuit Glue

When making a biscuit joint it is advisable to get enough glue into the holes, rather than put it thickly on the biscuits. It will give a better spread where it is needed.

279. Gluing Splits

Most wood glues will not flow into narrow openings and a split that cannot be sprung open can be a problem if you want to fill it with glue. This method will get glue into most of the depth, if not all the way. Put some glue on the split (1). Cover it with masking tape (2) loosely, but stuck down at the edges. Use your fingers on the top of the tape to knead the glue into the crack (3), increasing pressure progressively. Remove the tape before the glue hardens, let the glue harden, then level the surface (4).

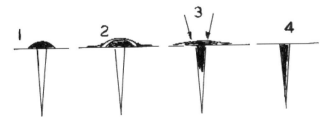

280. Use It All

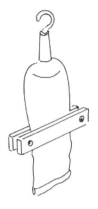

Tubes of glue and other substances used in the workshop and home may be metal or plastic. Most metal tubes can be rolled from the bottom as the contents are used, but plastic tubes resist this and it is difficult to use up everything.

Two pieces of wood with their ends screwed together can be used progressively to work the remaining contents upwards. A screw hook makes a good stopper and can be used for hanging.

281. Seal It

Flexible tubes or plastic containers of adhesives and other semi-liquids tend to get messy and the contents may gel around the opening. A screw or nail in the hole will seal it and stop gelling and can be used to clear the end, if necessary. A screw eye in a flexible tube can hang on a nail. A galvanised clout nail, with its large head, gives you something to grip while galvanising minimises rusting, due to the corrosive effect of some glues.

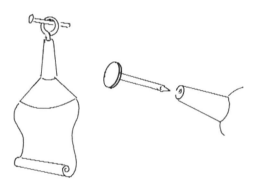

282. Last Drop

When glue is getting low in a container, it can be tedious and slow getting it out. If the container is stored inverted, the glue will be ready where you want it. Most containers have a screw cap. Drill a hole that will easily fit the cap. Make sure the nozzle is sealed, and you have what is left of the glue ready for use.

283. No Slide

If two parts are to be glued together over a large area, it is difficult to control the tendency to slide as they are brought together. One way of reducing this is to sprinkle a small amount of coarse sand on the glue before bringing the parts together. They are more likely to stay as you put them.

284. Keeping Glue

You may not use Superglue very often and may find it has gone off when you want to use it again. Its life can be lengthened by keeping the tube in the refrigerator.

285. Delayed Cleaning

It is often advised to wipe off surplus glue with a damp rag, but that does not work with all glues. In any case, it spreads dilute glue in the pores, which affects staining. With most glue, it is better to leave all that squeezes out of a joint untouched for a short time. When it becomes semi-hard, it can be removed with a chisel, without affecting surrounding wood.

286. Sawdust Economy

Work sawdust into a small amount of glue until it will not take any more. Use this to plug cracks or flaws in wood, or into mistakenly drilled holes, even screw holes drilled too large. When dry, you can work this stopping like wood. If you use sawdust from the same wood, it will sand to match.

287. Put Glue Right In

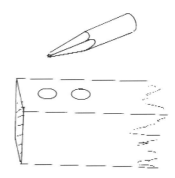

It is often difficult to get enough glue into the smaller dowel holes, but this is important for strong joints. Whittling the end of a piece of dowel rod makes a probe to do this job, uneven whittling is better than a round end made with a pencil sharpener.

288. Easier Screwing

Screws enter wood easier if they are lubricated. This is particularly so if you are hand driving and the screw is large. One of several ways of lubricating that will not stain the wood is to use candle wax.

One way of using this is to melt a candle into a small container and let it set. Dipping the first few screw threads into this should provide enough lubrication.

289. Safe Screws

The old idea of preventing a slotted-head screw being undone by filing away the sides of the groove is still a good one., if you are using slotted-head screws for securing bolts, staples or locks to a shed or workshop, but how do you treat socket-head screws? The answer is to use a hammer and centre punch to knock down the parts of the socket the driver engages.

290. Magnetic

When doing an awkward job with many small nails or screws, you can keep a few within reach if you tape one or more small magnets to your wrist to hold them.

291. Shortening a Bolt

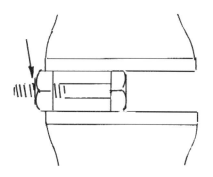

If you wish to cut the end off a bolt, there is a risk of damaging the thread and not being able to start a nut on it. You can reduce this risk if you cut as shown. Put a nut on the bolt, exposing the amount to be cut off. Grip the nut and the bolt head in a vice, and cut and file the end. Unscrew the nut and that should true any damaged thread.

292. Protect Threads

If you cannot avoid having to grip the threaded part of a bolt with pliers or a wrench, you need to avoid damaging the thread or you will be unable to fit a nut. If the grip is not intended to be too tight, you can wrap on a few turns of masking or electrician's tape and grip over that. If a really tight grip is required, wrap thin wire around the thread.

293. Making T-bolts

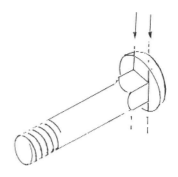

On some machines, such as a drilling machine, there are beds or other places slotted to allow bolting work on in several positions. It is not always easy or convenient to insert bolts from the far side and this is where T-bolts can be used. Push its head through the slot and turn it square across to stop it pulling out.

You can buy T-bolts or make them from coach (carriage) bolts which have a shallow 'pan' head and a square neck under it. Saw away the head on opposite sides, as shown, and you have a T-bolt.

294. Fit a Hanger Screw

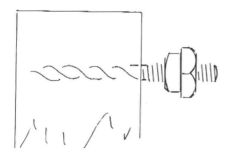

Hanger screws are treaded at both ends, one end for wood the other for metal. They are intended to allow something to be attached to wood by tightening a nut on the bolt part. The problem is how to drive one satisfactorily.

Put two nuts on the metal-thread part. Use two spanners in opposite directions to jamb the nuts tightly together. Drill a pilot hole for the woodscrew and enlarge its entrance to almost full-size. Start the screw with a hammer blow. Tighten fully with a spanner. Remove the jambed nuts.

295. Last-longer Abrasive

The abrasive sheet on an orbital sander often tears and becomes ragged around the edges before its abrasive qualities have worn away. This can be delayed by reinforcing the edges by putting strips of adhesive tape on the back on and near the edges.

296. Surprises

Nails, screws and other small items get dropped into the sawdust and shavings under the bench. Put the sweepings through a sieve or colander and you will usually be surprised at what useful things you can recover.

297. Abrasive Store

If you buy abrasive paper by the roll and cut off pieces as needed, a roll can get soiled or damaged if just left loose. One way of storing it while keeping it accessible is to use a sweet or biscuit tin, preferably round, although any other shape could be used. Cut a slot, as shown, so the end can project ready for cutting as needed.

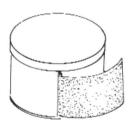

298. Wired Up

If your workshop ceiling or roof has exposed rafters or studs, one way of providing storage is to staple up wire netting. You can see what you put there and it does not accumulate dust in the way that solid shelving would.

299. No rust

If your workshop space is in a garage shared with the family car, beware of rust. If the car is brought in wet with the engine hot, the moisture on it vapourises with the heat and settles on any cold metal. Make a practice of always covering such things as the lathe, circular saw and band saw with plastic sheeting. Do not use cloth, as that will absorb the moisture and transfer it to the metal. A curtain between the car and machinery will also help.

300. Pot Again

When you buy small plants for the garden, they are often in throwaway plastic pots. They can be given at least one further use in the workshop. The hole in the bottom can be sealed with masking tape, which will be proof against most liquids, so the pot can be used for paint or varnish. A dry pot can hold nails and screws needed for the job in hand. An empty pot on the bench can take stray screws and other oddments.

301. Store

Small items, such as nails, screws and anything similar, can be stored in screw top glass jars. If they are clear glass, you can see the contents. If you put on a label, put a band of Sellotape over it and all round the jar, to hold it in place and keep it clean.

302. Anti-Freeze

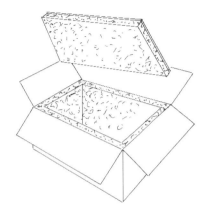

If your workshop is unheated and you leave water-based paint and other liquids there in the winter they could be spoiled by freezing.

This is an improvised container that will protect these items. It is a cardboard box lined with polystyrene, which has good insulating properties. Off cuts of builders' insulation board are almost as good. Line the box and put some more on card, hardboard or plywood to act as a lid.

303. Re-use Containers

It seems wasteful to throw away little plastic containers for 35mm film. In the workshop they can serve as containers for small quantities of such things as tacks, panel pins and small screws. They would be particularly helpful when you need to take these things to a job away from the workshop. To avoid temporary labels, put a small hole in each lid and drive a specimen of the contents into it, to show what is inside.

304. Pipe Storage

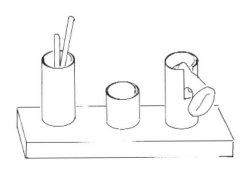

Off cuts of household rainwater down pipes have possibilities for storage items in the workshop. The usual diameters up to about 100mm can be mounted on end in holes in a block of wood to hold short pieces of wood or dowel rods. Very short pieces could make trays for nails and screws. Small cordless drills would fit with a slot to clear the handle.

305. Balanced Handle

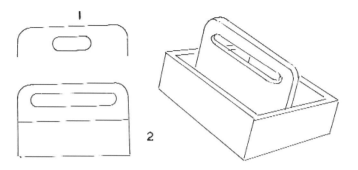

A box with a central partition with a handle usually has a central finger hole. This arrangement assumes the load will always be balanced, but quite often it is not, as when taking tools to a job. Instead of a slot just long enough for the hand (1). it is better to make a long hole (2) so you can slide your hand along to the point of balance when the load is uneven.

306. Wax It

If drawers move on wood runners in the usual way, rubbing the runners with candle wax will make the drawer slide smoother.

307. Improved Drawer Stop

The common way of stopping a drawer is to put a block on each runner and plane the rear of the sides of the drawer until the front is positioned correctly. Then wear takes place and it is difficult to set things right. This idea provides an adjustable stop, so initial setting is easy and later adjustment is possible.

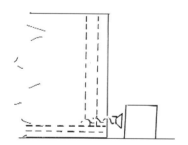

Drive screws into each side of the drawer so about 6mm is left projecting. Position the stop blocks so you can adjust the screws until the drawer is right. In some cases the back of the cabinet could be the stop.

308. Safe Drawer

If you have a power tool on a bench mounted on wheels or castors and one or more drawers in the bench, there is a risk that movement will cause them to slide and fall out. This could also apply to furniture which may be moved or tilted. You can use a simple idea found at sea to secure drawers when a vessel rolls.

Make a drawer with shallow notches in the sides behind a second front. Make the bench front opening so the bottom edge is above the level of the drawer runners and the top edge is high enough to allow the drawer notches to be lifted off the lower edge. This is all hidden by the overlapping front.

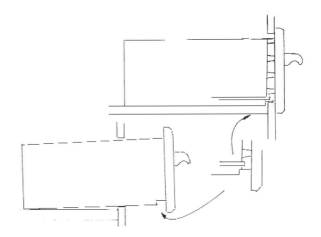

309. Moving Division

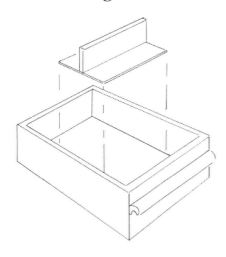

If you want to put a division in a drawer or box, where it's contents may vary from time to time, a division that can be moved or taken out is worthwhile. It also allows you to move things about and get the maximum capacity in a part space.

A simple division is shown. The base is plywood, an easy sliding fit in the drawer, and the division is thick enough to keep upright when screwed to it.

310. Simplify

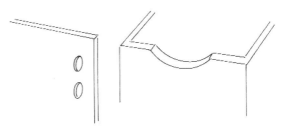

Most workshops are fairly crowded and anything projecting can be a nuisance, or even dangerous. One way of reducing this problem is to manage without knobs or handles on doors and drawers. Make finger holes in a door edge. These are all you need to open a hinged or sliding door. Hollow the top edges of drawer fronts, so you can put fingers over the edge to pull it out. There may be places around the home where you can use these ideas. You do not have to buy or make handles.

311. Drawer Lining

Makers of kitchen drawers, cabinets and cupboards, supply or sell rolls of lining material, which has a cushioning effect. This would be useful in tool drawers to protect your more important tools.

312. Resist Thrust

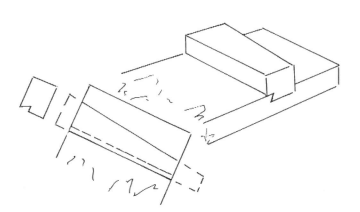

If you want to arrange a block to offer the greatest resistance to thrust, as in a shuting board or shop-made cramp, you can make a block, as shown, with the aid of a router with a dovetail cutter.

Arrange the block and groove so the working face is square across, but the other side is at a slight taper. Make the block too long, at first. Cut the leading edges of the block and groove with the dovetail cutter at the same setting.

Make a trial assembly by driving the parts lightly together, then apply glue and drive tightly. Trim the ends when the glue has set.

313. Winding

At one time, every craftsman made himself a pair of winding strips, often with special pieces of contrasting wood let in as sighting pieces. They are used for looking along a board to see if it has a twist in, described as 'in

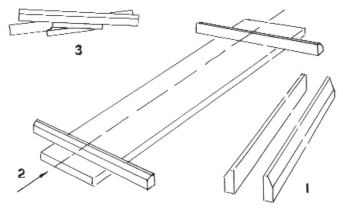

winding'. You may find it worthwhile making a pair, but they need not be elaborate.

Prepare two straight pieces of wood, parallel and thick enough to stand steadily, about three times as long as the widest wood you expect to test. If they can be two different woods of contrasting colour, that is a help. Thin the top edges from one side (1). Put them across the ends of a board and sight along them (2). The winding strips will exaggerate any twist, so it is obvious (3).

314. Accurate Wedges

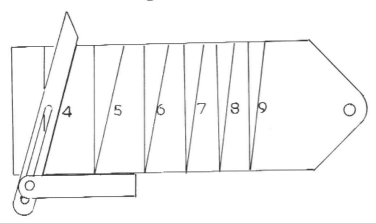

Wedges and angular cuts have to be made and usually there is a preferable angle. A steep angle, such as 1 in 4, gives movement with lesser power, while a shallow angle, such as 1 in 9, is more powerful, but there is less movement as it is driven. Dovetail angles can be chosen to suit the hardness or strength of the wood. Instead of guessing or marking out individually, it is a good idea to have specimen angles marked on a piece of plywood, then you can use an adjustable bevel to use across a cross-grained piece of wood. You are unlikely to need steeper than 1 in 4, and 1 in 6, 7 or 8 are usual for dovetails.

315. No rust

Many new tools come with little bags of silica gel crystals. These absorb any moisture that might otherwise settle on steel tools and cause rust. Keep them and put them in tool drawers or boxes, but remember there is a limit to how much can be absorbed. Dry the bags occasionally.

You can buy silica gel crystals. Place some in a plastic pot drilled with a lot of small holes and place it amongst your tools. You can also buy impregnated paper. Tape a piece inside a door and dry it if it gets damp.

316. Worm Holes

After eating its way around inside the wood, a woodworm emerges through a circular hole of a fairly standard size. If you are making reproduction antique furniture and want to simulate wormholes, use a 1.5mm bit. If you want to give an aged look to foot rails or other parts, give them a thrashing with a chain.

317. Extra Hands

Drawing a line around a curved spline is difficult when working alone. The method shown allows you to do the job accurately without help. Use two short pieces of dowel rod pivoted on screws at the end marks. Use a long spline and push it up to the centre mark with one hand, while drawing the curve with the other hand.

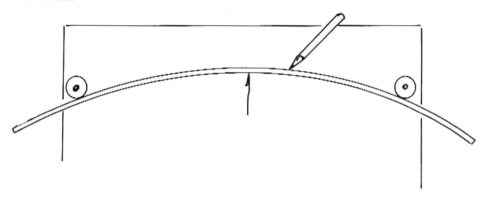

318. Milky Scoop

Milk containers seem too good to throwaway. You could convert some to scoops, useful in the workshop and in the home. Cut across a milk container to the size you want, either the wide or narrow side. You could just use scrap wood for temporary handles, or it may be worthwhile shaping better ones, as shown. Put washers under the screw heads to prevent them pulling through under a loaded scoop.

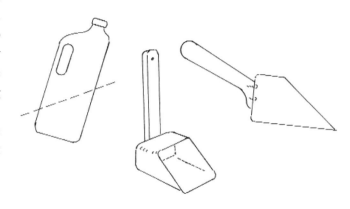

319. Plugless Bracket

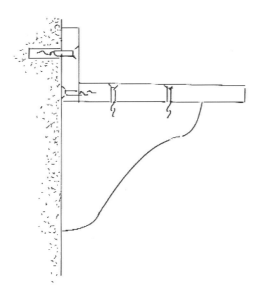

If a shelf has to be attached directly to the wall, it can be arranged so it is held only by screws and wall plugs above, and you do not need to attach the brackets to the wall. They will support the shelf without attachment to the wall.

Join the back piece to the shelf; not the other way round. Make sure the joint is square. Slightly obtuse is better than slightly acute. Join the brackets to the shelf and fix to the wall.

320. End Laminating

If the design needs a curved end on an otherwise straight piece, there is no need to cut waste from a wide piece or splice a shaped part on the end of the straight part. It is possible to make a sawn lamination, as shown. Make enough saw cuts of sufficient depth to allow the wood to flex. In most woods you can bend dry, but soaking in hot water may be necessary.

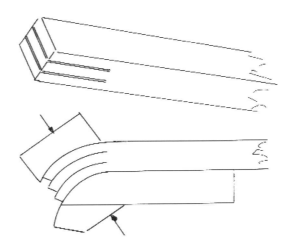

Lever the saw cuts open enough to squeeze glue in, then, bend and cramp round a former. It helps to allow some waste to trim away later. Long curves, such as sledge runners, can be made this way.

321. Other Lubricant

If you need lubricating grease and have none in the workshop, look in the medicine cabinet. Vaseline is a petroleum product, which is a good ointment, but it will also serve as a light lubricating grease.

322. Paper Towels

Kitchen rolls are standard in the kitchen and should be in most workshops. Besides similar uses to those in the kitchen, a paper towel will mop up paint, pick up glue before it hardens, wipe away oil and keep surfaces clean. Sling a roll on a cord from the ceiling temporarily, then make a proper roll holder.

323. Reach Out

A hook on a long handle can extend your reach, such as to the back of a cupboard or to the floor without bending. Keep one hanging on the end of the bench.

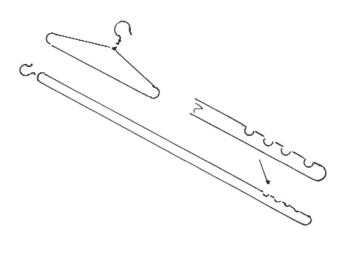

Cut the hook off a wire coat hanger, including the twisted part. This gives a greater area for epoxy adhesive to hold it in a hole in the end of the handle, which can be about 14mm square, with rounded corners. At the other end, put a few grooves across to show which way the hook is pointing, without having to look, and to provide a grip. A second one will have uses about the house.

324. Cap It

Precautions can be taken to avoid breathing in dust in the workshop, but dust in your hair can be a nuisance. If you do not regularly wear a cap in the workshop, it is worthwhile having a shower hat ready to put on for the dusty jobs.

325. Washing-up Rescue

The usual treatment for a seized up nut and bolt is soaking in penetrating oil, but if you do not have any, try undiluted washing-up liquid, which is very slippery.

326. Useful Junk

Before dumping junk mail, check it for pieces of paper with blank backs. These have uses in the workshop. Clip some to a piece of plywood for notes and use the rest for sketches. You might use the printed-paper to stand pots of glue, paint or varnish on.

327. Level Ply

If you have to fit plywood or other material over assembled parts, so its edge is level, possibly for the addition of moulding, it has to finish flush and you do not want to risk cutting through the other plywood below. Even if the joint is square, it helps to have a guideline on the top surface. If it is sloping, a line on top is almost essential, especially if the slope alters, as it does near the bow of a boat.

Use a piece of scrap wood, wide enough not to wobble when it is pulled along and long enough to stay flat on the lower part. Make the cutout large enough to give a good clearance to the cut edge.

328. Dowel Tapers

A good tool for putting tapers on the ends of dowels is a pencil sharpener. Many of them will take up to 8mm.

329. No Steam

If you borrow the family electric iron to press down veneer or edging, make sure you remove every bit of water. If not, it will spray unwanted steam on the work.

330. Putting in a Screw Insert

Starting a screw insert unaided is awkward. If it starts askew, the thread made in the wood is inaccurate, and when it is corrected the strength of the fastening is not as good. It helps if the wood is prepared with a suitable hole, and a piece of scrap wood is drilled with a hole to match the outside diameter of the insert, which can be used on the surface to keep the insert upright.

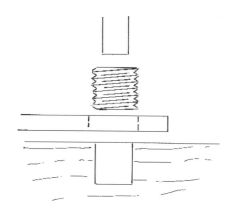

331. Strong Catch

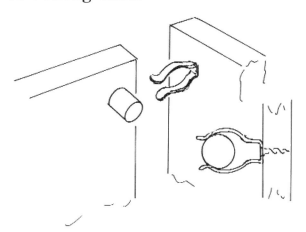

When a stout catch is required on a cupboard door, one can be made with a tool clip and a piece of dowel rod, as shown. The door will not rattle or fall open and there are no knobs to turn.

332. Gravity Catch

A fastener for a cupboard door can be made to fall into the fastened position, if it is made with a thicker heavy end, as shown. In this form it could close a plywood front to shelves under the bench, and it could be used on a door closing at the side, when the catch would drop over the side of the cutout.

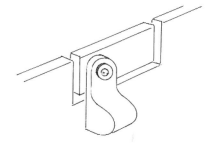

Make the catch from hardwood. Mount it on a block as thick as the overlap of the door front and wide enough for it to be swung clear. Pivot it loose enough to swing easily, on a screw with washers.

333. Flat Tests

If you need a flat surface for testing or holding bent wood for flattening, thick MDF sheet (25mm upwards) remains accurately flat enough for all practical purposes.

334. Tight Knob

If you have a doorknob held with a central screw from the back and it tends to rotate loose, take it off and drive a fine nail or panel pin into the back. Cut it off so only a short amount is left projecting. Re-assemble and this will press into the door and hold the knob in place.

335. Unstick

If you leave a partly used roll of masking tape, electrician's tape or similar tape in the dusty conditions of a workshop, dust and debris will stick to the flat sides of the roll. To clean this off, tear a length off the roll and use it, sticky side down, to wipe off the dirt.

336. Double Trough

Troughs are mostly used to hold square wood when planing the corners off and to support round pieces while being drilled across. This combination trough suits both purposes. It can be used upright on the bench or in the vice, or sideways on the drill press.

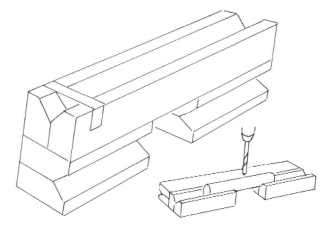

Prepare wood with 45° chamfers four times as long as you will need and with pieces that will join together as square sections. Join two strips to the length you want and fit a stop piece. Join two more pieces cut at the centre to leave a gap for drilling and join these to the first trough. Check their alignment before the glue sets.

337. No Threaded Wood

Most of us do not have the means of cutting matching screw threads in wood and not many woods are suitable for screw cutting. This is an alternative, using the threaded top and stopper of a plastic bottle. Choose a reasonably stiff type of plastic and a round stopper.

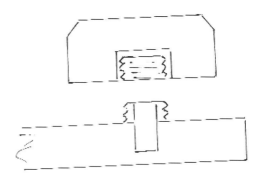

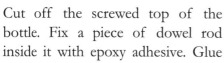

Cut off the screwed top of the bottle. Fix a piece of dowel rod inside it with epoxy adhesive. Glue the dowel into one wood part. Drill the other part to take the stopper or lid. Use a Forstner bit, if possible, for a flat-bottomed hole. Use epoxy adhesive in that part. The job should assemble as if the wood was threaded.

5. Joints

Although many modern glues are claimed to be as strong as wood, cut joints are still essential parts of most projects. They were originally intended to provide mechanical strength with no glue or the poor glue available. Even modern glues do not hold well on end grain. Cut joints still contribute mechanical strength, but they also provide side grain meeting surfaces for gluing. You should know how to make mortice and tenon, housing, halving and dovetail joints.

338. Barefaced

Traditionally, rails are joined to legs with tenons cut one-third the thickness of the rail (1). It is stronger and simpler to have the tenon barefaced, half the thickness, at one side (2). At a corner joint the tenon is longer and has a greater glue area (3), and you do not have the problem of making sure opposite shoulders match. If you want the rail and leg flush, mortices are more nearly central (4).

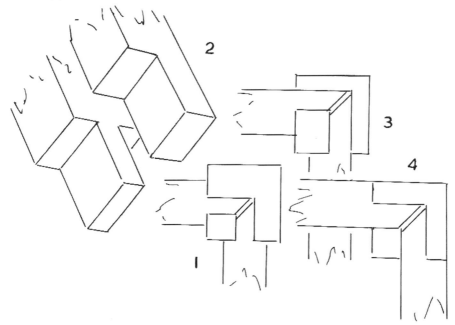

339. Strong Mortice and Tenons

If two pieces have to meet in another piece, such as fence rails into a post, cutting the mortice the usual width and then cutting the tenons to half this thickness leaves them weak. It is better to cut them as shown. Both tenoned parts have full-width tenons where they enter the

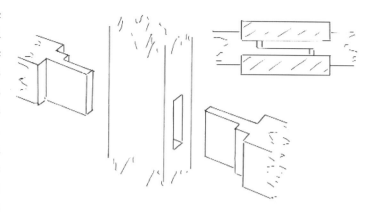

mortice, giving close strong wood to be glued, with the extensions overlapping.

340. Partway Shelf

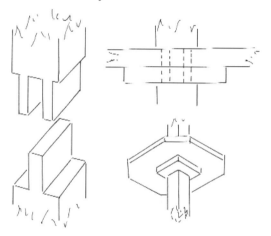

I wanted to put a shelf partway up a square pillar. The problem was securing it without weakening the pillar. I did it by thickening the shelf with a piece below and using interlocking tenons on the pillar through a mortise in the shelf and its support. The tenons were cut as shown. The width of the central tenon was almost as much as the combined double tenons, to give comparable strength. The tenons are slightly short so the shoulders fit closely and the break in the wood is not obvious.

341. Bent Tenon

If you cut a tenon at an angle, assembly with it unaltered would result in the parts being out of true. There is no need to discard the part. Leave the acute side, at first. Cut a little more off the obtuse side and glue on a piece thicker than needed for the final tenon. When the glue has set, cut squarely into the new piece, then trim the other side parallel to it.

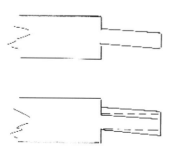

342. Sash Window Joint

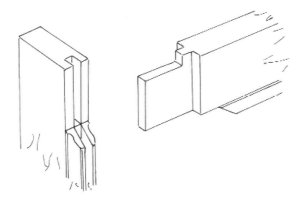

The material for making sash and other windows, as well as paneled doors, comes with molding and grooving included on one or both sides. This may seem to complicate making corner joints. The solution is to mark out the sizes and cut off the molding so it meets with mitered corners, leaving plain wood to cut normal haunched mortise and tenon joints.

343. Haunched

The old-time cabinetmaker did not like any part of a tenon showing at a corner, but ensured as much strength as possible with a tapered haunch (1). Such a corner joint is often made today without any haunch (2). With modern glues this is probably satisfactory, but it is not craftsman like. If it is a corner with grooves

for a panel, the groove in the mortised piece could run through, with a haunch filling the groove (3), but the groove could be stopped at the joint and a tapered haunch used, for a traditional craftsman like job.

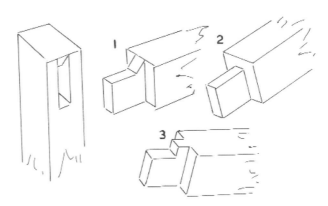

344. Unmarked Marks

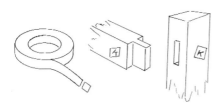

Identification marks for joints are often pencilled on and will have to be cleaned off later. It is a better idea to use pieces of masking tape, which will stay there as long as you need them and can then be peeled off without leaving any marks.

345. Split Limit

When you wedge a mortise and tenon joint there is a risk of the saw cut splitting further when the wedge is driven. This can be prevented by drilling a small hole and stopping the saw cut at the hole.

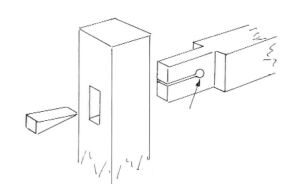

356. Tenons Both Ways

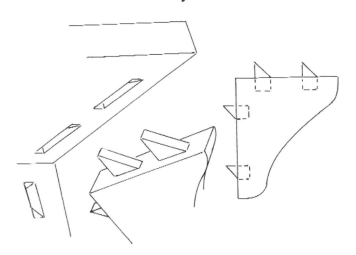

If you need to fit a bracket or other part into a 90° space, you cannot use normal tenons as assembly would be impossible. You might use mortise and tenon joints one way and screw or dowel through the other way. To keep the outsides clear, the only way is to use the method shown. The tenons can go into the piece to be fitted in the normal way, but so that they will go into the other parts their exposed ends should be cut at 45° and the mortises made to match. With modem glues the reduced glue area should not matter.

347. Takedown Tenon

When making furniture that can be taken apart, tenon joints can be made to lock strongly but are able to be dismantled and re-assembled as often as necessary. The tenon is long enough to extend and it is notched to

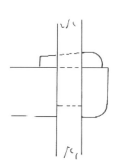
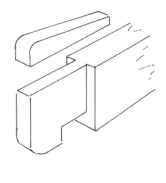

the mortised piece. The mortise must be made deep enough for the tenon to be inserted, which is held tight with a wedge that can be knocked out to take the joint apart.

348. Accurate Mitre

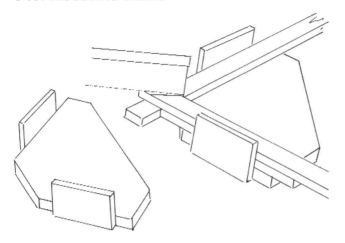

If the two parts of a mitre joint are cut together, they must match even if there are slight inaccuracies. The jig shown holds strips together to be sawn to get perfect results. The size of the jig can suit your needs, but use a stout flat board. Put guide pieces high enough to support any wood you expect to cut. Allow for one piece being packed up with a scrap piece so it fits over the other. Cramp the pieces to be cut to the jig. Mark the mitre on the top piece. Use a fine saw.

349. Accurate Mitres

Mitres can be cut accurately by hand with an old-style mitre box, but the saw slots will probably be worn near the top, although accurate lower down. In this case, you can give the saw better guidance and prevent further damage by adding blocks, as shown, to the tops of the mitre saw slots. Beech is the traditional wood. To ensure accuracy, glue on the blocks with their edges almost touching. When the glue has set, run a saw through opposing sets of blocks, so that they match. Modern glue should hold unaided if the surfaces are good, but if you have to attach to a worn uneven surface use screws as well.

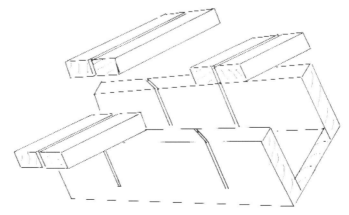

350. Picture Frame Jig

Most cramping arrangements for rabbeted corners, as in picture frames, put the

pressure centrally on the solid part below the rabbet. This cramping jig allows the pressure to be spread, to give a closer and tighter joint. Use wood of stout section to suit your needs. The best way to join the parts is with a bridle joint. Cut rabbets bigger than any you expect to cramp. In use, one cramp each way should be sufficient.

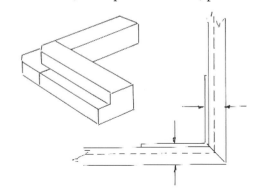

351. Squaring Jig

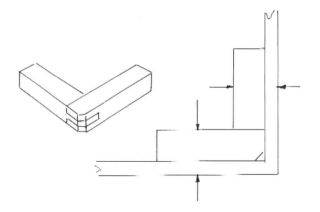

If two pieces you are joining need to be exactly square, it is possible to test with a try square, then find after the glue has set that the joint has moved. This jig is intended to hold such a joint until after the glue has set. Make it stout enough to stay in shape, with arms about 150mm for average use. A bridle joint is probably most suitable. Check before gluing, then test and true afterwards. Take a small amount off the corner to keep the jig clear of glue oozing from the joint.

352. Mitering

In the days when just about everything was done by hand, every carpenter's and cabinetmaker's workshop had a shuting (shooting) board (1) and a donkey (2) for planing mitres. If you regularly deal with mitres, it would be worthwhile making one or both. The shuting board is used to plane mitres on fairly narrow pieces, in either direction. The donkey is for planing wider pieces. In both cases the plane is guided while sliding on its side.

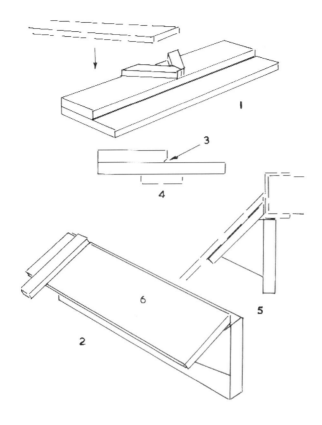

Make a shuting board at least twice as long as the plane you will use. The top board should be thick enough to support a piece of wood of average thickness near the centre of the sole of the plane. Undercut its lower edge (3) to prevent any build-up of dust or chips impeding the plane. You could put a piece below to grip in the vice (4). Fix the guide pieces accurately and securely with dowels.

Make the donkey longer than any wood you expect to plane and longer than the length of the plane. The support piece (5) should be thick enough to form a steady guide for the side of the plane. The guide piece (6) should be flat. Plane one edge to 45°. Mount it on brackets to hold it at 45° and at a height that will bring the edge of an average-thickness piece of wood near the centre of the sole of the plane. For right-handed planing, put a stop strip at the end shown. Leave the centre of the support piece clear to grip in the vice.

353. Squared Frame

A picture or other mitered frame must have opposite sides matching and corners square. It is worthwhile making a jig, as shown, for checking squareness. The corner is cut off so you can cramp a frame in the jig and work on a corner. It has a stiff plywood base and two sides high enough to come above any frame you expect to make. Cut off enough corner to clear an average frame corner and make the sides long enough to provide good support.

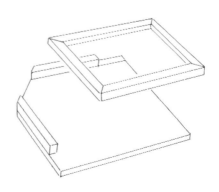

354. Butterflies

The butterfly joint is a specialised one used mostly for holding large mitres together. The mitered parts meet in the ordinary way, then a piece cut to the shape shown is let in to about one-third the thickness. The grain should be lengthwise and the waisting at the centre should not be excessive.

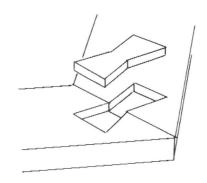

355. Mitred Corners

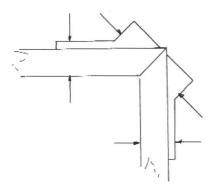

It is difficult to get cramp pressure square to the surfaces of a mitered joint. To avoid using glued blocks, where there is space for the extra cramps you can make blocks with extending arms to cramp to each part. Make the arms thin so the corner cramp pressure can come about in line with the centre of the mitre joint (arrowed).

356. Tight Mitres

One way to get pressure where it is needed when gluing mitres is to glue temporary blocks outside to take the cramps. Cut blocks at 45° large enough to allow the cramp pads to put their thrust in line with the centre of the joint (arrowed). Use paper in the block glued joints, so they can be prised off and the surface cleaned.

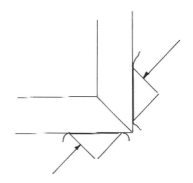

357. Matching Wedges

Besides haunch tenons, wedges are used elsewhere in furniture, either to allow it to be taken apart or just as decorations. A slope of 1 in 6 or 7 should suit, and should be standardised in take-down furniture, so that they are interchangeable. Make wedges too long at first. Drive one and mark the projection above and below for cutting off. In take-down furniture you can expect wedges to go a little

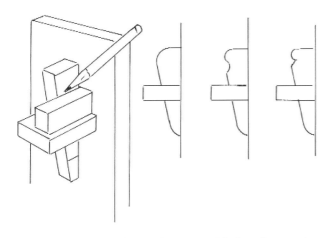

further in later drivings, so allow a little extra projection at the top. Drive wedges with a piece of wood as a punch, to avoid marking the wood with direct hammer blows.

For utility purposes, as in the workshop or garden, wedge ends can be left plain, but elsewhere there could be decoration, from simple rounding, to moulding to match the furniture. If the wedges are vertical only the top need be decorated, but if they are horizontal both ends need treatment.

358. Hand Halving

To cut a halving joint or other groove as accurately as possible follow the proper sequence. Mark out with a marking gauge and a knife (not a pencil). Cut the surface grooves deeply (1). Use a chisel to pare on the waste sides of the lines (2) to guide a fine saw (3). With the wood in a vice remove some of the waste by paring up towards the middle with a chisel (4). Turn the wood round and do the same from the other side (5), then level the bottom (6). Use a mallet on the chisel for the bulk of the waste, but a slicing hand action will get a smooth surface. It is better that the bottom finishes slightly hollow, rather than being rounded

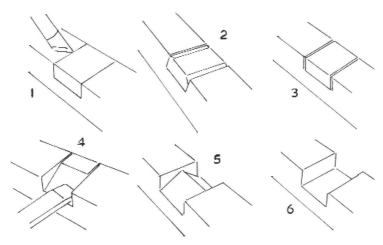

359. Bridle Cuts

In a bridle joint (1) the inner part is a tenon and can be cut with a router or other means in the usual way, but if you want to cut the open part with a router, in the same way as a mortise, leave some waste when you mark and 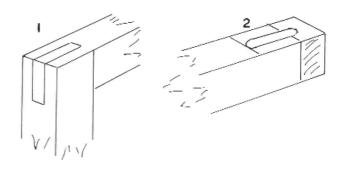 cut the wood. You can then cut like a mortise (2) and remove the waste later. If the pieces are not too long, you can mark out two rails end-to-end, cut like a long mortise, then separate them.

360. Traditional Gauge

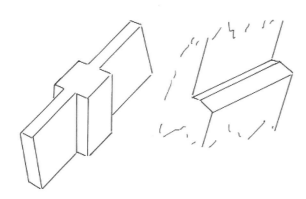

One of the simplest dovetail gauges to make and use is the traditional type shown. Cut it as if making tenons, but with a dovetail angle at the shoulders. To ensure a close fit on the workpiece, it is a good idea to undercut inside the angles.

361. Basic Dovetail Gauge

Most dovetail gauges, whether bought or shop-made are small, so the bearing against the wood is also small and the gauge tends to wobble, with inaccurate results. It is better to have a long stock, to spread the contact, thick enough to hold comfortably. The blade can be thin. If this extends at the opposite side, it can be used for squaring down the marks. A 1 in 7 angle will suit all dovetails today.

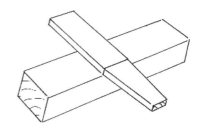

362. Holdable Dovetail Marker

Most markers for hand cut dovetails are small. Although most dovetails are small, it is better to have a large marker, so that it has more bearing on the wood and is less likely to wobble and spoil the marking out. The one shown is about 75mm square, with a piece of plywood let into a groove in a strip of wood. Set the angles after gluing. One end could be a slope of 1 in 7, which is

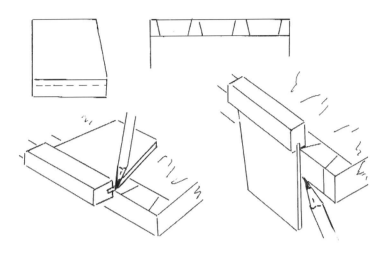

the accepted dovetail angle today, and the other end at 90° for squaring down.

363. Any Dovetail

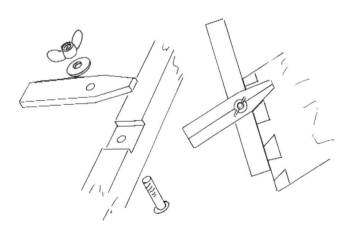

There are many designs of dovetail markers, but most will not deal with dovetails on an end that is not square. This tool will mark normal dovetails, but can also be set to suit any angled end. The blade can be shaped at one or both ends, if you use

different angles for soft and hard woods. Cut a shallow slot in the stock to hold the blade squarely for normal use. Hold the parts with a bolt, washer and wing nut. Draw a permanent centreline on the blade. For dovetails on a sloping end, put the blade on the other side of the stock and adjust it so the centreline is parallel with the sides of the wood.

364. Drawer Front

Drawer construction is sometimes shown with a full dovetail at the bottom of the drawer's side at the front to take the drawer bottom in a groove. It is better to use a half-dovetail, as shown. This is simpler to cut and there is plenty of room to arrange space for the groove.

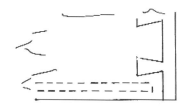

365. Dovetail Trimming Jig

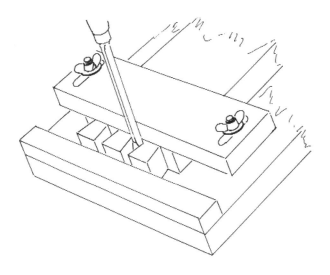

Hand cut dovetails can have their appearance spoiled if they are trimmed unevenly. This jig can be used to keep the inner cuts of both parts of a joint in line when being trimmed with a chisel. Make it wide enough to take the widest wood you expect to use. Put a stop piece squarely across the end. Keep it thin so it does not interfere with your view. The clamp piece needs slots for adjustment. They need not be very long, as the thickness of wood you deal with will not be great. Use coach bolts, with washers and wing nuts.

In use, put the work piece tightly against the stop and position the cramp piece in line with the parts to be trimmed with a bevel-edge chisel.

366. Skew Does It

The inside corner of a dovetail is difficult to cut clean as it is at an acute angle. You might cut the fibres with the point of a knife, but a skew turning chisel is the ideal tool for the job.

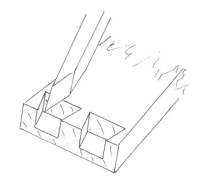

367. Dovetailed Tenon

The mortise and tenon joint shown has good resistance to pulling apart, even if no glue is used. The tenon is made in the normal way and a dovetail slope cut on one edge. The mortise is cut sufficiently deep for the tenon to be inserted and given matching dovetail cuts at both ends. Make an overlong wedge at this angle. Insert the tenon and drive the wedge to lock it. If the joint is to be permanently glued, cut off any extending parts of the wedge.

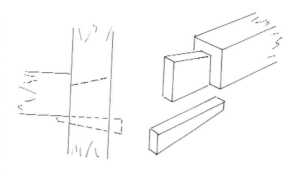

368. Attractive Shelving

The usual way of making a groove for a housing joint is with a straight cutter in a router and this is easier done right through. However, for most shelving, the appearance of the joint with the parts level (1) is not usually acceptable for a piece of furniture. A stopped housing joint could be used, but it is attractive to have a shelf projecting a little forward with rounded corners (2). An even better appearance, but involving more work, is to shape the curved part of the shelf level with the outside of the upright (3).

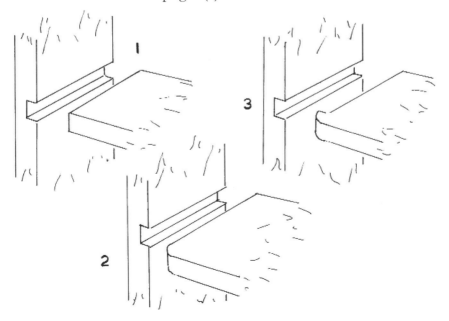

369. Mortise Template

If you make much framed
furniture or similar
assemblies, you will find
you use much wood of the
same section and you
frequently mark out and
cut identical mortises. You
can reduce this work if
you make a thin sheet
metal template of a
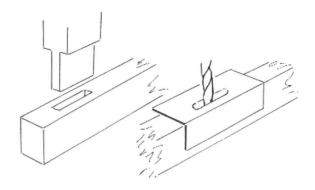
mortise to cramp on, then drill most of the waste through it with a twist drill,
leaving only a little trimming to be done with a chisel.

370. Strong Tenons

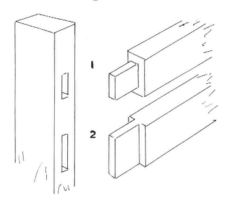

When marking out and cutting mortise
and tenon joints between parts of the
same thickness, it is usual to make the
tenons and matching mortises one-third
the thickness of the wood. This is good
practice, but another common practice,
which is unnecessary in many positions
and weakens the joint, is to cut away the
tops and bottoms of the tenons (1). This is
extra work and reduces the amount of
wood in contact for gluing. The joint is
stronger and easier to cut if the tenons are kept the full depth of the wood {2}.

371. Better When Different

It is usual to make tenons one-third the
thickness of the wood. This is satisfactory if the
parts being joined are the same thickness, but
the joint will not be as strong if the tenoned
part is to join something thicker, as in most rail
to leg joints. In that case, the joint will be
stronger if the tenon is more than one-third the
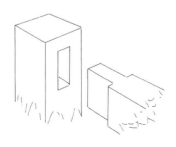
thickness of the rail, possibly up to one-third the thickness of the post.

372. Staggered Shoulders

When a part has to be tenoned into another part with a rabbet, the shoulders of the tenon have to be staggered. They have to be marked and cut accurately for a good fit. It is a help to have a short off-cut made when the rabbet is cut. It can be used as a gauge to get the shoulders right. It is shown held against the short shoulder, so the position of the other shoulder can be squared across, but it could be used the other way round.

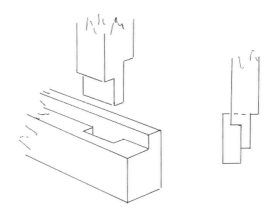

373. Tenon Development

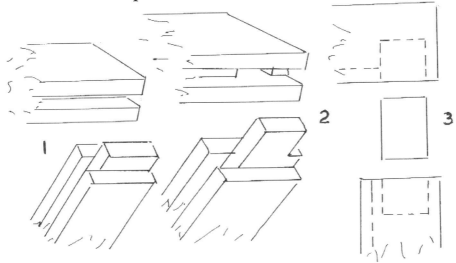

Mortises and tenons form the most used joints, but tradition has been overtaken by modern glues and routers. Most commercially produced panelled parts have tenons no deeper than the groove, so the joint depends on a good fit and the glue (1). This contrasts with the traditional haunch mortise and tenon, which is mechanically stronger (2) and therefore less dependant on glue. An alternative, using a router, is to have a separate tenon fitting into two mortises (3). The groove does not have to run through and if the tenon has rounded ends there need be no chisel work on the mortises.

374. Multiple Mortices

If you need to cut many end mortices for inserted tenons, they are better cut in batches for shared support to the router base. This cramping arrangement is shown with four pieces being cut. It could be used for many projects. Make the two parts thick enough for strength and to

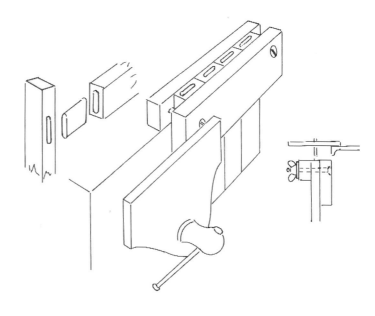

give good support to the router. A narrow piece rests on the bench top. A deeper piece can be gripped by the vice. Arrange bolts through the ends, with washers and wing nuts. Make sure the router fence will clear the top of the vice.

375. Dowel Wedges

A tusk tenon makes a strong joint that can be taken apart, so it is suitable for take-down furniture, though it is often used in more permanent assemblies. Instead of the usual wedge with a rectangular section, it is quicker and just as satisfactory to use a tapered dowel. Drill the tenon at the same angle as the bevel on the dowel.

376. Hide the Tenon

If a rail that is tenoned into legs becomes broken, you will be unable to fit a new one with normal tenons. A way to do it without the repair showing is illustrated. Make a normal tenon on one end of the rail. At the other end,

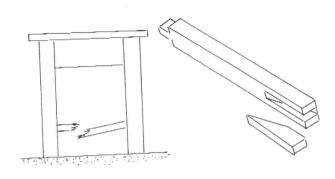

make a loose tenon with a part to fit a long-angled groove. Glue the tenon into the mortice, fit the other end and lower the glued slotted part on to the loose tenon. The repair will not show unless the furniture is turned upside down.

377. Multi Mortices

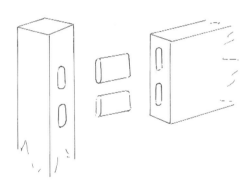

If you make mortice and tenon joints with inserted tenons and have to make a joint with the end of a wide board, it is stronger to use two or more short mortices than one long, because of the solid wood remaining between the mortices, as shown. If there are many of these joints, cut a specimen mortice, then make enough wood for the tenons to match it, in a long piece.

378. Flat to Round

If you have to join a flat rail to a round post, you could cut a mortice in the post and make the end of the rail with curved ends, against a tenon. It is stronger and simpler to cut a notch in the post as wide as the rail, then the joint becomes a normal mortice and tenon, with extra support from the notch.

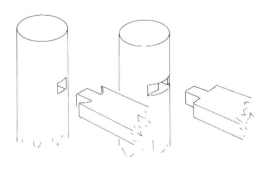

379. No-pull Halving

A plain T-shaped halving joint has no resistance to pulling apart, except for glue. It can be given a mechanical resistance by cutting it in steps, as shown. Make the division near the middle of the joint and make one part a little above the middle of the thickness and the other the same amount below it.

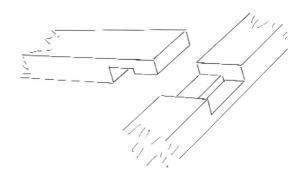

380. Strongest Post Halving

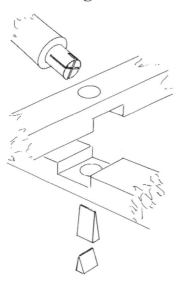

When the strongest possible joint is required for a post with a turned plug/tenon at the end, this can depend on the method of wedging. Make the halving joint in the usual way and drill for the end of the post. Have the end of the post slightly too long, for trimming after fixing. Make two saw cuts across it, square to each other; one almost full depth and the other about half depth. Glue all surfaces and assemble the joint with the deep saw cut square across the grain of the upper piece of the crossing parts. Put glue on a long wedge and drive it in the deep slot. Split it with a chisel and glue and drive in a short wedge. Leave until the glue is dry, then trim level.

381. Taper Leg Shelf

One way of attaching a shelf to a tapered or sloping leg is to notch it in as shown. Do not cut a notch more than halfway across the face of a leg. Glue should hold the shelf, but screws could be driven diagonally from below.

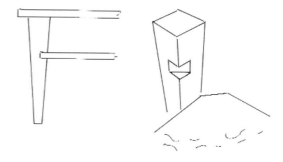

382. Long Halving

When joining two pieces lengthwise to form table legs or something similar (1), the crossing is often made as a long halving joint (2). There are long parts with little support. To improve this, make shallow grooves extending from the notches and fit the mating parts into these (3).

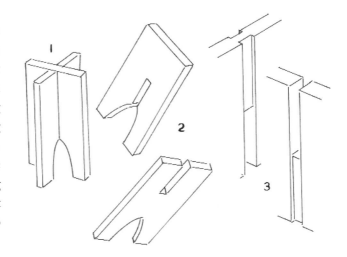

383. Other Housing

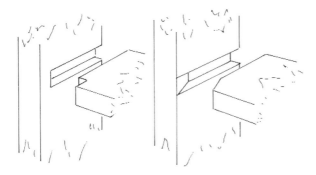

When shelves are to be fitted level with an upright, as in a typical bookcase type of construction, the traditional joint is a stopped housing, with the groove stopped and the shelf notched. Another, and probably easier, way is shown. This has the advantage of supporting the shelf right to the front.

384. Big Housing

If you have to fit a thick horizontal piece into an upright with a housing joint, cutting away for the full depth weakens the upright (1). It is better to cut away the end in two steps so less has to be cut from the upright (2).

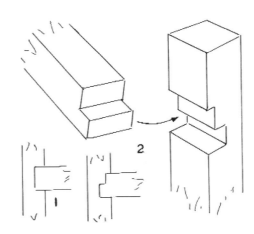

385. Dowel Tools

This tool will make a groove along a dowel if driven through and it provides a guide to making an accurate central saw cut in the end. Use square-section wood. Drill for the dowel and saw through to provide spring. Use a large gauge screw, for a good point. Make the end saw cut with the same saw you will use on a dowel.

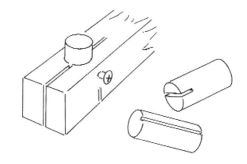

386. Dowel Grooving

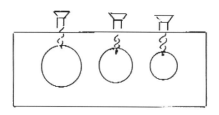

In a dowel joint it is advisable to groove the dowels to let air and excess glue escape as the joint is assembled. A simple way of making the grooves is to drive the dowel through a hole with the point of a screw projecting into it.

To make a permanent holed block, prepare a piece about 18mm thick with holes of the size you expect to use for dowelling. Make it a suitable size to rest over the jaws of your vice. Drive screws projecting into the holes. These can be adjusted to vary groove sizes. Drive each dowel through with the next.

387. Dowel Cuts

shop-made dowels are cut from a long length of rod, then the ends tapered roughly with a chisel and a groove sawn lengthwise to allow air and excess glue to escape. Preparing these dowels can be awkward, and an adapted bench hook will help to make the work easier and more accurate.

A little V-block can hold a cut

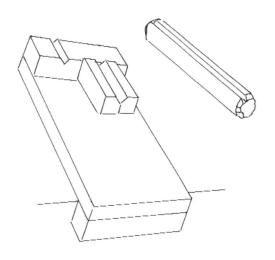

dowel with its top above the end of the bench hook for sawing the groove. A V groove across the end of the bench hook forms a place to steady a dowel while its end is tapered with a chisel.

388. Dowel Saw

It is always advised that dowels should be grooved to allow air and excess glue to escape and there are various ways of doing this. For dowels over 12mm diameter, sawing is probably the only satisfactory way of doing this, but holding the dowel and saw can be difficult and tedious. This tool keeps dowel and saw together, so that the cut is easy and accurate. The dowel enters a fitting hollow and is pushed against a piece of hacksaw blade, which makes the groove.

Use close-grained hardwood. The length of the sole could be about 100mm. Allow for drilling a hole along the grain of the diameter the dowel is to fit, with a thickness of wood to allow enough wood outside the hole. Cut through the hole to make the hollow. Saw along the hole to take a piece of hacksaw blade. Use a blade with moderate teeth. The blade need not be new. Cut off a length of about three-quarters of the length of the hollow, by making grooves across on the edge of a grinding wheel and snapping. Make the cut for the blade at a depth that will leave the teeth projecting the amount you want, probably between 1 mm and 2mm. Fit this in, with teeth pointing forward, with glue or epoxy adhesive, leaving the plain hollow ahead of it. The block could be left plain, or shaped, as shown, for a comfortable grip.

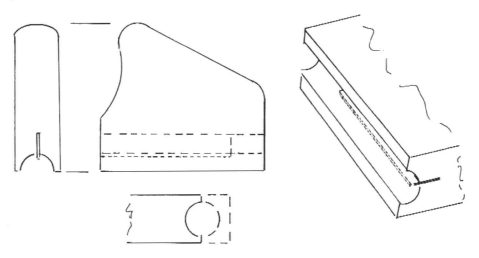

389. Dowel Grooves

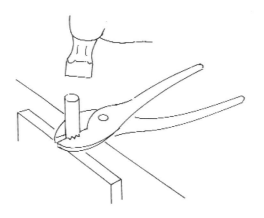

For the best dowel joints there should be a few grooves in a dowel so excess air and surplus glue can escape. Grooving can be done in several ways, but a simple way is shown, using a pair of pliers. Most pliers have teeth to grip round stock. You can use these to make grooves if you grip the dowel and hold it over a hole in a block of wood or a partly open vice, while you drive it through the tight pliers with a hammer.

390. Pressed In

There are several ways of preparing a dowel so air and surplus glue can escape as the dowel is driven into its hole. This method has the advantage of making a groove without removing wood fibres and will probably close after the joint is made. Have a wire nail longer than the dowel

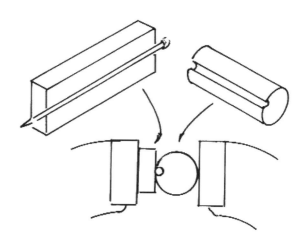

and back it with a piece of scrap wood. Put this and the dowel in a vice and squeeze tightly, preferably just before using the dowel.

391. Dowel Cutting

The jig shown will hold pieces of dowel rod securely with their ends upwards without the risk of flattening, as happens when held directly in a vice.

Drill holes of the size you need through a block of wood, then saw through to past the last one. Leave some uncut wood past the end of the cut. Small strips each side of the sawn part will help easy location in a vice. Keep the uncut part outside the vice, then the other part will have enough spring to close on the dowel rod being worked on.

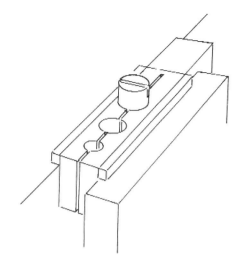

392. Better Dowel Grip

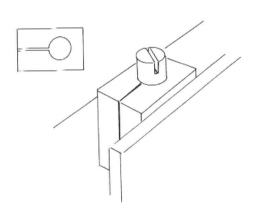

You may need to grip a piece of dowel rod to cut a slot for a wedge or to do other work on it. If you put it directly in the vice, that has to be tightened to prevent movement, so it flattens it. For a one-off job you could cut a piece of scrap wood as a holder, but if you expect to need to grip many dowels, it is worthwhile making a few of the holders shown, with holes to suit the size dowels you will use. Drill a hole squarely in a block of wood and make a saw cut into it. When the vice tightens, the dowel will be gripped, but it will keep its shape.

393. Dry-test Dowel

In a joint with many dowels it is advisable to have a dry test to ensure all holes line up, but if you use ordinary dowels, it is often difficult to remove them. Some dowels cut as shown have enough spring to make testing accurate and release easy.

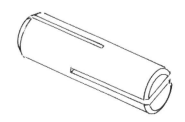

394. Accurate Dowel Spacing

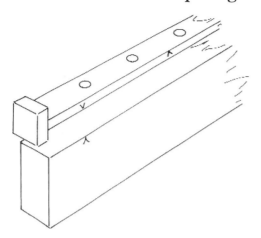

When two parts are to be joined by dowels, it is important that holes are exactly lined-up. This becomes increasingly difficult to maintain if it is a long row of dowels. As an alternative to trying to do this with careful marking out, a jig can be made, as shown. This might be short or any length to suit the job.

Use a strip of wood cut to the same width as the thickness of the parts to be joined. Mark out and drill the dowel holes on this. Put a stop block on the end. Put identifying marks on its edge. Drill through the first part and put mating marks on its edge. Turn the jig over and do the same on the other part. The holes will now be in perfect alignment.

395. Dowel Centres

If you need to find the centres of dowel rods, as when cutting wheels for small toys, use a drill with a long point to make a hole in a piece of scrap wood until you see the point break through. Use a drill of the same diameter as the dowel rod. Put the rod in the hole and mark through the centre with an awl or spike.

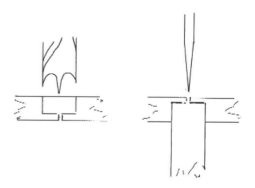

396. Easy Dowelling

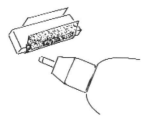

It is not always easy to get dowels into their mating holes, particularly if you are making an assembly where some joints have two or more dowels. Getting the parts together quickly and correctly will be helped if the dowel ends are tapered, preferably evenly all round. You can prepare dowel ends in this way if you hold each dowel in a drill chuck and hold some abrasive paper wrapped round a strip of wood against it briefly while it rotates.

397. Test Dowelling

If you wish to test the alignment of dowel holes before final assembly, using normal dowels may result in difficulty in getting them out. It is a good idea to make a few test dowels in the sizes commonly used. Crossing saw cuts will give spring to the part of a dowel to be first pushed into a hole, while a taper (preferably made in a lathe) helps lining up the mating part. Both ways should release easily.

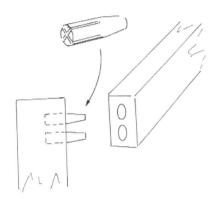

398. Assembly Help

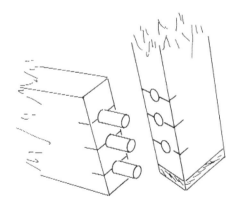

If you use dowel joints in a framework or other assembly, you will have to get several glued dowelled parts lined up and cramped within the setting time of the glue. Any help in lining-up will speed accurate assembly.

It is usual to mark the positions of dowel holes across the meeting surfaces only. It is a help in getting a joint lined up and assembled if these lines are squared over a short distance on the exposed surfaces. This is particularly helpful if you are working alone.

399. Exact Dowelling

It is not always easy to get all dowel holes in line, yet for easy assembly and final strength, they should be. To avoid having to carefully mark out both parts, you can use nail heads as markers.

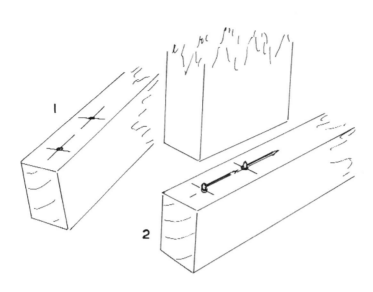

One piece is marked out and deep centre punch marks made at each position (1). Lay nails with their heads in these dots and hit or press the other part on them (2). The impressions the nail heads make are the exact positions for holes in that piece.

400. Dowel Lengths

Most dowelled assemblies need many dowels of the same length, which have to be cut from a long rod. This gauge can be set to the length required and used to guide the cutting on a band saw or by hand.

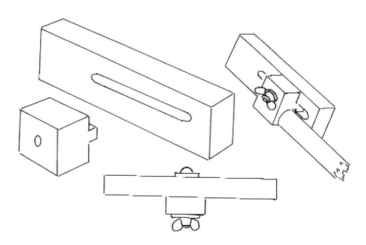

For the usual sizes of dowels and a gauge that will be stable in use you could use 50 by 25mm wood. Make the groove to adjust for the greatest length you expect to need and have one end long enough to hold. A 6mm bolt can go through washers to a wing or knurled nut.

401. Shrinked Dowels

If you find dowels are too tight for the holes, try giving them a very brief heating in the microwave oven to dry out the moisture. Drive them straight away. They will absorb moisture from the glue and expand to make a very tight fit.

402. Prise Out

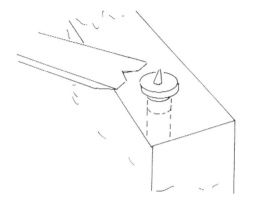

Metal dowel locators have to be tight fits in the dowel holes. but this makes them difficult to pull out. A piece of flat steel filed to a chisel end with a nick in it makes a good lever for prising a locator out.

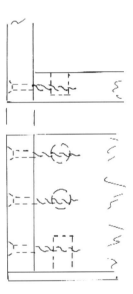

403. Hide the Dowels

To give a screw a stronger hold in end grain a dowel may be put across so the thread of the screw will get a better grip in its cross-grain. If you wish to avoid the ends of dowels showing on a surface, they can be stopped in the thickness of the wood, either in holes drilled from inside or upwards from the bottom. A Forstner bit will let you drill deeper than one with a point.

404. Single Dowel Screwing

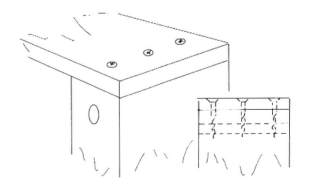

Where screws are driven into end grain, it is usual to put dowels across so the screws get a stronger hold in the cross-grain. If the end-grain piece is thick, a single dowel can be used for all dowels to grip. Choose a hardwood dowel, if possible.

405. Easier Screwing

At one time a cabinetmaker lubricated a screw before driving it by pulling it through his hair to extract a little lanolin from it. A better alternative today is to draw the screw across a piece of candle, which will lubricate without leaving a stain on the wood.

406. No Cramps

This method of edge-to-edge jointing was once common practice and could be worth using today. It will pull a joint together tightly without using cramps and add strength to it. This is secret slot screwing.

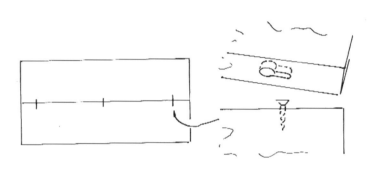

Drive screws at intervals along one edge, but leave the heads standing high enough to leave a little of the neck showing. Go a short distance along the other edge and drill holes large enough to clear the screw heads and deep enough to take their projection. Use a drill the size of the screw neck to remove waste and make a slot at least as far back as directly opposite the screws.

Assemble the pieces by putting the screws into the holes and driving one board over the other, so the screw heads cut along the slots until the boards are in line. Knock the boards back and separate them. Give each screw a half turn, then apply glue and make the final assembly.

407. Hidden Screwing

If you wish to fit something, such as a bracket, to a very thick post or something already in place, without screw heads showing in the bracket, you can use the method known as 'secret slot screwing'. Drive screws into the post, but leave the heads and a short part of the neck showing. On the other piece, go a short distance down at each point and drill a hole large enough to clear the screw head and deep enough to allow for its projection. Use a drill the size of the screw neck to remove waste and make a slot the same depth back to a point at least opposite the screw head. Put

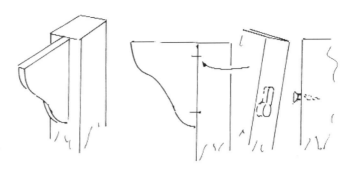

the parts together closely and drive the bracket down until it is level and the screw heads have cut along the slots. Knock them back and separate them. Drive each screw a half turn, apply glue and drive them together again for the final assembly.

408. Hidden Screws

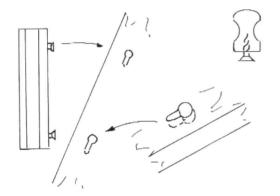

A wood handle of the bar type can be securely attached to a door or lid with secret slot screwing. Drive two screws so their heads and a short amount of the neck are still projecting. Mark on the door or lid where they are to be positioned.

Go along the grain and drill holes that will admit the screw heads, going slightly deeper than the screw heads are projecting. Use a drill the same size as the screw necks to remove the waste for a slot extending at least as far as the final position of the screws. Put the screw heads in the holes and drive the handle along to its final position. Drive it back and remove it. Tighten the screws a half turn, then apply glue and assemble the handle again.

409. Safe Screwing

If you wish to drive slot-head screws with a power driver, the bit is liable to jump off the head, and this can happen with some socket-head screws. You can keep the driver in place with a block of wood about as deep as the length of a screw and drilled to clear the screw head and the driving bit. Start the screw with a

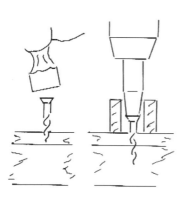

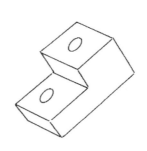

hammer, then put the block over it to guide the power driver. A stepped block with two holes will suit most applications. A hole with a diameter of 8mm or 9mm suits most common screws.

410. Pointless

When assembling screwed jobs, there are occasions when screws are needed of non-standard lengths, possibly so they will not go through. This involves taking the points off screws. If a screw is gripped in a vice, its thread may be damaged. If held in pliers to grind the point off, it probably moves. A safer and more accurate way is to drive it through a piece of wood so the required amount projects and hold that to grind or file off the point. With the help of a power screwdriver, changing a number of screws does not take long.

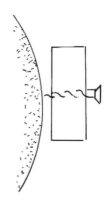

411. Screwing Oak

Avoid using steel screws in oak, unless they have a protective coating; black marks will develop around the screw and creep along the grain. Steel fittings may have a similar effect. If there is no alternative to steel, put a layer of wax paper or plastic bag material behind them and use brass or plated screws through them.

412. Neat Screwing

In the best furniture making brass screws are used. These are softer and the heads more easily damaged than steel. To avoid spoiling appearances with damaged brass screw heads, drive a steel screw of the same size first, then withdraw it and drive the brass screw for a neat finish.

413. Painted Screws

When dismantling screwed parts that have been painted, paint on a screw head can be softened with nail varnish remover. Leave it for a short time and the end of a screwdriver can be pushed through it into the slot or recess.

414. Tighter Tapers

Plug cutters for cross-grain plugs for counterbored screw holes, that make tapers, are worth having, but the plugs are usually longer than you need. If you drive the glued small end and trim off the rest, the part of the plug in the hole will not be as tight as you wish. It would be better to cut off the top part of the tapered plug and use that, leaving just enough to trim level after the glue has set, then the finished tighter plug will be less obvious.

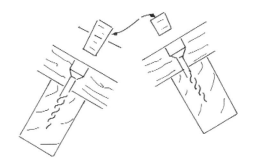

415. Will It Move?

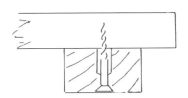

If a solid wood table top or some other wide board assembly is to be supported with parts having their grain crosswise, allowance has to be made for expansion and contraction in the wide part. This is often done having slots for the screws, which is necessary when using very wide boards. For more moderate widths, where you do not anticipate much expansion or contraction, a simpler way is shown.

Drill the reverse way into the screw hole, using a much bigger drill bit. This gives clearance for the screw to bend in the hole, to allow for movement in the wide part.

416. Straight Pins

Driving panel pins into hard wood can be frustrating, as most of them bend. It is unlikely that you will have a drill fine enough to make a hole, but one can be made from a panel pin. Flatten its point by hammering on an iron block. File a diamond shaped point and cut off the head. Grip this in the chuck of a hand drill and this will make starting holes for the pins, so they should enter the tough wood accurately and straight.

417. Inserting Inserts

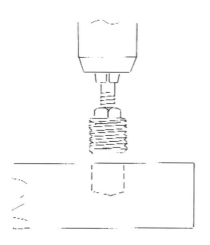

A screwed insert for use in wood has a coarse wood thread on the outside. Inside there is a thread to take a metal-thread screw or bolt. It is not easy to fit an insert by hand, but one can be driven with an electric drill on slow speed. Drill a suitable size hole for the insert. Mount the insert on the end of a screwed rod or bolt with its head cut off. Lock it there with a nut. Put this in the drill chuck and drive it. Unlock the nut and withdraw the rod.

418. Equal Nail Spacing

If there have to be a number of nails driven, as when fixing plywood to framing, it looks best if the nails are equally spaced. They should also be the same distance from the edge, and this can be difficult if plywood is to be fixed and then cut level with the frame.

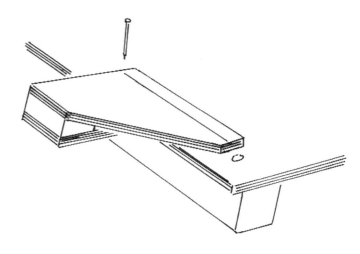

The gauge shown can be made to ensure even spacing. The piece below will go below any overhanging plywood. The top piece settles the nail spacing and a line on it lines up the nails.

419. Strongest Nailing

A plain nailed box corner is not always very secure. A much stronger nailed joint is shown. It cannot come apart without breaking the wood. Cut rabbets on the ends of two sides and nail as shown.

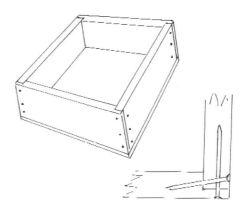

420. Nail Lengths

Nails and pins are sold in metric lengths, so you should allow for the difference if the project is being worked in inches. For instance, the nearest size to ¾ inch is 20mm, which is longer. Allow for this in the thickness of wood, to avoid points going through.

421. Nail Holding

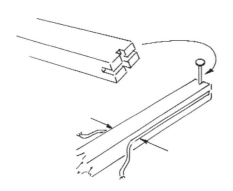

If you have to drive a nail or panel pin in a place where it is difficult to hold, or just want to avoid hitting your fingers, this is a simple way of holding. Cut a short slot for the nail in a thin piece of scrap wood and another deeper to take a thin piece of string. Put the nail in its slot and tighten the string around it. Hold tight as arrowed, then when the nail is started, pull it all away.

422. Stronger Clench

For some work, especially in the garden, it is acceptable practice to use long nails and clench their points. Trellis is usually nailed in this way. The common way of clenching is to support the nail head on another hammer or an iron block and knock the nail end along the grain. This may be neat, but it is liable to split the wood and the point is usually left exposed (1).

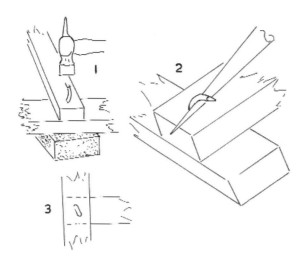

It is better to turn the nail end to a curve over a spike (2) or a stout nail and then bury it diagonally (3), so it goes across the grain lines, giving greater strength, reducing the risk of splitting and getting the point out of the way.

423. Level Nail Head

If you are driving nails and wish to get the heads level with the surface without the hammer marking the wood, but do not have a nail punch or sett within reach, use another nail as shown.

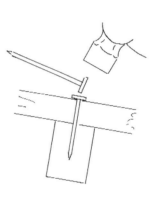

424. Stay-put Nails

Large nails used for outdoor work, such as fencing, need all the strength possible

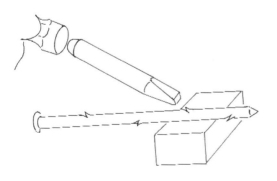

to do their job. You can increase the grip of a nail by cutting teeth in it, pointing towards the head, so they resist pulling out after driving. This can be done with a cold chisel with the nail held on an iron block. Stagger the teeth so they pull on different grain lines.

425. Nail Holding

We tend to just drive nails and assume all will be well. If the wood splits, all the strength of the nail has gone, so avoid nailing near an edge or drill a pilot hole first. If you are nailing two pieces of wood together, it is the grip in the lower piece that matters, which has to pull the top piece with the nail head. Drilling an undersize hole at least partway through the top piece makes driving easier, as well as reduces splitting, and does not affect strength. Staggering the nails so they go through different grain lines is stronger. As is driving at different angles instead of straight. Nails with ridges around can be as strong as screws.

426. Strongest Nailing

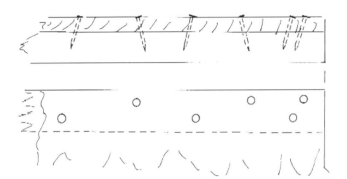

Nails driven straight in, and in sufficient numbers, will hold in most cases, but if you want the strongest nailed joint, without any more effort, there are a couple of ideas that will help.

If you drive the nails at alternate slight angles, there is a dovetail effect and a greater resistance to the joint coming apart. It helps to reduce the risk of splitting and therefore makes a stronger joint, if nails are driven into different lines of grain in the lower piece. It will improve strength if you put an extra nail near the end of the joint or reduce the spacing of the last few nails.

427. Stronger Corners

If three strips have to be nailed together at a corner, as is often the case in outdoor woodwork, the strongest joint is made if the parts overlap, as shown, so they support each other.

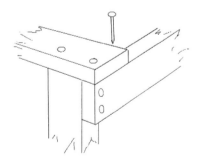

428. More Credit

An old credit card can be used to prevent a hammer marking the surface of the wood, if you drill some holes through it. When you drive a panel pin, do it through one of these holes. If you lift off the card, the pin can be levelled or sunk with a punch.

429. Lookalike

Nails used in old furniture would have been cut nails with a distinctive oblong head showing on the surface (1). If you are using nails in reproduction furniture they will be round wire nails with round heads. You can get something like the appearance of traditional nails if you file off the sides of the heads (2).

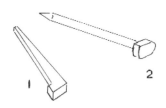

430. No-warp Top

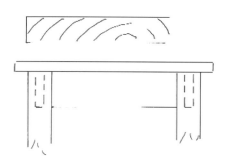

If you are fitting a solid wood top to a table or similar assembly, consider its future possible tendency to warp. If the grain lines on the end are very curved, any warping will try to straighten these lines so the section shown would try to curl up at the edges. Your best plan is to mount the board so the edges can be secured and any attempt to warp will hold the centre down.

431. Will It Warp

You can learn a lot by looking at the end of a piece of wood. You can use this information in selecting the piece for a job. The boards have been cut from a log, nearly always by making

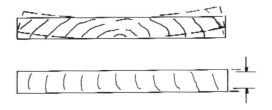

parallel cuts right across. The grain lines on the end will show you at which part of the diameter that board was cut.

If the cut was made some way from the centre the lines will curve towards one side. If the wood warps, it will do it by appearing to straighten the lines. If it shrinks as moisture dries out, this will be in both directions.

If the cut was made across the middle of the log, or close to it, grain lines at the end will be through the thickness. This board will not warp. Any shrinkage will be in the thickness and negligible in the width.

432. Warp Limitation

Wood will warp according to variations in its moisture content. To check the warping tendency, look at the annual ring lines on the end of the wood. If the wood warps, imagine the lines trying to straighten (1). If the wood has been cut radially from the log, so the lines go through the thickness (2), it will not warp. If you join several boards to make up a width, alternate the end markings to minimise the overall effect of warping (3).

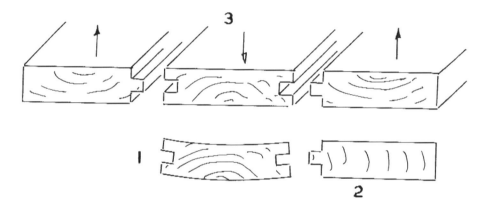

433. Relieve It

In places where either a tight or close fit are needed, it is advisable to relieve one part. Two situations are shown. If you make clamping pads for a picture frame, drill a hole at the corner before cutting the internal angle, so the angle of the frame is not damaged. If a half-round or other moulding is to be fitted into the angle between two pieces of wood, plane the corner off the moulding. This will keep it away from anything, such as uncleared glue, and ensure it fits closely.

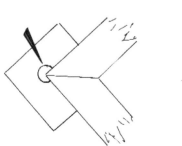

434. Better Butts

If boards are to be joined edge-to-edge, the surface left from machine planing is not the best for glue penetration. Even the sharpest rotating cutters will pound the surface and case-harden it. Give at least one stroke with a sharp hand plane on each surface, before making the glued joint.

435. Removable Marks

Identification marks on joint parts are often done with a normal pencil, but these are difficult to remove after assembly. It is better to use a wax pencil. It makes a prominent mark that can be easily wiped off. These pencils are sold as Chinagraph (for marking on glass), or as cosmetic eyebrow pencils.

436. Safer Brackets

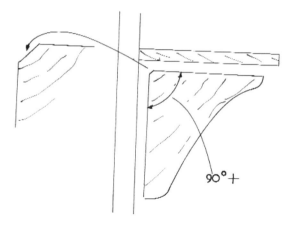

A shelf under load may sag forward in use and there is a risk that anything on it may roll or fall off. To discourage this it is advisable to make brackets slightly more than at right angles: only a degree or so more that 90° is enough and will not be noticed. To get this benefit, a bracket must fit closely on both surfaces and it helps to take off the corner, so it goes closely into the angle.

437. Drawer Fit

When you make and fit a drawer, try it in position first with the bottom loose. If the front does not close level or parallel to its framing, you may have to manipulate the body of the drawer, slightly sideways to match the carcass, before screwing the bottom to the back. Bevel the rear ends of the sides slightly for easy entry and to prevent grain breaking out.

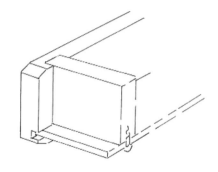

438. Curved Rail

If you want to make a curved rail under a tabletop, the longest segment you can cut without exposing too much end grain, is about one-sixth of a circle. The

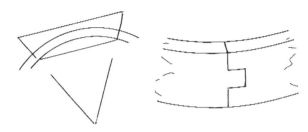

deepest you can expect to cut with the usual band saw is about 75mm, so if you cannot design to suit, you will have to make up with overlapping parts.

A suitable joint is the version of the bridle joint shown. You could vary it with two or more tenons.

439. No Warp

If it is important that there should be no risk of a square post warping, when it is standing free and there are no brackets or struts to keep it straight, one way of ensuring it will resist warping is to cut it down the middle, then glue together what were the outside surfaces. Grain lines that would have warped with each other are now in opposition, so any tendency by one group to warp is resisted by a similar set the opposite way.

440. Best Corner

When making a corner joint in a box or similar assembly, whether just glued or nailed or screwed, you can reduce the risk of the edges opening at top and bottom if you arrange the end grain the right way. For the best results, any tendency to warp should press the edges closer together and not away from each

other. When the end grain lines go straight through, the wood will not warp. When the grain lines on the end are curved, if the wood tries to warp, the effect is as a straightening of these lines. If you can arrange the wood so the heart side is outwards, as shown, when the wood tries to warp, it will push the edges tighter together.

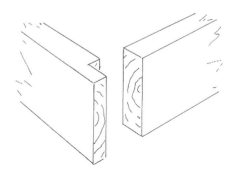

441. No Cramps

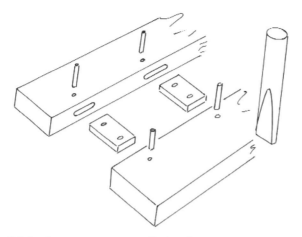

Boards can be pulled together edge-to-edge, with or without glue, without using cramps, if wedged dowels are driven through tenons. Cut a series of matching mortices along the meeting edges. If they are made by drilling or with a router cutter, there is no need to square the ends.

Make loose tenons to fit in the mortices, but they need not reach the curved ends. Drill through the mortices at what will be about the middle of the tenon penetration. Drill the tenons, but stagger the positions of the holes so they are nearer the edges of the boards. Cut dowel rod pieces to fit the holes, but about twice as long as the thickness of the boards. Plane tapers, as shown, to about half thickness. Drive the dowels with their tapers outward at the same time in each tenon, so the tapers act like wedges and pull the tenons tighter into the mortices which draws the boards tight. Finally drive the dowels through far enough for the tapers to be clear and both ends can be cut off.

442. Less Glue Scrape

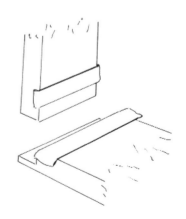

If you put enough glue on the parts of a joint, some of it oozes out and has to be removed. This is difficult inside an angle and can be reduced or eliminated by putting strips of masking tape across what will be the inner angles, to peel off, with the surplus glue, after it has set.

443. Enough Glue

There should be a good spread of glue in any joint, but in dowel and biscuit joints it is not easy to check that there is enough glue over the meeting surfaces. To check this, it is a good idea to put glue in the joint, then insert the dowel or biscuit and twist or move it about, before withdrawing it. You can then see how the glue has spread and if you need to add any more before making the final assembly.

444. Three Way Joint

If three pieces of wood of the same section meet at a square corner, it is impossible to make a joint of much strength. The example shown has about the same strength in each direction.

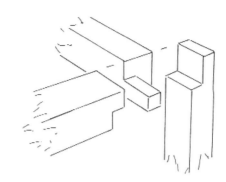

445. Accurate Drawer Back

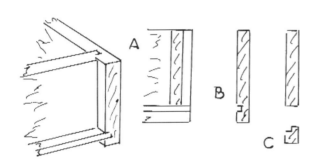

A drawer made in the traditional way has its back above the drawer bottom (A), so that can be slid in after the other parts are assembled.

If you are making several drawers, it may be worthwhile grooving the back the same width as the sides (B). The upper edge of the groove will be at the top level of the drawer bottom (C) and that forms a guide to cutting it off to finish exactly right.

446. Shut The Door

If a door or gate is to open and close properly the knuckles of the hinges must be exactly in line. This is extra important if there are three hinges. Check with a straight edge during assembly.

447. Self Closing

If you want a door or gate to swing closed when you release it, fit the lower hinge so its knuckle is further out than the top one.

448. Hinge Jig

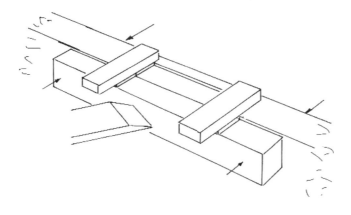

When making a recess for a hinge by hand, the cut most likely to go wrong is removing the waste for the thickness of the hinge. This jig provides a guide to stop the paring chisel going too deep or tearing the wood fibres.

Make two packings the same thickness as the depth you have to cut. Sandwich them between two crosspieces spaced to suit, and a piece extending long enough to cramp to the job and wide enough to guide the chisel level.

449. Hinge Stop

If you want to limit the amount of movement of hinged parts, as in a box lid, you can use some sort of stay, but this method provides the stop at the hinges. There are plates behind the flaps of each hinge arranged to project and meet behind the knuckle when the required opening angle has been reached.

Use sheet metal, preferably of the same type and thickness as the hinge. Cut pieces to go behind each flap, with enough projection to provide a stop when their edges meet. Drill to match the hinge screw holes. You may have to experiment to get the width right for the tilt you want. Let these pieces into the wood with the hinge flaps.

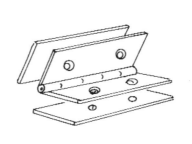
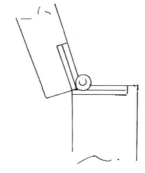

450. Plywood Hinges

If you want to fit hinges to plywood, there is a problem either way. There is not enough thickness to give screws a good grip. If they can go through into solid wood, that gives secure screwing. If you have to fix to the plywood only, the only safe way to do so is by riveting. Drill for nails the same diameter as the screw holes. Put nails through and cut them off a short distance above the hinge. Support each nail on an iron block or another hammer and spread the end in the countersink with a ball pein hammer.

There is enough depth if you need to screw to an edge, but even if a pilot hole is drilled the ply tends to break and the grip is weak. For the strongest screwing, put dowels across and use screws long enough to go right through the dowels.

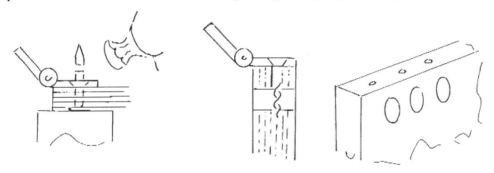

451. Buttoned Rail

It is usual when making large tables with solid wood tops to join the top to the framing with buttons engaging with slots in the rails to allow for the wood expanding and contracting. If the rails are too thin for grooving or you want an easier way, a simple and satisfactory alternative is to fit narrow strips inside the rails and let the buttons engage with them.

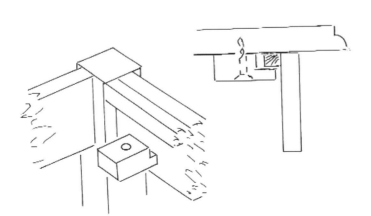

452. Better Button Grip

A common and satisfactory way of securing a solid wood tabletop, which allows for expansion and contraction of the wood, is to join the top to the rails with buttons that engage with the grooves. This is satisfactory in most cases, where the usual button does not extend far behind the screw (1). Having a greater length behind the screw gives more leverage and a much stronger grip with the button (2).

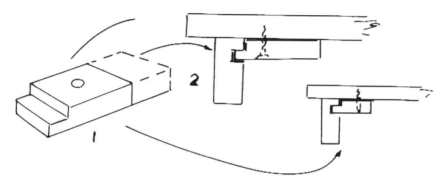

453. Pocket Screwing Accuracy

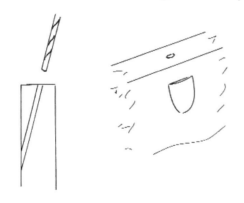

When attaching a tabletop to its framework with pocket screws, the screws should exit from the top of a rail in its centre. Instead of cutting the pockets first, start by drilling all the holes at the same angle from the top (1). Now make the pockets, which will all be at the same level (2) and the holes will be true.

454. Ply Spline

Plywood will make a good spline to join wood edge-to-edge with matching grooves. Cut it so the veneers are diagonal to each other, as shown by the arrow, for maximum strength.

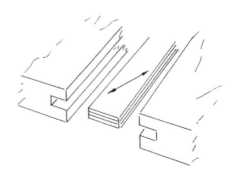

455. Drawer Bearing

Nowadays we usually rout a groove in a drawer for the plywood bottom (A), which is satisfactory if there are side runners or the drawer is to be only lightly loaded. Otherwise there is a risk of wear on the drawer sides or the supporting pieces. Traditionally, drawer bottoms were held in strips glued on (B) and this doubled the wearing area. For a workshop, or other drawer, which you expect to be heavily loaded, an alternative way of getting a broad bottom area is to rabbet the bottom in and fix a wider strip over it (C).

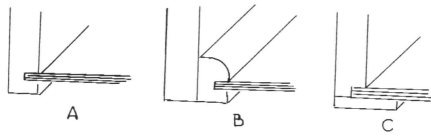

456. Joint Marks

If several boards have to be joined to make up the width you want, meeting surfaces have to be matched and identified for assembly. One common way is to put letters on each pair of edges. The traditional way is to draw freehand diagonal lines in a V formation across the lot, although lines of different numbers across the joints are less conspicuous. If the final surface is important, pencil marks will have to be cleaned off later. One way of avoiding this is to put the marks on pieces of masking tape, which peel off cleanly. Another way is to put mating marks on the actual meeting surfaces, so they disappear.

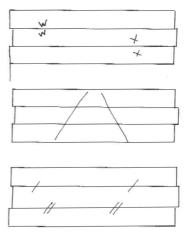

457. Breadboard Joint

If a wide board, either one piece or glued strips, is to be prevented from warping with crosspieces at the ends, allowance should be made for expansion and contraction, otherwise something will break or crack. The joint is usually called 'breadboard', from its common use in the past. A tongue and groove joint is used, but it is inadvisable to glue it. Instead, one or two tenons can be arranged at the middle, as shown. They can be glued and the whole joint cramped tight. When used, any movement of the wide board occurs each side of the middle.

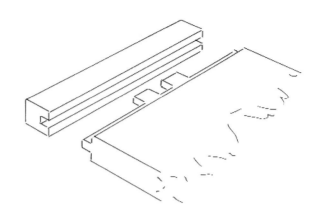

458. Good Looking Cleats

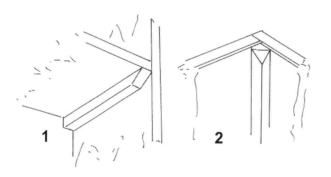

In some circumstances there is no need for cut joints. A shelf might be supported on cleats attached to the uprights, but the front of the cleat can be made less conspicuous by cutting it back at an angle (1). In other places, such as the corner of a plywood box, it would look better cutting diagonally (2).

459. Even Spaces

If several strips have to be laid on crosspieces with spaces between, uneven spacing will be very obvious. Instead of relying on measurement, it is wiser to use a spacing piece, as shown. For a very long assembly, it could be in sections over each fixing part. If

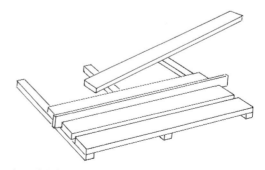

you can arrange the spaces to match the thickness of a piece of plywood or other sheet material, the making of the spacing piece is easy.

460. Pre-biscuiting

When planning biscuit joints, you have a choice of three sizes of biscuit, and can arrange spacing as you like. It is helpful to have a block with the three sizes projecting, to hold against the job to arrange the most suitable size and spacing. When making the gauge, it will be easier to hold, while

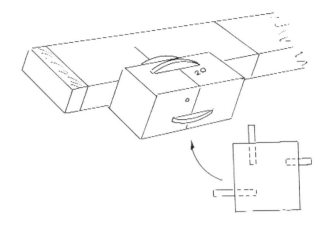

making the biscuit slots if it is longer, and then cut down to a size to handle. Mark clear centrelines around it.

461. Biscuit Buttons

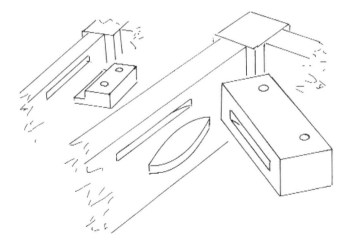

A solid wood tabletop is usually attached to the rails with buttons that engage with slots, to allow for expansion and contraction of the wood. You may find it simpler to use biscuits in the blocks, instead of buttons. Cut biscuit notches in the table rails and prepare blocks with matching notches. Drill them for screws upwards into the tabletop. Glue biscuits in the blocks. Position the blocks so there are gaps between them and the rails, so the dry extending biscuits can move in the rail slots if the table top absorbs or releases moisture and expands or contracts.

462. Ply Gauge

When plywood, or other sheet material, is to be fixed to a frame, it is good practice to cut the plywood slightly oversize and trim its edge after fixing.

Getting nails or screws central in the framing and marking for trimming the edges can be helped with a thumb gauge, as shown. This is especially important if the edge is not straight. Notch a small block of wood, so its lower edge can run against the framing and the top edge will guide a pencil to draw a line for the nails or screws. When that is done and the plywood fastened, cut the top edge of the block level with the bottom and use it to mark where you have to cut the plywood.

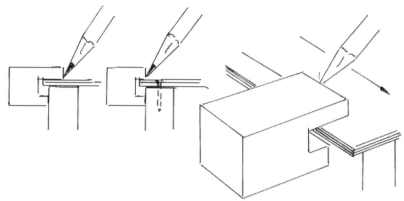

463. Flap Door

There are places on a wall cabinet or cupboard where it would be preferable to have the door opening downwards to form a near horizontal flap. An example is a bathroom cabinet, where what is needed can be laid out on the flap. The weight is taken by the hinges, which should be securely screwed. There is no need to let them in. When the door is down its projecting bottom goes under the bottom of the cabinet. To get the opening angle you want, put a strip along behind the hinges. To stop things falling off, it should open to a slight upward tilt.

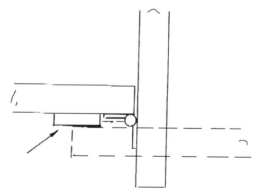

464. Identical Sides

When making a framed plywood box, of the type used for waste paper beside a desk, you could form opposite sides and join others to them. In the method shown, all four sides are identical. If you are making several boxes, this will

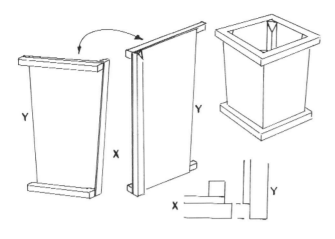

simplify and speed the work. Cut four identical plywood sides. Put an inside corner strip on one edge of each (X). Put top and bottom outside strips on each side. On the edge with the inside strip let them project by the thickness of the plywood and on the other edge (Y) more than enough to cover their ends (see section drawing). Assemble by attaching edge Y to edge X all round. Add a plywood bottom, and then trim edges and overlaps.

465. Lid Limit

A simple way to limit the amount of opening of a box lid is to put a strip along the back. It need not go the whole length and could be in two parts on a long box. It could have a square section, but is better chamfered, as shown.

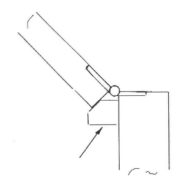

466. Non-slip

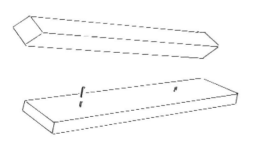

If two parts are to be glued and exact position is important, you have to take precautions against slip when cramping. One way of doing this is to drive two panel pins into one piece and cut them off so a very short amount is left projecting. These ends will engage with the other part when you press it on, so there can be no movement.

467. Piped Glue

Pipe cleaners will put glue into places that are difficult to get at otherwise, such as dowel and biscuit holes. Use the end of a pipe cleaner straight or fold the end back if that will go in places such as narrow but long slots. You can cut off a used end and get several uses out of one cleaner.

468. Clean Glue Removal

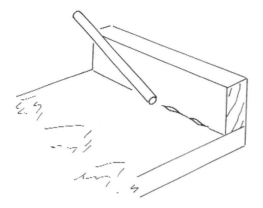

You cannot avoid some glue squeezing out of a joint and this should be removed without spreading, if possible. Leaving it to dry and remove with a scraper or chisel tends to lift fibres. One way of removing most of the glue in one pass is to use a drinking straw, which can get into the angle and scoop the glue without spreading it.

469. Tidy Glue

Squeezing glue through the nozzle of the usual container is not very precise and can result in an excess where you do not want it and nothing where it should be. Glue may be squeezed out on to a scrap of wood and scraped up to put into dowel or biscuit holes or elsewhere with a sliver of wood or a small brush. If you have many of these situations to deal with, the temporary glue pot shown will hold what you need. Cut it from the top of a discarded cleaner container. Support it in

a hole in a wood block. Put enough glue in it and dip the wood sliver in it. When you have finished, you can unscrew the cap and run any remaining glue into its container. A similar container could also be used when you only need to have available a small quantity of paint or varnish.

6. Cramping

In most constructions, pressure has to be applied to pull parts together. Glues only hold best if the meeting wood surfaces are close fitting. Weights can be used and there are many improvisations, but every workshop needs a variety of cramps in several sizes. Keep cramps clean of glue and any screws lightly lubricated.

470. True Cramping

The corners of a tenoned or dowelled frame have to be pulled tight with cramps. When you check squareness by comparing diagonal measurements (1) there may be a slight error to be corrected. This can be done without taking the cramps off the job. Slacken one cramp and move it to pull diagonally in the direction of the diagonal measurement to be reduced (2). Adjust it until the frame is true. Leave the other cramp pulling squarely.

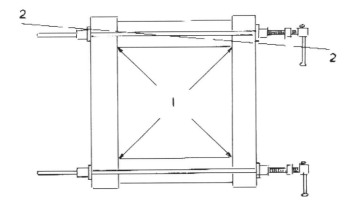

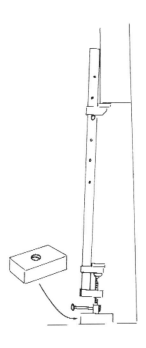

471. Push It

Most bar cramps allow the sliding head to be removed and reversed, so it faces outwards, to let the cramp be used for a push or lift. The push at the other end has to be taken by the outside of the head of the adjusting screw. To keep your hand clear, it is advisable to make a block with a hollow drilled to stop the end moving, as in the example shown.

472. Assembly

Most woodwork assemblies have to be square, usually in all directions. Any error will be apparent to any viewer. A correct order of assembly is important. Trying to assemble all parts at the same time is not usually successful. Parts must be accurate and matching. If there are four legs, they should finish exactly the same. Rails in a side should be exactly the same between shoulders. So far as possible, mark out all parts that should match together. Legs should be correctly marked, but left overlong to trim after assembly. If there are panels, they should be square, but size should allow a little space in the grooves for squaring adjustment of the framing.

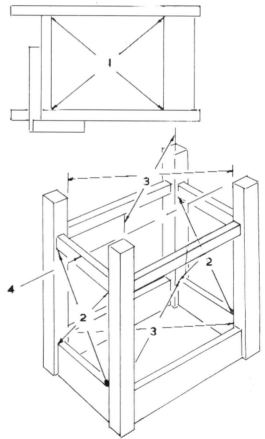

Assemble opposite sides and check against each other. Assemble and cramp on a flat surface. Sight across to look for any twist and correct this before the glue sets. Square with your largest try square, but also compare diagonal measurements (1). Trim tops of legs level. Assemble with the rails the other way. In most cases, have this assembly upside-down on a flat surface, so the top will be true. Bottoms of legs can be trimmed level later. Check squareness in the new direction (2) and in the view from above (3) at both levels. Before leaving for the glue to set, sight across the rails (4). They should be parallel, especially the top set, if a top is to be fitted.

Leave this assembly cramped for the glue to set. Add the top after any cleaning up, leaving trimming the legs to length until then in case the top has caused slight distortion. You could make a door slightly too large before this stage, or make it now. Getting a door to make a good fit is best left until other construction has been completed.

473. Reverse Cramping

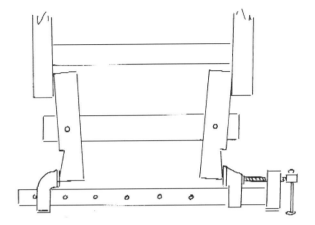

If you need to apply force outwards as in removing a rail from chair legs make the device shown from scrap wood. The two arms pivot on bolts. For greater pressure increase the lengths of the arms on the cramp side.

474. Cramp Pedestal Feet

Pedestal feet are usually joined to the upright with dowels or tenons and the joints have to be cramped while the glue sets. The pressure points on the feet would be sloping and a cramp would damage the surface and slip. One way of getting parallel pressure is to cramp strips each side of the feet, as shown. Put a packing slightly thinner than the feet under where the strips are cramped together. Arrange the strips so pressure with the bar cramp comes near central over the joints.

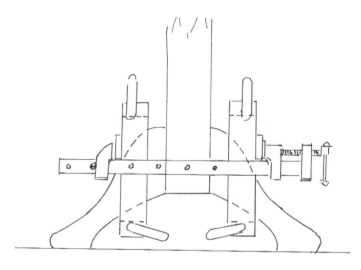

475. Trestle Cramp

Where workshop space is limited, something dual-purpose is worth having. If you make a trestle with a board on the edge of a suitable thickness to fit cramp heads, you can drill it to suit and this will not affect its use as a trestle, but give you a cramp as well.

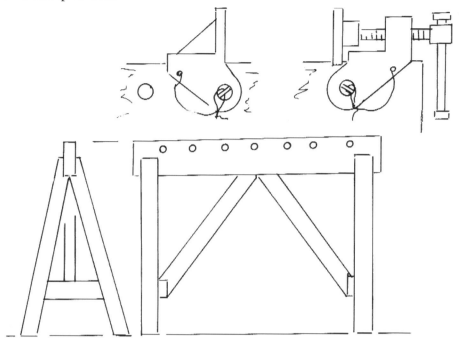

476. Sweeping Curve

If you spring a spline or batten to draw a large curve on a panel and it is only long enough to reach the sides, the curve you draw tends to flatten towards the ends. It is better to spring the curve further than the width of the panel, so the flattened ends of the curve are outside the width needed. Instead of trying to hold the batten by hand or with nails, it is better to do the squeezing with a bar cramp. Besides holding, this gives a fine adjustment.

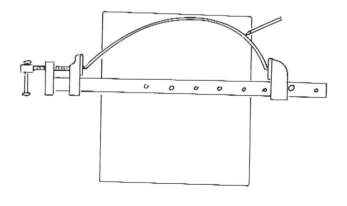

477. Bar Cramp Pad

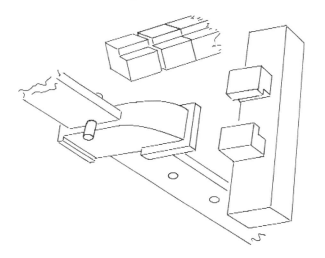

Positioning a scrap wood pad against the jaw of a sash cramp or similar cramp can be a nuisance when you are putting together the parts of an assembly. It is a help to have pads that grip the jaws. A simple way of doing this is shown. Cut rabbets on a strip of wood, of a size to fit over a jaw, then cut off pieces to glue to pads.

478. Stay-put Cramp Pads

It is a nuisance having to locate scrap wood pads under cramp jaws when you are also fitting parts together in a job. These pads will fit on a bar cramp and stay in place while you assemble parts and tighten the cramp. In each pad, a strip a

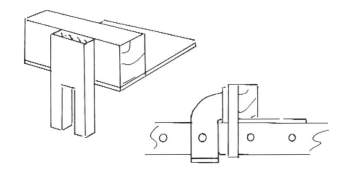

little wider and higher than the cramp head takes the thrust and keeps the pad in place. A softwood pad spreads the pressure and below it is a piece of hardboard. This keeps the job above the bar. It tends to get fouled with glue after a little use and can be removed and another piece pinned on.

479. Adjustable Cramp

You may never have as many bar cramps as you need for a job and one or two of these wedged cramps can supplement them or take their place. Make to a size to suit your needs. Fix a pressure block securely to one end and cut a long slot

that will just clear a
coach bolt. Make the
moveable pad long
enough to spread the
pressure and secure
the bolt in it. Use a
large washer under
the wing nut – a
'penny' washer on a
8mm bolt would be
suitable. Cut two
identical wedges at
about 1 in 6 slopes,
to fit together and provide the pressure.

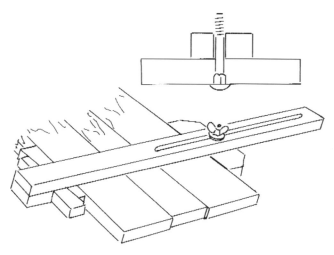

480. Stay Put Wedges

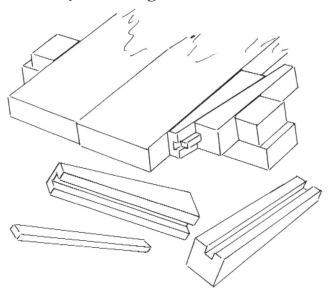

Folding wedges form
a convenient way to
put on pressure or
provide lift, but there
is sometimes a
problem keeping them
in line. A method of
preventing unwanted
movement is shown.
You could use a
tongue and groove
joint, but this method
only uses one straight
router cutter. It is
simplest to make the
grooves on the edge of a wide board, then cut the wedges off. Make the spline
an easy sliding fit in the grooves.

481. Strong Wedge Cramp

The cramp shown could be made in any size. The jaws should be stout enough
to resist bending. They are shown with pressure pads, which are optional. Drill

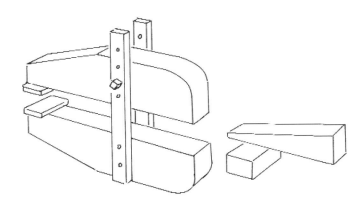

the matching uprights to allow several positions for a pivot bolt. Fix them to the lower jaw. Tightening can be with one wedge and several packings or you could make thicker wedges.

482. Ratchet Cramp

This bar cramp, tightened with folding wedges, uses a ratchet arrangement instead of pegs in holes to provide adjustment. Arrange a fixed pad and wedges at one end. Further along the underside of the bar cut a series of notches at about 30°. Make the moveable head (1) with cheeks each side of the bar and a slope the same as the notches. Put a spacer between the cheeks (2) and a shaped piece at the bottom (3). Arrange the pad so when the pad is tilted (4) the bottom piece clears the notches and allows adjustment (5).

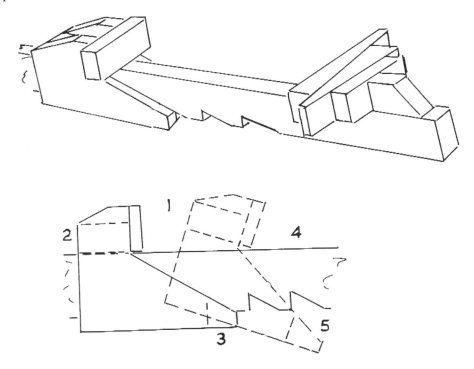

483. Best Edge Cramp

Veneer and plastic laminate needs tightly securing around the edges while the adhesive sets. Notched wood is often used, sometimes with a wedge, as a cramp. A better cramp is shown. The body is large enough to resist pressure. A lower notch holds a strip to spread the pressure. This 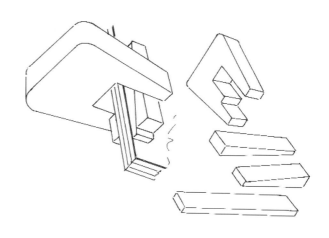 could be a long piece, inside several cramps. Pressure is applied with a pair of folding wedges, which have a parallel action to spread contact.

484. Not Square

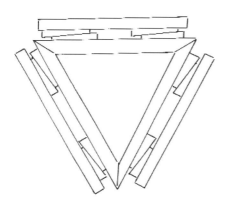

There are several cramps intended to pull together mitered frames with square corners, but what about other shapes, such as three, five and six, or four uneven sides? One way of cramping these is shown, using folding wedges to apply pressure. Use a stout plywood piece as base and position straight strips far enough away from the frame outline to admit folding wedges and fix them down securely. Make sufficient pairs of folding wedges to go fairly near the corners. Put newspaper or other paper under the corners to prevent excess glue sticking the frame down.

485. Mini Cramp

Most wedged cramps are intended to supplement or take the place of large bar cramps, but smaller ones are worth having. There are always jobs where G and other small cramps cannot cope. This cramp could be about 300mm long. Fix a solid block at one end and have a slightly deeper moveable one. Use a plain pad

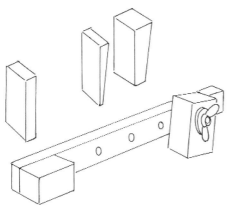

at the fixed end to apply pressure, but it is worthwhile making wedges of different thickness to use at the other end. The moveable block on a bolt will pivot to suit.

486. Reversed Wedge

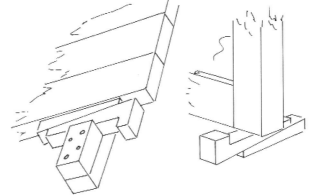

A pair of plain folding wedges will put on considerable pressure and may be all you need for many jobs. If you want to adjust movement by reversing a wedge, as you may when using wedges to lift a door to an exact height when fixing hinges, it is a help to prepare one wedge, as shown. The knob helps when you have to apply a little backwards pressure and when you have to release the wedges after use.

487. Longer Cramp

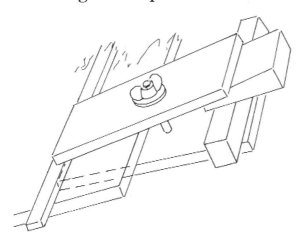

There is a limited reach to most cramps, which is adequate for most purposes, but if you need to cramp something further from an edge, this is an idea taken from boat building, when clinker was a common way of building small boats (overlapping planks). Two matching pieces of wood form the cramp. Put a bolt and wing nut through far enough from one end to allow the reach you want. If you arrange a wedge and packing at the other end a combination of tightening the wing nut and driving the wedge will put pressure on the other end.

488. Edge Cramps

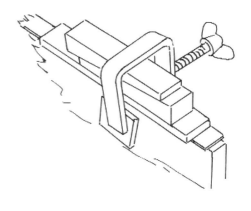

If an edge has to be covered with veneer or other thin material, it is important that it is held tight while the glue sets. One method of cramping is shown. Use a stiff piece to spread the pressure. This could be long, under several cramps. It is possible to use single wedges, but a pair of folding wedges under a cramp provides a wider and greater pressure.

489. Wedge Control

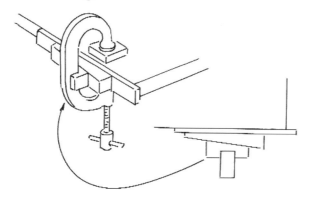

Driving a wedge inside a G cramp to hold wood to an edge is common practice. Instead of driving the wedge against the inside of the cramp itself, it is easier to control and more accurate if a matching block is notched round the cramp, as shown.

490. Further Cramp

If you need to cramp boards together, but do not have bar or other cramps long enough, it is possible to do the job with shorter cramps, as shown. Hold blocks securely to both sides of one

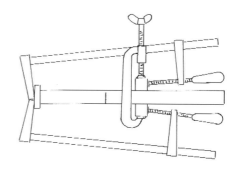

piece, close enough to the far edge to allow the cramps you have to reach. This should tighten a joint just as well as long cramps.

491. Further Out

Normal G cramps do not extend very far. Sliding cramps will go further, but

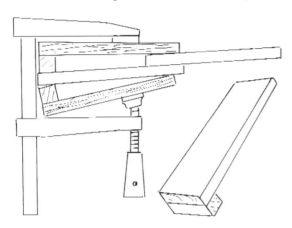

sometimes you need to put on pressure even further from an edge. It is possible to extend the reach of a cramp with a pair of pressure pads, as shown. They can be made to reach some way from the jaws. Although the pressure at the ends is reduced as the reach is lengthened, it should be enough to hold glued parts in contact.

492. Better Pads

To help keep pads under cramps, you can rout grooves that take the ends of the jaws to the centre of the blocks. If it is a close fit, a block is helped to stay in place. It is easier to hold the wood if the routing is done with the blocks marked on a strip of wood.

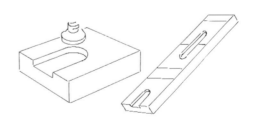

493. Secure The Pad

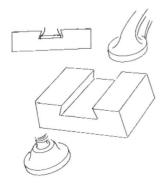

When assembling a job you need both hands for several purposes and locating scrap wood pads under cramp heads can be a nuisance. This idea allows the pads to be loosely attached to the cramps. Use a router dovetail cutter to make recesses across a pad at a width that will stop the cramp head lifting out. Without a router you could do this by hand sawing. Both parts of most small cramps should fit similar grooves.

494. Secure Pads

To hold scrap wood pads to cramp heads without reducing the thickness of the pad, you can add retaining pieces as shown. Rabbeted pieces will hold on a rectangular head. A circular piece can fit a round end.

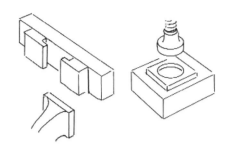

495. Retained Pads

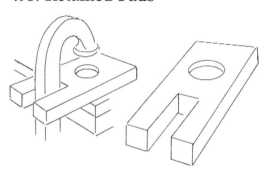

It reduces hassle if pressure pads will hold in place in a cramp. Those shown are suitable for G cramps and others used for the same purpose. It may be possible to cut a pair of pads to suit more than one size of cramp. Make the pads large enough to spread the pressure and long enough for a slot to go well over the back of the cramp. Drill shallow holes to locate the cramp pads. Top and bottom pads should have the same spread on the workpiece for even pressure.

496. Bed It

Coil springs in a sprung bed mattress are tempered to be quite powerful. A spring from a discarded mattress can be converted into cramps for several purposes. The steel is too hard to cut, but it can be broken off after grinding hollows on the edge of a grinding wheel. Grind points on the cut ends to grip the job. A spring cramp can be used on a picture frame mitre, as shown, as well as many other thinner glued assemblies.

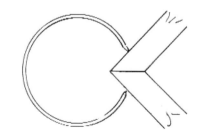

497. Mitre Corner Grip

This is a way to arrange cramp blocks at corners of a picture frame allowing adjustment to many sizes. The four sides are the same. Make strips longer than

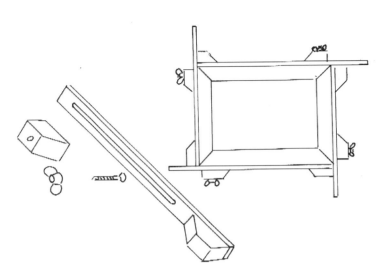

you expect to need. Cut slots to pass a counter-sunk bolt and bevel the inner edges to allow the bolt to come level. Make blocks to go at an end and similar blocks to slide. Cut the blocks so a cramp across the 45° end will press centrally over the corner of an average frame. Glue a block on the end of a strip and drill the other to take the bolt.

498. Tighter Mitres

Most cramping devices for mitered frames rely on pulling the whole frame tight, rather than squeezing the mitres close. It would be better to have cramps at the corners, especially for fairly substantial assemblies. The cramp pads shown are intended for use with G cramps, or others with similar action. They are adaptable to many sizes of frames. Make four pairs, wide enough to take cramp pads. Cut the faces the cramps will grip at the mitre angle, but have the end faces on each piece cut back slightly. In use, cramp a pair of pads to each side, with the working ends a short way back from the corners of the frame. Apply glue and assemble the frame on a flat surface. Use cramps in the directions of the arrows.

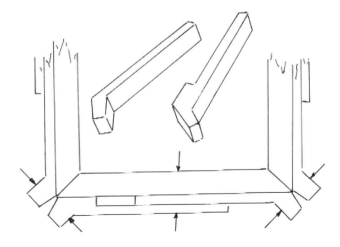

499. Mitre Cramp

The corners of a light picture frame are usually glued and panel pins driven both ways. This shop-made mitre cramp forces a corner tight and holds it while pins are driven. Size will depend on your needs, but a base about 150mm each way should suit most needs. Cut off the corner to give clearance for driving the pins

and make the outer blocks higher than the thickest moulding you expect to use. Fasten them with glue and screws from below, as they will have to take plenty of thrust. Cut the wedges the same. A slope of 1 in 6 would be suitable. Make them thin enough to go inside the rabbets of the frame moulding. Cut the slopes of the adjusting piece to match them and with a slot to give all the adjustment you need. A 6mm or 8mm coach bolt through the base tightens with a wing nut on a large washer.

500. Corner Cramping

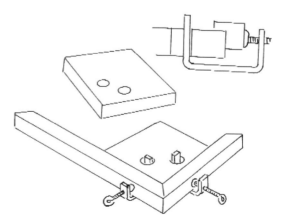

Picture frame corners can be difficult to pull tight. The corner cramp arrangement shown will pull and hold small rabbeted frames, using two strip metal fretwork cramps. Make a square-cornered block at least as thick as the rabbet depth. Drill holes that will clear the cramp ends. In use, adjust the height of a cramp so pressure comes near central on the rabbet.

501. Wedge and Cord Cramping

Most modern synthetic cord and rope (except nylon) has negligible elasticity, so can be pulled very tight. Used with a wedge, it can put on pressure as much as a cramp. To pull a joint together, tie a cord tightly over scrap wood pads and the end of a wedge, as shown. Drive the wedge under the cord. This will also drive the cord diagonally across the work, which helps to tighten it on the job.

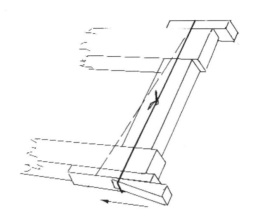

502. Square It

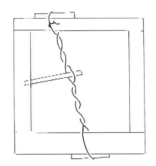

If you assemble a frame and it will not keep in shape while the glue sets, you can use a piece of rope or cord to give an easily regulated pull in the right direction, whether there are cramps on the joints or not. Tie a loop of rope over scrap wood, to avoid marking the job. Slope it in the direction you need the pull and twist it until the frame is square, then lodge the lever against a side.

503. Cramp with Rope

An alternative to conventional cramps, which can be used if you do not have suitable cramps for the job, is the use of rope in a Spanish Windlass. It can put on considerable pressure, with quite a strain on the rope, so use strong rope and protect the edges of the wood

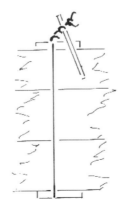
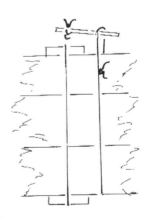

with scrap wood pads. Tie the rope around the job loosely and push a stick through at one side. Use this to twist and tighten the rope. When the pressure is enough, you may be able to lodge the end of the stick against the job, but otherwise you can put another rope or cord round to prevent it unwinding.

504. Cord Cramping

Modern synthetic cord has considerable strength and can be used to put on as much pressure as a cramp, as in the example shown, but you have the problem of locking the cord when the pressure is on. One method is borrowed from camping, where much lighter guy ropes are used today. Make a runner with holes as shown. Make the holes an easy fit on the cord and cut the middle one to the side to form a slot. Thread this on the cord and pull the job tight. Now put the cord from the single side through the slot. This should lock it, but as a further step, pass it behind the protruding knot.

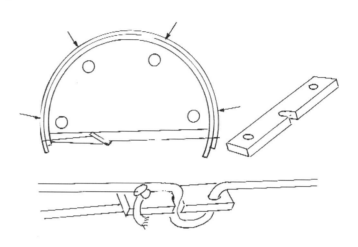

505. Rope Cramps

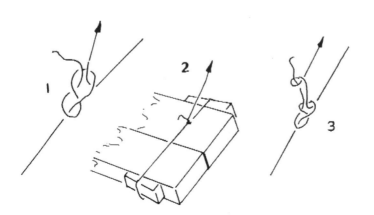

Rope or cord can be used to put on considerable pressure. To avoid it pulling in to edges, use scrap wood pads. If you make these wedge-shaped, you can drive them to get a bit more tightening after the rope is tight. Take the rope round and make a figure-eight knot in one end around the other end, which will be pulled (1). Pull as tight as possible (2). Friction in the knot should stop the rope slackening. Lock it by putting a half hitch with the working part around the projecting end (3) and close this down against the original knot.

506. Closer Curves

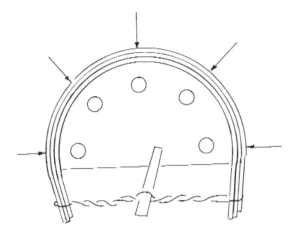

When you bend solid or laminated wood around a former, the ends may not follow the curve and tend to straighten. To avoid this it is best to have the wood long enough to extend. Cramp it as shown by arrows, then use rope on the extended ends to pull them in. Twist the rope in a Spanish windlass and lock the tightening stick against the former.

507. Even Tighter

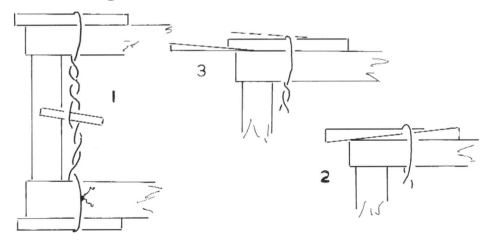

Using a rope as a Spanish windlass (1) can put on as much pressure as a cramp. Use scrap wood pads to prevent the rope pulling into the job. One way of getting even more pressure is to use a pair of folding wedges instead of scrap wood, then drive them together after the rope is tightened (2). Another way is to drive a wedge under one or both pieces of scrap wood (3).

508. Spanish Pull

If you need to move a heavy load, there is a version of the Spanish windlass that can be used with strong rope. There must be a fixed point to take the strain. You need a stout pole a metre or so long. It could be 50mm to 100mm in diameter.

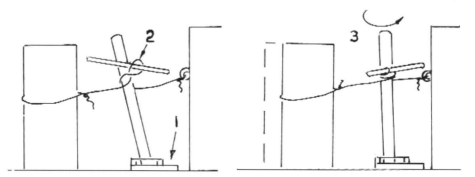

You get more movement with a large diameter and greater leverage with a small one. If the rope will reach, the fixed point could be at any distance - maybe a tree. The foot of the pole must not move in use. On soft ground you could push it into a hollow. On a hard floor use a crude box with the bottom extended to put your foot on (1). The lever could be wood or metal of a size you can handle.

Attach the rope to the fixed point and fairly low on the load to be moved with enough slack to allow you to twist a loop round the lever (2). Tilt the pole towards the load and use the lever to twist the rope round the pole, while its foot is secured and you hold its top. Once you have a tension on the rope, one turn of movement around the pole will move the load a distance about the same as the circumference of the pole, which will become more upright in the process (3). If you need more movement, shorten the rope and start again!

509. Grip Round

If you use parallel-action wood cramps, you can add to their usefulness without affecting their grip on flat surfaces. Cut V grooves, as shown and the jaws will grip round items across and end-on.

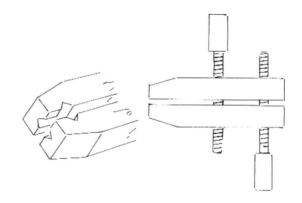

194

510. Better Corner Blocks

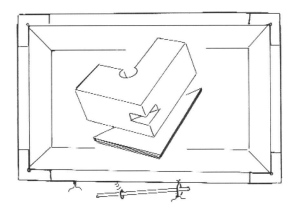

Corner blocks with a cord around are the usual way of pulling a mitered frame together, but with plain blocks there is a risk of the blocks or cord slipping. You can improve blocks by cutting grooves for the cord as shown, and a piece of plywood below the block helps to keep it in place. A cord around can then be twisted to tighten, without anything slipping.

511. Quick Grip

If two pieces of the same thickness have to be held together, a convenient way of holding them for nailing or screwing is shown. Pad under the cramp ends, if you wish.

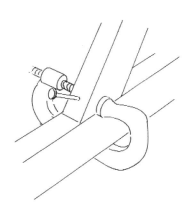

512. Joiner's Dogs

 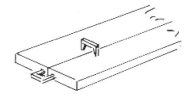

These seem to have disappeared from the market, but if you can find them, they are the simplest form of cramping. They look like large steel staples. The sloping inner surfaces of the legs pull parts together when they are driven. The assembly has to be one that will not matter if the small holes remain after use. They could be especially useful in edge jointing, to hold ends when other cramps are used across.

513. Better Small Cramp

A wooden spring clothes peg has a powerful spring and, within its limits, a peg can make a small cramp but the unaltered pressure area is rather small. The holding power can be improved, as shown. With thin pieces of hardwood about 50mm long glued in the small cramp will grip wood up to about 12 mm.

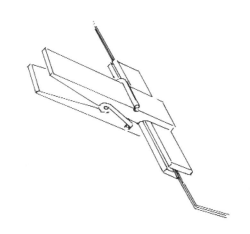

514. Press The Edges

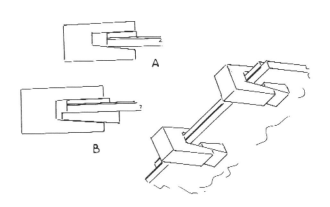

Edges of veneer or plastic laminate tend to lift when being glued and pressure is needed all round. This is often put on with a number of notched pieces of scrap wood (A). You can get a more even pressure if you make the notch deeper so there is space for a separate wedge to be driven (B).

515. Tube Cramps

Off-cuts of large plastic tubes, such as rainwater pipes, can be used as cramps. If rings are cut across, there is enough spring to grip thinner jointed parts. Modern glues do not require excessive pressure and a row of these will provide all that is needed.

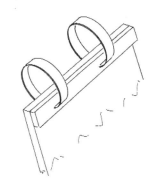

516. Round Cramp

If you need to pull together the parts of a round object, such as a wheel or barrel, and have some Jubilee clips, they can be unscrewed and joined end-to-end to make a circle of any size, with many points of adjustment.

517. Masking Tape Cramping

There is enough strength and grip in masking
tape to allow binding parts while glue sets. Have
long overlaps and several pieces to give the
adhesive good gripping areas. You can nail
through the tape, if necessary, and pull it away
afterwards.

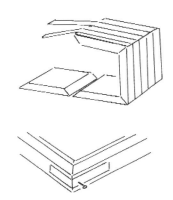

518. Non-stock Former

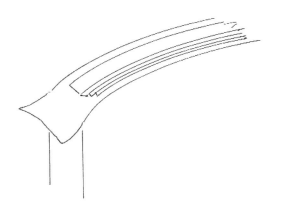

When laminating strips, cramps
cause glue to ooze out and some
of it may get on the former and
stick the workpieces to that. To
prevent this happening, cover
the former with plastic wrapping
tape. The glue will not stick to it.

519. Multi Grip

The device shown
can be used to grip
pieces of irregular
outline when
drilling or doing
other work on
them. Sizes should
suit your require-
ments. The two
sides are identical
and chamfered on
their inner sides.

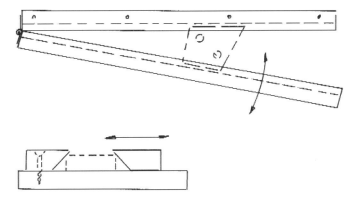

Hinge them at one end. Fix one down to a board, then the other can be swung
to accommodate the job and either held by one hand or a cramp can be put
across the two sides, while work is being done.

520. Weighty Cramping

Glued parts can always be held sufficiently tightly under a weight, if the circumstances are unsuitable for cramping. A problem comes if one surface is shaped and you do not want to risk damaging it. One way of applying an even pressure on an uneven surface is to use a plastic bag full of sand or soil from the garden, as the bottom of this will conform to the shape underneath.

521. No Cramp!

If parts have to be held tight while glue sets and it is a job where you cannot use a cramp or do not have a suitable one, there is a way of invisible cramping using super glue. Put a few spots at the ends or other vital spots and spread the normal glue elsewhere. Hold the parts together for a short time, then leave them for the normal setting time for the ordinary glue.

522. Balloon It

It may not be often that you need to provide inside pressure, but consider the use of a child's balloon when you do. For instance the inside of a cylinder could be veneered and pressure applied evenly by inflating and pushing in a balloon, then deflating it after the glue has set.

523. Soft Grip

When anything with a shaped section, such as moulding, has to be cramped, care is needed not to damage the surface. One material that will conform to a shape under pressure without damaging it is a pencil eraser, which is a fairly hard rubber, and transfers enough pressure.

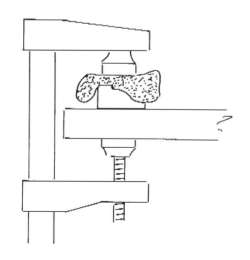

524. Tied Pads

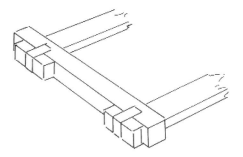

There are several ways of retaining pads when cramping by attaching them to cramp heads. An alternative is to hold them on the workpiece with one or two pieces of masking tape, as shown.

525. Small/Large Cramps

If you do not have sash cramps or other long cramps and need to cramp large frame sections, as when making a framed cabinet, the arrangement shown can be adapted to any size and you can use small cramps to put the pressure on a frame of any size. There are two lengthwise strips and two longer than the frame the other way. One is screwed to the lengthwise strips and the other free to apply pressure. Blocks fixed to the lengthwise strips are spaced to suit available cramps, which can be fitted and used to compress the free strip against the job, with as much pressure as you could get from sash cramps.

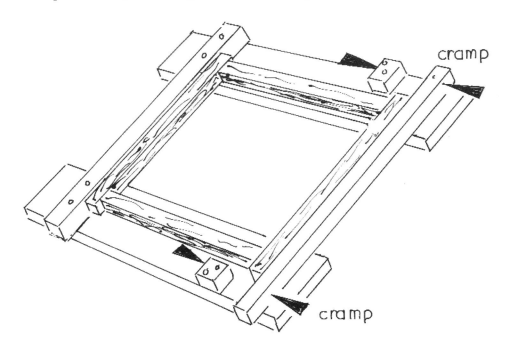

526. Vice Holdfast

When wood has to be held down to the bench or on top of the vice this arrangement can take the place of a bench holdfast or supplement its use. Use a stout piece of close-grained hardwood. Cut at an angle of about 1 in 7 to take the wedge and make a wider wedge to match. In use, set the height so the wedge enters a short distance, tighten the vice and either squeeze the wedge in with a cramp or knock it in with a hammer.

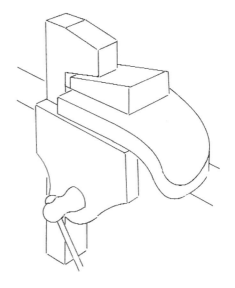

7. Hand Power Tools

Compact reliable electric motors have made possible the hand power tools so common in all workshops. For some purposes they cannot do the work of static power tools and it is unwise to attempt to use them outside their capabilities. Keep the batteries of cordless tools fully charged to avoid strain on them and to prolong their life.

527. More Torque

A drill chuck with a key may be difficult to get really tight on large drills, particularly those oversize drills with reduced shanks, resulting in the chuck jaws marking the slipping drill. You can get more leverage on the key, and find it more comfortable to use, by putting 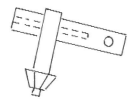 pieces of drilled dowel rod on it and extending the rod on one side. The long end could be drilled to hang on a nail or have a string loop through it.

528. Quick Stop

A simple drill depth stop can be made from a rubber water tap washer. The standard hole may stretch to many sizes, or it can be drilled larger.

529. Simple Depth Stop

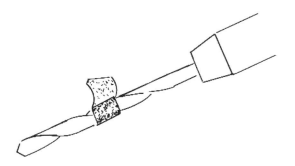

When you want to drill a hole to a certain depth, a quick and simple way of marking the required depth is to put a few turns of electrician's tape round the drill and leave a short length flapping. If you use coloured tape, it will be even more obvious.

530. Clean Holes

You can drill right through into scrap wood and the far side will be clean in many woods, but it could be splintery in others. For the best result use the method common in the days when holes were made with a bit in a hand brace. If it is a bit

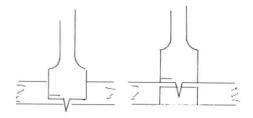

with a central point, stop when the point shows through and reverse the wood to drill back the other way.

531. Small Drill Grip

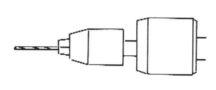

The chucks of most power drills will grip drill bits up to 9mm or more, but they may not grip the smallest drill, such as 2mm. You may have a hand-operated wheel brace, that has been superceded by the power drill. Its chuck will almost certainly have three spring-operated jaws that will go down to the smallest sizes. You could retain this for very small holes. If you want to use the chuck in a power drill, cut off its spindle to grip in the power drill chuck, by removing the bevel gear or, if that is impossible, sawing through.

532. Faster Forstner

Forstner bits have their uses, but they do not cut very quickly. One way of getting through the job quicker if you need to drill deeply with one, is to make a start with the Forstner bit and take it in a few millimetres, then change to a flat or another bit of lesser diameter to remove some waste. Take it as far as you can, but if the reason for the Forstner bit is to make a flat-bottomed hole that does not go through then watch that the point of the other drill does not. Change to the Forstner bit to complete the required hole.

533. Freehand Plugmaking

Plug cutters are intended for use in a drill press. In a handheld electric drill they will move about and not enter to make plugs unless guided. If you are away from your drill press or do not have one, this method will allow you to make plugs to go over counterbored screw heads.

Have a block of wood about as deep as the body of the plug cutter and make holes in it that the cutter will enter easily. This could be cramped to the wood for the plugs, or you could add a piece of plywood, as shown, to grip in a vice. The hand-held cutter will work effectively through it.

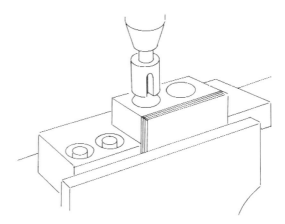

534. Drill Sizes

If you need to measure the diameter of a drill with twisted flutes with a micrometer or vernier calliper, do not measure at the cutting end or anywhere along the flutes. Measure at the solid shank, for a correct reading.

535. Grip a Keyless Chuck

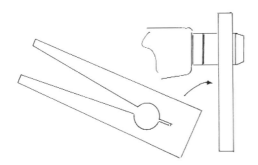

Keyless drill chucks are convenient, but it is often difficult to grip and tighten them sufficiently and then release them. Using a steel wrench may damage the surface of the chuck. A wooden wrench will do the job without marking the chuck. Use fairly thick hardwood and make a hole that fits the chuck. Cut into it to provide the handles and make a saw cut at its far side to provide spring.

536. Nut Check

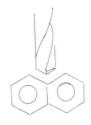

The common Morse-pattern drill should be sharpened so both cutting edges are at the same angle. If not, one cuts more than the other and the hole may be larger or that edge blunts first. The end should be at 1200, or each side at 600

to the centreline of the drill. A simple way to check this is by putting two hexagonal nuts together, preferably glued or cramped. The combined angles are what you need.

537. Perpendicular Drilling

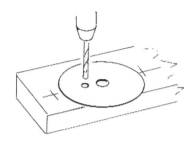

When drilling a hole with a hand-held electric drill, it is not always easy to see if the hole is being made perpendicular to the surface. A discarded CD can be made to help. Its playing surface is sufficiently reflective to be used as a mirror. Drill a hole in the CD, either the same size as the drill bit you are using or a little bigger. Put this over the spot to be drilled. The drill will be reflected in it. When the reflection is in line with the actual drill bit, you are drilling perpendicularly.

538. Drill Squarely

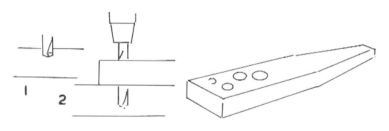

If you need to drill holes square to a surface and have to use a hand-held power drill, it is risky to depend on just sight. Make a guide from thick wood, drilled on a drilling machine with holes of a size you expect to use. Extend one end as a handle. Drill a shallow locating hole in the work piece (1). Put the drill through its matching hole in the jig and find the locating hole with its point, then drill fully and squarely (2).

539. Other Way

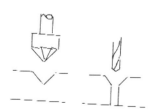

It is usual to drill a hole for a screw and then countersink it. It is too easy with a countersink bit in a power drill to overdo it, or the bit may snatch and make an uneven outline. You get better control and a more even effect if you countersink first. The bit that makes the hole has a positive position to locate it centrally.

540. Better Small Countersinking

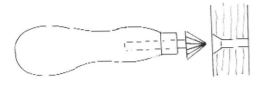

If you use a countersink bit in a power drill, or even in a hand drill, it is too easy to overdo it on small screw holes, so the screw head finishes below the surface. In soft woods you have to allow for the head pulling in, so countersinking has to be slight. For sinking small screw heads accurately, the job can be done with a rose countersink bit mounted in a file handle, a specially turned one or even a piece of dowel rod. A few waggles should make an adequate countersink. It is also useful for removing raggedness where the drill breaks through at the far side of a hole. Lock the bit in its hole with epoxy adhesive.

541. Drilling Guide

If holes have to be drilled squarely, using a hand-held drill, a try square may be stood on edge and sighted, but it is easily knocked or shaken over. A better sighting object is made from two square-cut pieces of wood nailed together, as shown.

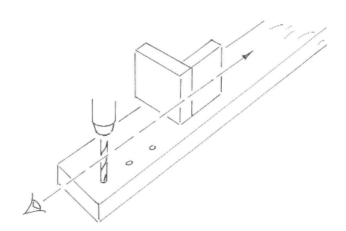

542. Longer Screw Driving

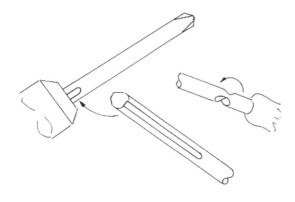

Screwdriver bits intended to be gripped in the chuck of an electric drill are usually quite short, yet there are places where you need a longer reach. A longer screwdriver bit can be made from the blade of a cheap hand screwdriver. To cut the hardened steel, use the edge of a grinding wheel to make nicks on opposite sides of the blade near the handle and snap it off. Grind the cut end flat and grind three flats at equal distances around the end that will go into the chuck to help the jaws grip.

543. Mortising Jig

A drill can be used to remove waste wood from a mortice, but without guidance the amount is limited. The jig shown controls the drill and most of the waste can be removed (1), leaving not much for the chisel. Drill separate holes in a block, with the drill to be used. Make their overall length half a hole with a diameter

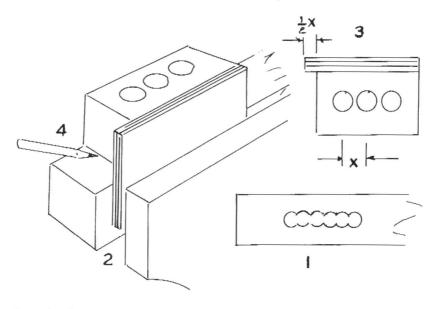

less than the final length of the mortice. Attach a piece of plywood to grip in the vice (2) and project at one end half the distance the hole centres are apart (3). Put the block in position and mark on the workpiece the position of its end (4). Drill the holes through the jig, then move it along so the edge of the plywood is on the line. Drill through again and this will remove the wood between the first holes.

544. Stop Wandering

There are no problems when cutting crossgrain plugs in a drill press, but if you have to do it with a handheld electric drill, the cutter will not stay in position, but try to wander across the surface. If you want to make crossgrain plugs without using a drill press, first drill shallow holes, preferably with a Forstner bit. They can be the same size as the plug cutter or the nearest size larger. The cutter will stay put and you make and remove plugs in the usual way.

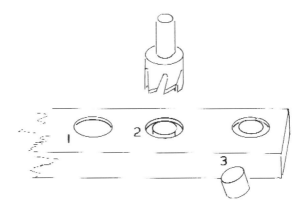

545. Safer Screwing

Screwdriver bits for use in a power drill are often reversible. The end for socket-head screws works very well, but the end intended for slot-head screws is not so successful, as it is difficult to keep the end in the screw slot. If it jumps off, surrounding wood will be damaged. It is a help to use a guide, as shown (1). The holes should be only a little larger than the diameter of a screw head or the bit,

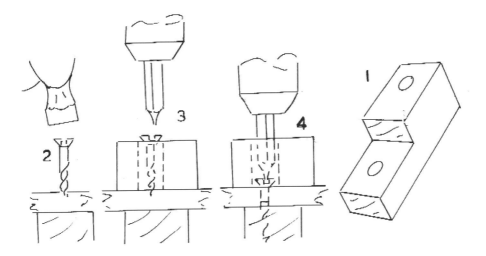

which will be about the same. In hardwood you will need to drill a pilot hole, but usually in softwood, you can let the screw cut its own way in. Start a screw with a hammer (2). Use the thick part of the guide in early driving (3). The hole will stop the bit straying enough to matter. Go all the way in that hole, if you can (4), or if the bit is short, change to the other hole. Keep a good grip on the guide, while driving.

546. Drilling Plastics

If you try to drill plastic with a metalworking drill, it will snatch in most plastics and cause a ragged hole as it breaks through or shatters the material. For safe clean drilling, grind the cutting edges in line with the drill for a small amount. Drill slowly. Heat is generated by fast drilling and some plastics will soften enough to go out of shape or seize on the drill, causing an inaccurate hole.

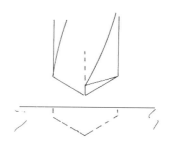

547. Jigsaw Control

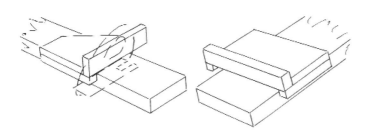

A jigsaw is not designed to cut straight unless there is some form of control. You could use a similar operation to that used for a router across a board when using the tool for cross cutting. Alternatives are shown. The single-side one fits against the board like a bench hook and can be held or cramped there. This allows right-handed cutting, but if you want to be able to turn the gauge round you can make the two-sided one. Make it longer than the widest boards you expect to cut.

548. Straight Jigsaw Cuts

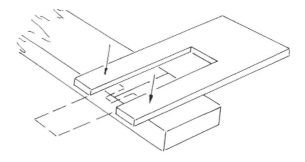

Jigsaws have become more powerful and most are capable of cutting quite thick wood. They are intended for freehand cutting curves. Guidance is needed if you want a straight cut. You can, for instance, use your jigsaw for crosscutting boards. Even if you cramp on a single guide strip, the saw will try to wander from it. The guide shown, cramped on as indicated by the arrows, will help you make a straight cut across a board. Use plywood thicker than the jigsaw base. Cut the slot an easy fit on the base and longer than the widest board you expect to cut. Allow an extension to hold the sides parallel.

549. Jigsaw a Circle

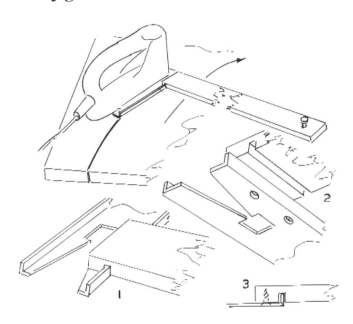

If you try to follow a line with a jigsaw to make a circle or an arc freehand, the edge will not be perfect and considerable work with other tools may not get the result you want. The answer is to make the jigsaw into a compass, but the usual tool is not equipped to take a radius arm. One can be improvised as shown. Most jigsaws have a base made from sheet metal with turned up edges. A wooden radius arm of any length can be attached to it, and removed without affecting the use of the jigsaw in other ways. Notch the end of the radius arm loosely over either edge of the base (1). Drill and countersink holes for two screws into it through the base (2 and 3). Use a nail or awl as the pivot and feed the saw slowly for the best edge.

550. Jigsaw Stand

The vital part of a jigsaw is the blade. If you are unlucky when you put the tool down, you could bend or break the blade. The stand shown provides a rest when you want to put the jigsaw down between cuts and could act as permanent storage. Spare

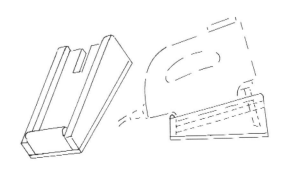

blades can be stored in the space underneath. For most jigsaws you could make the stand from 12mm wood. Allow enough slope for any blade and cut the support to be a loose fit on the bottom of the tool.

551. Better Shaping

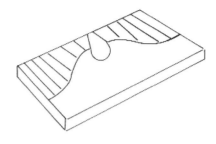

When cutting a shaped part with a band saw, jigsaw or scroll saw, you will get better results if you make some cuts into the waste part first, so pieces break away as you progress. If there are points in the pattern, approach them from opposite directions to get a sharp finish. In the shape shown, cut into the hollowed part from the edge, to remove its waste, then cut the outline curves towards it.

552. Minimum Tearout

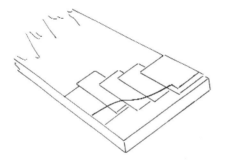

A jigsaw cuts on the up stroke, so it tends to leave the cut ragged on the side where you are following a line. This can be reduced by marking out on overlapping pieces of masking tape and cutting through them. They will peel off without leaving marks.

553. Turn It Over

A jigsaw cuts on the up stroke, so any roughness is on the top and dust may obscure the line. This is unsatisfactory when cutting small or intricate shapes. One way to avoid this when making small shapes, is to mount the saw upside-down in the vice, as shown. The wood is being cut downwards, so the top surface stays smooth and there is little dust.

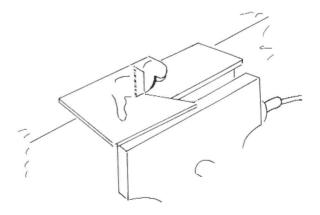

554. Tidy Blades

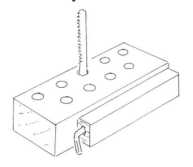

Jigsaw blades are easily lost in the clutter on the bench. If you store them in a box, they may blunt each other. A block like a drill stand will keep the blades apart and easy to select. If your jigsaw needs an Allen key, it can be held in a block at the front.

555. Cut Uptight

A jigsaw is normally used on wood held horizontally, but it is just as successful at other angles. An example is cutting a hole in weatherboarding. This would be a job for a reciprocating or sabre saw, if one is available, but a jigsaw can be used vertically in the same way. Choose a coarse blade and work slowly.

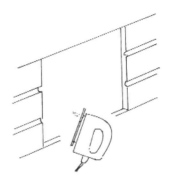

556. Belt Cleaner

A sanding belt tends to clog before it has worn out and can be cleaned with a material sold for the purpose, but hard rubber is quite effective. Try using a piece of garden hose or discarded rubber doormat.

557. Inverted Orbit

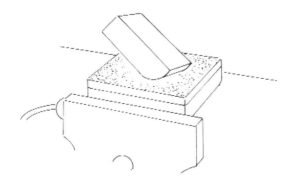

An orbital sander is intended to be used on areas larger than its working surface. To sand small items, most sanders can be inverted and the body gripped in a vice, so the wood can be moved on them, as shown. Make sure the moving part is clear of the bench and vice and do not tighten the vice excessively.

558. Sanding Line-up

Many orbital and other sanders need the ventilating holes on the disc lined up with those in the backing plate as it is fitted. It helps in getting this right if you keep two short pieces of dowel rod that fit the holes available to press in the backing plate and slip the disc over.

559. Punch Plate

Many orbital sanders have holes for dust to be extracted through the abrasive paper and suitable matching perforated paper can be bought. If there is no perforating plate supplied for making your own, this template can be made. Put a piece of paper on the pressure pad and mark its outline and holes. Use this for 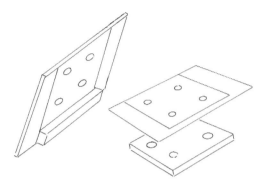 marking and drilling a thin plywood template, with a piece to rest against an edge and extensions, if end pieces are needed, for attaching. Push an awl through the holes when marking the paper. There is no need for precision holes.

560. End Biscuits

 If biscuits are to be used in a corner joint, such as a box, care is needed when cutting the slots in a surface near an end, particularly if it is end grain and there is a risk of it breaking out. Hold a thick piece against the end, with cramps or a vice and check the angle is 90°. Cutting biscuit slots should then be as free of risk as possible.

561. Dry Biscuits

Biscuits for jointing are made to be absorbent so they soak up glue in a joint and expand. This means that if they are left exposed to moist air, they will absorb water and expand, possibly to the stage where they will not go in the cut slots. Keep them from exposure to air in sealed plastic bags or closed metal or plastic boxes.

562. Short Biscuiting

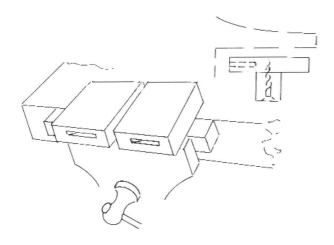

If you need to make cuts for biscuit joints in the ends of short strips, there is a problem of holding them so the biscuit jointer can do its job. Short pieces can be held as shown, so there is nothing to restrict the end of the jointer. Two or more together will give a wider bearing for the jointer. Screw through a block that can be held in the vice. The small holes left by the screws can usually be hidden inside the assembled job.

563. Saw Guide

To cut squarely with a hand-held circular saw you can use a T-square guide similar to that used with a router, but with a thicker strip. Use a thick straight strip, so the saw base is unlikely to ride up on it. Attach a strip stock to it, but do not cut it to length yet. The guide strip

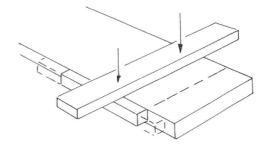

should be square to it, projecting a short way behind it,. and be further than you expect to cut in front of it. The first cuts you make will also cut the stock to length.

564. Tighter Screws

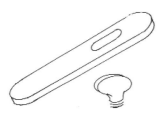

Some thumbscrews on power tools are not easy to tighten sufficiently by hand. Where there is no restriction of space, a slotted lever made from thin plywood will give you more leverage. Make the slot a loose fit over the screw head.

565. Toggle It

One way of keeping a coiled cable tidy when out of use is to hold it with a toggle loop close to the power tool. This is a piece of cord with a loop at one end and a wood toggle at the other; the whole thing being long enough to go round the coiled cable and allow the toggle to be pushed through the loop to lock it. The toggle could be turned or a piece of dowel rod. The loop and wrap round the toggle could be bound with thread or electrician's tape.

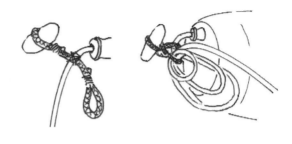

566. Tidier Leads

If you have several hand power tools with leads, the maze of these cables can be a nuisance on the bench. A way to reduce this problem is to cut each power tool lead quite short and fit a plug to it. Have one long extension lead with a socket on its end and plug into this as needed.

567. Secure Cable

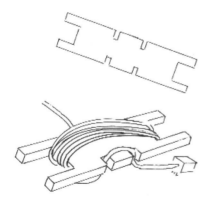

Electric cables to power tools are often wound on shuttles, but there is usually nothing to stop them uncoiling. This shuttle will lock the cable, but it can be released for use easily.

Make a shuttle, as shown, with widely spaced notches in the sides. These can be wider than the cable diameter, as when the cable is bent it will grip the openings.

568. Tighter Wing Nuts

Wing nuts or screws are used on many machines, but it is often difficult to tighten enough, particularly if machine adjustments mean the wings are awkward to reach. Using pliers or other long means of leverage could overdo it or even cause damage. The wing spanner shown helps you get a little more torque

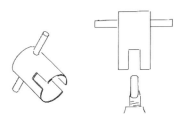

without straining yourself or risking damage. Use a piece of metal tube that will go over the wing and cut a slot that makes an easy fit. Drill across for a metal rod handle, which may just push in or be soldered there. Keep the whole spanner short, so it can go into restricted places.

569. Tighter Knobs

Some power tools have plastic knobs that do not offer a very good grip when tightening or loosening. A way of getting more leverage without affecting the appearance of a knob is to drill a hole into which a nail or awl can be pushed.

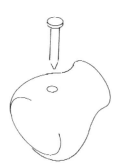

570. Allen Handle

It is difficult to get much leverage with the usual bent steel Allen key, especially when turning with the short end. It needs a handle. A simple one can be made by ploughing a groove to fit on the edge of a wide board and cutting off a strip, as shown. Drill for the key and fix it with epoxy adhesive, if you want it to be permanent. Round off edges and corners for comfort.

571. Better Looking

Bought wooden handles with dowel ends are convenient when you need a set to match, but the method of manufacture leaves a dimple at the centre of the knob, just where it shows. You could get rid of this by sanding it in the chuck of a lathe,

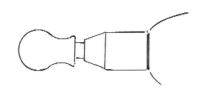

but you could also do it by gripping the dowel end in the chuck of a power or hand drill and rotating the knob against a piece of abrasive paper held in the palm of your hand.

572. Much Charge

If you have a cordless power tool, you have a charger. If you have several cordless power tools, you have several chargers, and until chargers are standardised, you will gather more. Label them to avoid confusion.

8. Machine Tools

Most workshops contain static machine tools, most of which are self-contained and designed for their purpose, and it is unwise to consider modifying them, so most work done to or for them is in the form of additions. Such modifications are usually concerned with the feeding of wood to or from machines or finding more convenient ways of using them.

A machine tool is designed with a certain capacity and it is unwise to try to exceed its limitations. Overloading can be dangerous and will reduce the life of the machine, particularly the motor.

573. Safe Chuck Key

To protect your knuckles when turning a chuck key hard, knock out the lever so you can put a rubber washer on the shaft, then refit the lever.

574. Easier Tightening

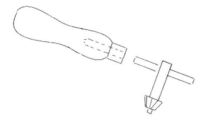

The key for a drill or other chuck does not offer much leverage and it may be difficult to get the tightness you want. A drilled out file handle, or one specially turned, can put on the extra leverage needed, without affecting the key for normal use.

575. Drill Press Table

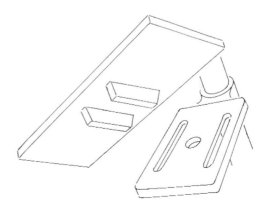

Many pieces to enlarge a drill press table involve using bolts. This is a quick-fit extension that can be fitted or removed easily. It depends on the two blocks, which should be tapered, so when they are pushed into the grooves in the metal table they hold securely when fully down.

576. Cylinder Cramp

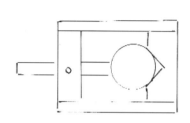
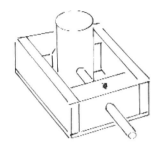

If a cylindrical piece has to be held endwise on the drill press or for other work, it is not easy to keep it exactly in position. This cramping box will hold a cylinder or tube of any size up to its width. Make a box of the size you need, with two thick ends. Notch one end and drill the other for a dowel rod. Both should be cut squarely for a true hold. Drill for a screw to hold the dowel rod. Flatten its end for a better bearing on the rod. To hold a cylinder, push the rod tight against it and tighten the screw.

577. Drilling Support

The usual drill press we use was originally designed for metalworking and does not have as big a table as we often need for woodwork, so pieces of wood may be difficult to keep level. An extended table can be made with a piece of flat

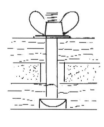
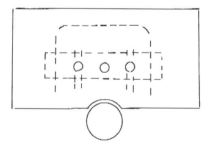

wood of the size you want, held with two counter-bored coach bolts through the metal table slots to wing nuts and washers on a cramping strip below. A hole below the chuck gives clearance for the drill. A notch around the pillar provides location, if the board is removed and replaced.

578. Lined-up Holes

When using the drill press to make a series of holes to remove the waste from a mortise, or making a series of holes for rails, it is helpful to have a guide to keep the holes in line and the same distance from the edge. The guide shown extends each side of the drill table and provides plenty of support.

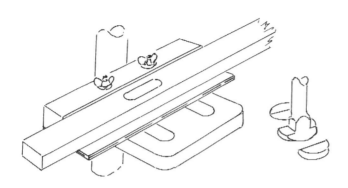

A square strip fixed to a plywood base is held to the drill table with two coach bolts through washers and wing nuts. So the bolts can be put through the table slots from the top, saw off the sides of their heads. A bolt can be slid through and turned to grip below.

579. Drilled Ball

To make a hole centrally through a ball, it is unlikely to be accurate if you rely only on eye. The arrangement shown will hold the ball and show you the centre. Drill two matching pieces of wood with holes not more than

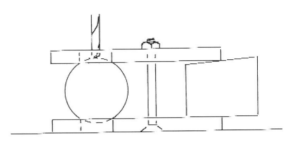

half the diameter of the ball and holes to take a bolt, which should countersink into one of them. Grip the ball between the holes using a packing to keep the pieces of wood close to parallel when a nut is tightened on the bolt. If you drill centrally in the top hole, using a drill press, the hole will go through the centre of the ball.

580. Accurate Drill Location

It is not always easy to enter a drill exactly where you want it, either by hand or using a drill press. It helps if you centrepunch the positions, in the same way as is done for metal. When you buy a centrepunch it is sharpened at 60° for metal. It is better to grind it to a finer point for wood, as this offers a better guide to a wood drill point.

581. Smaller Drills

The chuck on a drilling machine is designed to take drills up to 9mm or more, which it does very well, but if you want to hold very small drills, it is not always successful. If you have a discarded hand drill, its smaller chuck, which will take the smallest drills, is on a parallel shank. Grip this in the large machine chuck and the drill in the small chuck.

582. Hole Saw Clearing

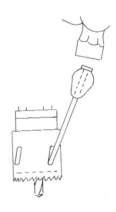

When a hole saw is used in a pillar drill to cut circles out of sheet material, the waste material removed tends to jamb inside it. A large nail with its end filed flat can be used through the slots provided to drive it out, but can be awkward to hold. It is easier to hold and control if you turn and drill a block to form a handle, as shown.

583. Line-up Drill

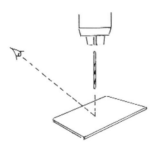

The chuck on a drill press takes large drills with no trouble, but although it will hold a small drill, it is difficult to line it up at the centre of the three jaws. It can get locked between two jaws and runs out of true. An aid to getting a drill in line is a mirror laid on the drill table. If you hold the drill up to the chuck you can see when it is central to the jaws.

584. Evenly Spaced

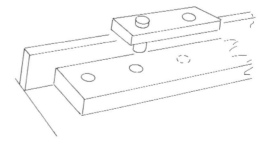

You may mark hole spacing evenly, but the drill may not enter exactly on the mark every time. If precise spacing is important, this jig will ensure good results. It uses a fence on the table of a drill press. Drill two holes at the distance needed from the edge and at the spacing required. Put a piece of dowel rod in one of them. After drilling the first hole in the workpiece, put the dowel in it and drill the next hole through the other jig hole, and so on along the wood.

585. Drill Stop

One of the simplest ways of providing a stop as well as a depth gauge for drilling is to first drill through a piece of dowel rod, so the drill extends the right amount.

586. Double Trough

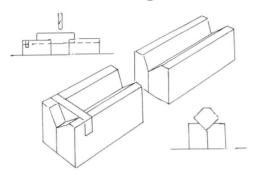

The long trough we use to hold square stock when planing it octagonal or preparing it for the lathe can be improved by cutting it in two. The parts can be separated to support longer square pieces and used on the drill press, with a gap between, to support round pieces being drilled.

587. Tighter Plugs

When a screw is counterbored, it is not usually sunk very far below the surface, but a plug cutter makes a crossgrained plug longer than the depth of the hole. If it is a tapered plug and you just drive the glued small end in (A), it may not make a fit as tight as you want. If you cut off a piece from the thicker end of the plug, leaving a little extra for levelling (B), and glue that in, it will fit closer and be less obvious.

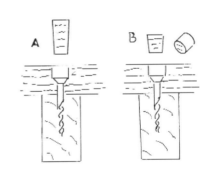

588. Plug Release

If you use a plug cutter to make plugs for counter-bored screw holes randomly in scrap wood, they have to be broken out, probably with the narrowest chisel you have, bevel downwards. This is unlikely to be narrow enough, particularly for the smallest plugs.

You can make a tool for the purpose from a screwdriver intended for the smaller screws of the slot-head type, or from a piece of steel rod about 3mm diameter fixed in a handle or just a piece of dowel rod. File or grind the end to a chisel shape. It will not be tempered hard enough for use as a chisel, but it will lever out plugs.

589. Trim Plugs

When levelling crossgrain plugs over counterbored screws with a chisel, make a preliminary cut with the chisel bevel downwards (1). This will show you if the grain in the plug slopes into the hole and might break below the surface, so you can check the best way to take a slicing cut with the chisel bevel upwards (2).

590. Drill Sanding

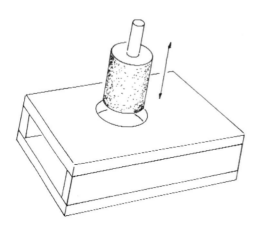

Mounting a sanding drum in a drill press can be successful and economical. Make the hollow box shown, to cramp on the table of the drill press. Make it deep enough for the sanding drum to go down its full length. Have a hole to clear the drum. Grip the sanding drum in the drill chuck. The drum can be used at a fixed height for work held against it or used up and down for economy and a smoother finish.

591. End Drilling

To make holes accurately in ends of rectangular stock, the piece should be supported. A simple way is shown. The L pieces should be parallel and square and large enough to be held steady.

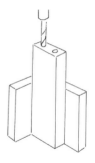

592. Accurate Tapping

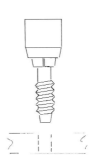

To cut a thread in a hole in wood the tap has to be kept square to the surface, particularly on entry, otherwise the thread will be damaged. A good way to keep the tap straight is to grip it in the chuck of a drill press. Pull the chuck round by hand, or pull round one of the belt pulleys, as you feed carefully downwards with the handle.

593. Wood Mitre Fence

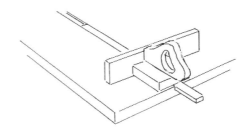

The standard mitre fence supplied with most machines is small and inadequate. It is rarely used on a circular saw for any but square cuts. This fence does not adjust, but gives a wide push. With support nearer the saw you have better control.

If possible use a metal strip in the groove, although hardwood should also be satisfactory as it will last for a long time. Make the face piece as deep as you expect to need and take the end fairly close to the line of the sawcut. Have a stout supporting block. The handle could be a piece of dowel rod or something more elaborate. You could fit a discarded saw handle.

594. Stop Kickback

When you feed a short piece of wood into a circular saw, it will kick back if the leading edge rises as it starts the cut. One way of preventing this is with a featherboard used vertically. The fence is probably not deep enough to allow

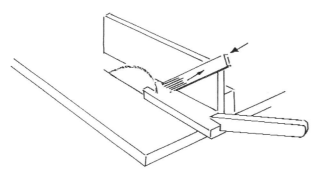

you to cramp a featherboard directly to it. Cramp on a board to provide extra width and cramp to it a featherboard that will hold down the wood as it meets the saw blade.

595. Splitter Alignment

If the splitter is not exactly in line with a circular saw blade it can cause problems as the wood runs through. It can be checked with two matching straight pieces of wood. The splitter is thinner than the set of the saw teeth. Have the saw near its 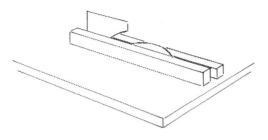 maximum height. Hold or cramp the strips each side of the saw. The splitter should come midway between them if it is set properly.

596. Saw Squareness

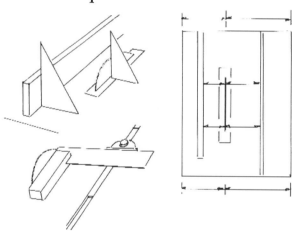 When you cut wood on the circular saw you count on angular settings being exactly what they should; in most cases 90° Maybe they are, but you should check your machine occasionally.

Put a try or set square on the table against the fully raised saw blade. Sight through and see that it is upright. Do the same with the fence. Measure from the ends of the exposed blade to see that the fence is parallel to it. Do the same the other way to check the groove for the mitre fence. Set the mitre fence to its 90° calibration and test a try square against it and the saw blade. If you use a sled or other shop-made jig that has to be guided by the table sides, check they are parallel to each other and to the saw blade. It is the relation of everything else to the saw blade that matters. If there is an error that cannot be corrected, you must allow for it when working.

597. Featherboards

A featherboard can hold and guide wood through a circular saw. Its commonest use is relieving you of the need to use a hand to hold the wood close to the fence, as shown.

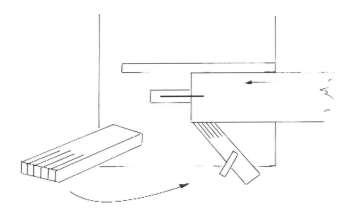

Use wood thick enough to not let the workpiece ride up on it. Cut the end at an angle (about 45° is suitable). Make several saw cuts in the end. How many and how long depends on the flexibility of the wood. Cramp the featherboard to the saw table, so it presses against the wood being cut.

598. Set Mitre Fence to Wood

To cut an angle on a circular saw exactly as required, it is advisable to rely on marking the wood and not the calibrations on the mitre fence. One way is to mark the angle on the face side of one piece, then to square it round to the other side. Set the inverted mitre fence to this, as shown, and the setting will be exact.

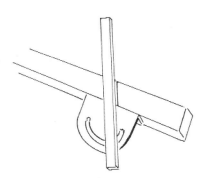

599. Adjustable Fence

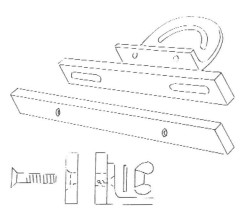

The sliding mitre fence supplied with most circular saws, band saws and router tables, does not give very wide support, so a workpiece may not stay steady on it. Additionally, you need the work supported close to the cutter for the best results. Putting a wider wooden face on the fence helps, but only has one coverage. An adjustable auxiliary fence is shown. Screw a strip to the metal fence, extending far enough each way for you to make slots to give the amount of movement you need. Put a longer piece outside this with countersunk bolts through it to fit in the slots and be locked in position with washers and wing nuts.

600. Depth Set Block

A square block of wood with notches at various depths can save time and trouble when setting depths of cut on several machines, such as a router and a circular saw. Make a block of hardwood of a size convenient to handle and cut rabbets around it at known depths. There can be as many as eight. Mark the depths over each rabbet.

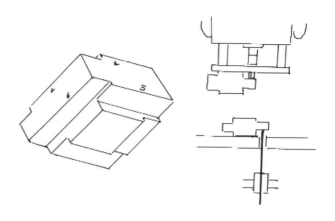

601. Non-slip Fence

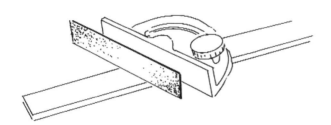

The face of a mitre fence for most machines is smooth metal. It can be improved by gluing on a piece of abrasive paper to give a better hold on the wood.

602. Tighter Fence

The body of the mitre fence is held at the angle you want with a screw through a slot. In many cases the screw head has a small knurled head, which is difficult to get really hand tight. It can be extended to give a more powerful grip. Use a piece of hardwood planed octagonal and drilled with a hole that makes a push fit on the knurled head. Fix it on with epoxy adhesive.

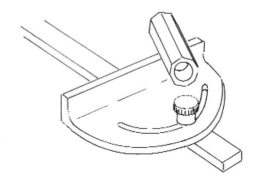

603. Squared Saw Cuts

The groove for the mitre fence in a circular saw table is parallel to the saw cut and should be square to the edge of the table. Check it. Much of the work of a mitre fence is pushing wood to make cuts at 90°. To set it accurately, you can turn it over in the groove and run the mitre head against the edge of the table before tightening the locking screw.

604. Really Square

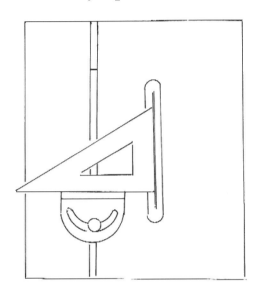

The mitre fence on a circular saw is mainly used to guide wood being trimmed square across, but is it truly square? The calibrations are rather coarse and the setting may be out of true. The guide groove may not be exactly parallel to the saw blade, which is what decides the actual direction of cut. The check for 90° should be with the saw blade, so it is worthwhile using a set square against the blade to get the fence correctly adjusted.

605. Permanent Side Pressure

If you can arrange a pivot point outside or at the edge of a saw or router table, you can have a side pressure pad permanently in position. Locate the pivot point towards the feed end of the table. Make the pad from wood 18mm or more thick. Mark on it where its end will come when cutting close to the saw and fence and where its edge should be when holding the widest board you expect to cut. Draw and cut a curve through these points. The pad should then allow you to swing and hold for any width board being cut or routed.

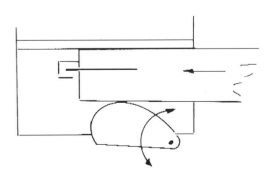

606. Saw Sled

For accurate crosscutting
on a circular saw the best
guide is a sled. This will
control long pieces of
wood and pieces of sheet
material. The width of the
sled is controlled by the
width of the saw table,
although you can extend
the width of the sled

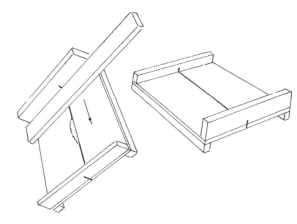

slightly. The length can accommodate any size you require, but too large a sled
becomes cumbersome and unwieldy when only cutting across strips.

The main part is a piece of sheet material, such as plywood. Underneath are
guide strips to slide against the sides of the saw table. There is a fairly high push
strip and a matching lower batten at the other end. Slide the whole assembly over
the saw to make the kert. In use, the workpiece is held against the push piece and
the whole sled moved across the saw.

607. Exact Saw Angles

The mitre fence supplied with most circular saws has calibrations that only give
an approximate angle – certainly not as precise as we need for accurate joints. It
is better to set the fence with two straight strips of wood and ignore these
calibrations. Mark on a straight moderately wide piece of scrap wood the angle

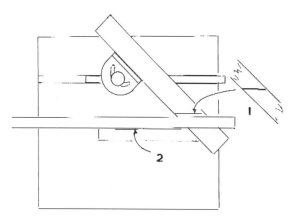

you want to cut (1). Put
another straight piece of
scrap wood against the saw
blade (2). Put the mitre
fence in place with its
adjusting knob slack. Hold
the marked strip against it,
as shown, then adjust
under the strip against the
saw blade until the pieces
match, lock the mitre fence
for a precise setting.

608. Double-action Push

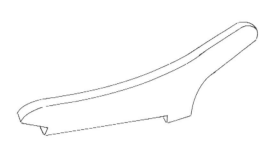

It is often necessary to hold down a piece of wood as it enters a circular saw. If you are only removing a small amount, there is nothing outside to hold. This dual-purpose push stick can overlap the wood and hold it down, then as it gets into the cut the notch in the end can be used to push in the usual way. A distance between the notches of about 150mm should suit the common home workshop machine.

609. Four Pushes

A push stick for a circular saw soon gets damaged and, when there is only one notch, it may be dangerous to continue using the damaged end. A stick with four notches, as shown, gives you alternatives ready to take over if the notch you are using becomes broken. When all four are useless, you can cut them off and start again.

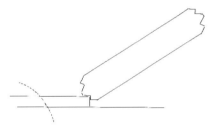

610. Short Push

When cutting shorter pieces of wood on a circular saw they tend to ride up, so they need holding down as well as pushing. This is further complicated if the cut

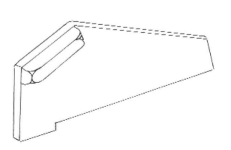

is fairly close to the fence. The push stick shown is long enough to hold the wood down and is high enough for the hand to be above the fence. The handgrip is on the side away from the blade to give ample clearance when pushing wood for a narrow cut. It is unwise to try to use the circular saw for very short pieces of wood.

611. Safe Push

When making a cut fairly close to the fence on a circular saw, this push stick is safer to use than the usual type. Make it high enough for the grip to come above the top of the fence. Allow a good overlap on the notched part, to hold the wood down.

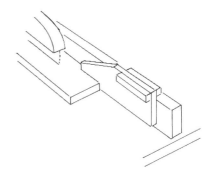

612. Multiple Push Stick

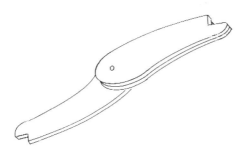

For safety wood should be pushed through the circular saw with a stick having as deep a notch as possible, but most push sticks have a rather shallow notch for use on all thickness of wood. The arrangement shown consists of three push sticks pivoted together. You can choose one with a notch to suit the wood being pushed. Make the three identical parts, except for the notches, preferably from hardwood. Make them long enough to grip where they join and of a size you can hold comfortably. The pivot could be a bolt through or a nail long enough to go through and be clenched.

613. Controller Push

The usual push stick for use on a circular saw is narrow and has a small notch. The wider one shown stops the job lifting and there is plenty of wood for re-cutting if the working end becomes damaged.

614. Safer Push

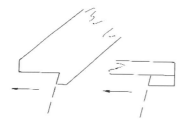

It is usual to cut the notch in a push stick for a circular saw or the angle of the thrust piece of a push stick for a planer at right-angles, but it will be less likely to slip if it is arranged at a few degrees less than 90° as shown.

615. Feathers

When you push a piece of wood through a circular saw or against the fence of a router table, you need to press sideways as well as forward. The sideways pressure is usually applied with a small block of wood, on which you tend to press mainly at its forward end. 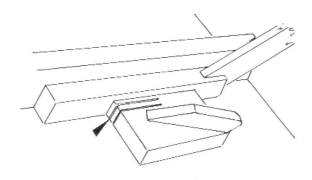 To cushion this it is a good idea to make some saw cuts, to give something like a featherboard effect.

616. Circular Saw Storage

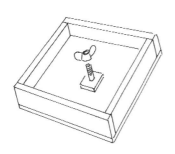

If you have several spare circular saw blades, they should be protected during storage. This need not be elaborate; a simple box is shown. Put a bolt through the middle. Anything available will do, it does not have to be the bore of the blades. Put a block of hardboard, plywood or MDF on the bolt to lift the bottom blade. Have several more of these to act as washers between the blades and under a wing nut holding them in.

617. No Pinch

When ripping some wood the board warps after passing the saw blade and the kerf may pinch on the saw. The far end of the fence is often the trouble. Cramp on a board to act as an auxiliary fence with its end opposite the centre of the saw blade, this will free the cut parts to warp or bend as they will.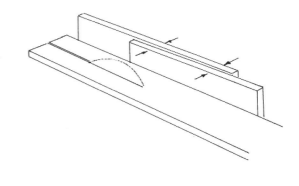

618. Accurate Diagonals

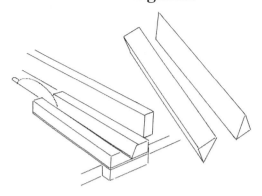

Triangular pieces cut diagonally from square stock are needed to reinforce corners. Cutting them accurately is not easy without support. This jig will hold a square strip so a diagonal cut can be made exactly. Two pieces planed at 45° are mounted on a piece of thin plywood. Make the assembly long enough to overlap the circular saw a short distance. A stop block underneath rests against the edge of the saw table. Have the inner strip wide enough to give the job clearance from the rip fence, when the jig is held against it. Prepare the jig for use with a preliminary cut against the saw at the bottom of the V.

619. Matching Wedges

When you need wedges, you usually need a set all at the same slope. You can do this on a circular saw, cutting cross-grain blanks with the aid of a simple jig/push stick.

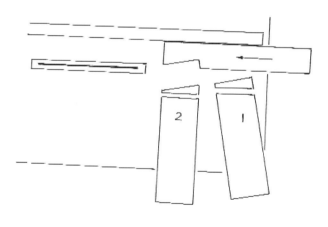

Make the stick long enough to keep your hands clear and with a notch the size of the wedge required. Push the square end of the blank into the notch and cut the first wedge. Turn the blank over and push it in again to cut the second wedge. Continue in these alternate ways until you have enough wedges.

620. Less Breakout

When cutting wood on a circular saw, particularly across the grain of softwood, slow the feed towards the end of a cut and there will be less risk of splintering and ragged grain at the edge.

621. No Kick Back

When feeding wood into a circular saw, it should be held absolutely flat on the saw table. If the leading edge tilts up, even slightly, when it meets the saw teeth it will kick back. It is better if the leading edge is at a slight downwards slope as it is fed in.

622. Accurate Tapers

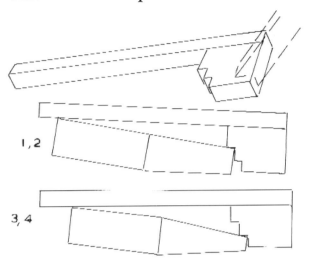

When cutting a set of tapered legs on a circular saw it is advisable to make a jig to ensure the legs match. The simple jig shown, controls the cut at the two stages of the work.

Draw a full-size outline of a leg with the tapers you want. From this you can get the positions of two notches. The inner one controls a leg when it still has one side straight (1,2), while the outer one is needed when you cut the other sides (3,4). Have the jig thick enough to stop the leg wobbling in the last cuts and push the jig and leg with a push stick.

623. Magnetic Featherboard

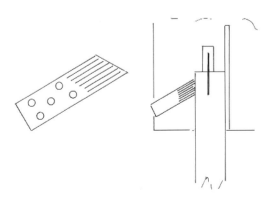

A featherboard to hold wood close to the fence while being cut on a circular saw normally has to be cramped to the saw table or held by hand. This featherboard is made in the usual way, but several small round magnets are let into holes on its underside, to hold it to the iron saw table, secure enough for most sawing.

624. Mitre Fence Setting

A mitre fence can be set accurately to the angle of cut you want by using a test strip. Mark the angle near the end of the strip. If there is a groove at the other side of the saw, line up the mark with it. Otherwise, line up with the edge of the table. Lock the mitre fence and any cut will be exact.

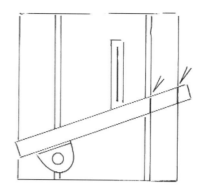

625. Band Saw Care

All band saws have some means of taking the thrust as wood is pushed against the blade and two guides to keep the saw straight at the point of cut. Patterns differ, but it is important that these things are correctly adjusted at all times the saw is in use. Check frequently as locking may not always stand up to use for long periods of use. Slackness may also cause wear and can result in less than accurate work.

626. Changing Blades

When you need to remove a circular saw blade you have to resist the loosening of the nut, and this is usually done by holding the blade with the risk of cutting your hand with the saw teeth. A safer and better way is to use a cramp on cloth wrapped over a few teeth. You can hold the cramp or lodge it against something.

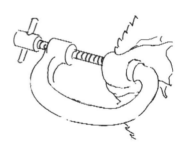

627. Small on Band saw

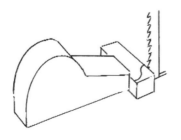

If you have to cut a small piece of wood on the band saw, you need a push stick that will guide it and keep your fingers away from the blade. Make one from scrap wood, as shown. Cut it long enough and high enough at the end to keep your hand out of the way and allow you to watch the cut.

628. Band saw Safety

If you release the tension on a band saw blade, to reduce strain on the blade and machine, you have to avoid switching on later without re-adjusting. Put a paper clip and a scrap of paper on the blade to provide a visible reminder.

629. Bigger Band Saw Table

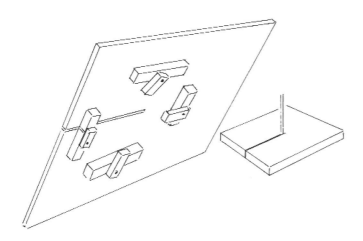

If you want to work on something of large size on the band saw, it will need supporting over a larger area than the normal table. You may arrange some outside support, but built-in support from a larger table is better. Use stiff plywood or other material. At one side it can take up the space between the existing table and the frame, then you can extend its area in other directions to suit your needs. Cut a slit to admit the saw. While in position, mark underneath the shape of the metal table. Fix guide blocks in these positions, with their thickness matching the table. Cut through the block over the slit and put turn buttons on the blocks to lock the auxiliary table in place.

630. Storing Blades

If you use several widths of band saw blades, you need to store those out of use carefully, without risk of distorting or damaging them. Hanging over several pegs, to hold a curve, is better than putting them over a single hook. Arrange the pegs as shown. This can usually be managed so other tools can be hung or fitted to racks within the loop. Hang a loop with its teeth towards the wall.

631. Round Squarely

If you want to cut across round rod or other stock, it is difficult to hold it squarely when cutting on a circular or band saw. The device shown has a bar to slide in the groove in the saw table and the V-block supports anything round squarely and without rolling.

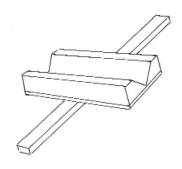

The block is cut from one piece of wood planed to 45° and halved to mount on a thin piece of plywood. Make the V-block long enough to come reasonably near the blade. If the groove in the circular and band saw tables are different distances from the blades, make the V-block reversible.

632. Run Off

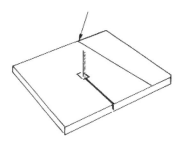

Most band saws cut with a slight run off. They do not cut quite squarely across the table. You have to allow for this if making a long cut. It is helpful if you draw a line on the saw table at the angle of the run off, so you can hold a job parallel to it when necessary.

633. Dowel Gauge

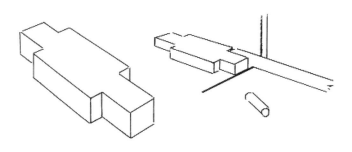

If you need to cut several dowels of the same length from a rod, with a band saw or other means, notch a piece of wood to the length needed and use that to feed the rod to the saw. You could make four notches of different length, as shown, to keep as a regular gauge.

634. Upright Cut

If you doubt if the band saw makes a cut square to the table, make two cuts close together in a thick piece of scrap wood. Lack of squareness may be obvious, but test with a try square.

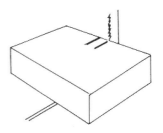

635. Better Sawing

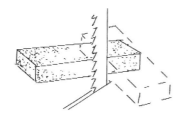

The rear edge of a band saw blade may be quite rough and this can affect the smoothness of sawing. When you fit a new blade to your machine, it is worthwhile holding an abrasive stone at an angle both ways against the back of a blade when you first run it. Do this briefly and lightly. You will notice the improvement when you back a piece of wood from the blade or have to make tight curves.

636. Extended Table

A small band saw does not have a very big table and there are many occasions when you need a bigger area of support. If you usually mount your band saw on a Workmate or similar folding bench, the extended table shown will support large pieces of sheet material.

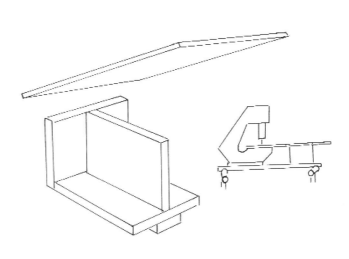

It will be best to start by making the top, of plywood or other sheet material stiff enough to remain flat. Have it as big as you need; the solid wood support can be smaller. Put a block underneath the same width as that used for the saw.

637. Circles on the Band Saw

To make circular pieces of sheet material on the band saw, you need a false wood top to the table. It need not be full-size, but it helps to have the front and one side level. Plywood is suitable. Make a cut to match that in the metal table and draw a line square to it. Hold this with cramps (1).

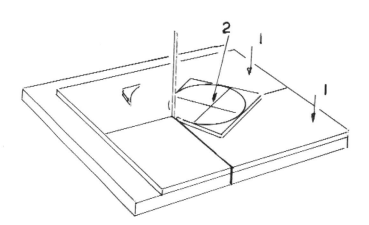

Make a square of the piece to be cut and draw lines square across it. Partly drive in a panel pin (2). Line up one of the lines across the square with that on the false table with one edge against the saw, then drive in the panel pin. Rotate the square on the pin to cut the circle.

638. Hold It Vertical

A band saw is convenient for cutting tenons, providing all cuts are vertical on the wood. If the wood is not flat or at an angle on the saw table and there is no vertical support, they may finish on the skew (1). In order to prevent

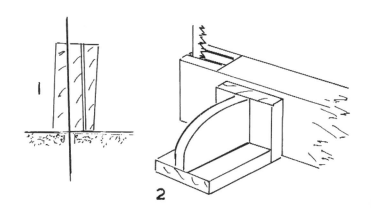

this happening it is advisable to always hold the wood against a hand-held fence or support (2). Slide it with the job.

639. Roll It

When cutting tubes of plastic, metal or even cardboard on a band saw, there can be a sudden snatch as the blade breaks through to the wall thickness. This could be dangerous or cause the cut to wander. To reduce this risk, roll the tube in a forward direction as you make the cut.

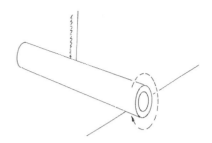

640. Band Saw Tenons

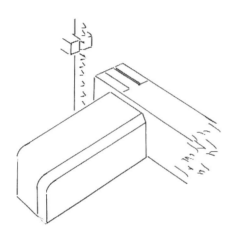

When cutting tenons or halving joints on a band saw the cut has to be parallel with the sides. If the wood is exactly square in section it may stay true, but to ensure parallel cuts, the guide block shown can be used alongside the job. Its ends and forward side are at 90° and the chamfer shows which side has to be in the direction of thrust, as the block and the wood held to it are moved towards the blade.

641. Band saw Fence

Most band saw cuts tend to drift a little to one side of square across the table, so although the saw will rip quite thick wood, it cannot be fed square and you have to allow for the drift.

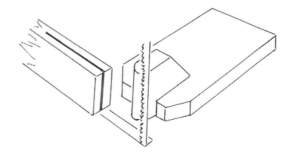

The saw has to follow a marked line, but the wood has to be kept upright. The fence shown has a rounded end to support the wood and allow it to be guided as needed. It can be cramped to the table or sometimes hand-held.

642. Softer Push

When making close cuts on a band saw, it is risky to use your fingers too near the cut and a notched type of push stick does not give exact control. A piece of dowel rod with a rubber tip intended for a walking stick can be used to push and direct a close cut in fine work.

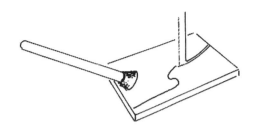

643. Pushing on the Band Saw

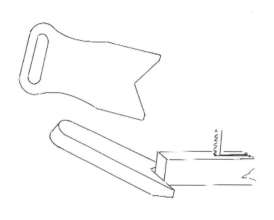

Many cuts on a band saw finish where it would be dangerously near your fingers if you continued to hold there as the saw broke through. It is wiser to have a couple of push sticks to hold, all the way or at the end of a cut.

For wood on edge make a push stick from 50 by 25mm wood with a deep notch in one end and a bevel underneath. For larger and wider work you could make a push stick from plywood with a hand hole. The working ends of both tools will suffer cuts, so allow some extra length for re-cutting the notches.

644. Plane Start

If you feed a piece of wood on to the cutter of a planing machine, the sudden grip of the blade can cause snatch and an uneven start to the work, especially if the wood is wide. This can be reduced if you start a cut slowly with the board askew to the cutter (1) and move to straight when the full width is being cut (2).

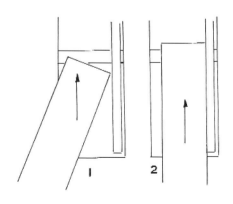

645. How Flat

If a board is to be put through a thicknesser, the top surface will reproduce variations in the bottom surface, and therefore must be flat. However, it is not always necessary to put the first surface repeatedly over the planer until every sign of unevenness has gone. If you remove the high spots sufficiently to rest on the lower supports of the thicknesser, its blemishes and hollows still showing will not stop the other surface finishing true.

646. Recycle Handle

A throwaway hand saw may last some time and conform to modern thinking, but the idea of discarding something that still looks satisfactory wrankles with craftsmen. Here is a way of using at least part of it. An ex-saw handle will make a good safe handle for a planer push stick. Your hand is not likely to slip and be hurt when holding this. Cut off the blade at a slope without disturbing the handle attachment. You can use the edge of a grinding wheel and cut a groove

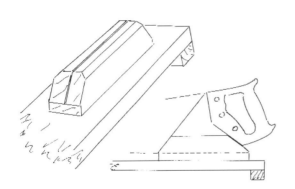

across, then snap it and grind the edge smooth. Make a block to match the part of the saw blade, with a saw cut to fit and attach it to the push stick. Make sure there is no grease on the steel and fix it in the slot with epoxy adhesive. Locate it so the handle gives thrust against the block.

647. Push Safer

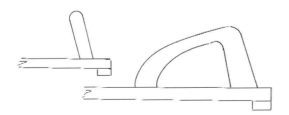

A common type of handle on a shop-made push stick for use on a planer is a length of dowel rod mounted at an angle. There is a risk of your hand slipping off on an awkward job and touching the revolving cutters. It is safer to make an enclosed loop handle, which gives greater protection and offers a better grip when a hard push is needed.

648. Safer Push

A push stick for use on a planer can be fairly basic, but if a wide push stick is used on narrow wood there is a risk of wobbling and your hand might hit the revolving cutters. To reduce this risk without affecting the use of the tool, you can put

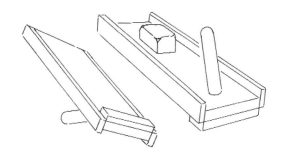

sides on a push stick – high enough to limit your hand movement.

649. Safer Push

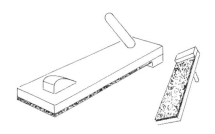

A large broad push stick should be used on a planer and it can be made less likely to slip, and therefore safer, if the contact surface is faced with cork. Suitable sheet cork is sold as cork floor tiles.

650. Replacable Push

The part of a planer push stick that wears out first is the crosspiece that actually pushes. If you have a router and a dovetail cutter, you can make a push stick where this piece can be changed. You could have push pieces of different depths to change to suit the work.

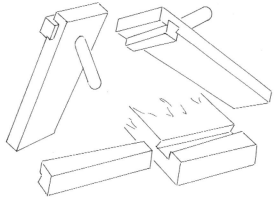

The upper part can be standard; underneath, square across for the point of push. Make a push piece too long at first and give it a moderate taper. Leave its rear edge square, but cut a dovetail-angled rabbet on the forward side to go slightly less than halfway through the main part. Mark a groove across to match the push piece. Cut it with its edges square at first, then use the dovetail cutter to undercut the forward edge. Drive in the push piece and trim its ends level. If you want to be able to change this part, do not use glue.

651. Surform Push

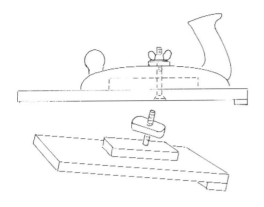

A safe and successful push stick for use on a planer needs a handle to push and a handle or knob to apply pressure. If you have a plane-type Surform tool, its handle and knob are in just the right positions for a push stick. You can add a push stick base to a Surform tool and still be able to change it back to its intended purpose. Make a plug to form an easy fit inside the body of the tool. Make the push stick part to a size to suit your needs. These pieces fit to the body of the tool with a bolt with its end through a wood turn button and a washer and wing nut. A 6mm or 8mm metal-thread countersunk screw would be suitable. It could go through the base and be deeply countersunk, or just the plug piece which is glued and screwed to the other part.

652. Reduced Ripple

The rotating cutters of a power planer, whether fixed or hand-held, make hollows or ripples on the surface of the wood, which may have to be levelled by hand planing or sanding. If you feed the wood slowly, these ripples are smaller and less finishing will be required to produce a cabinetmaking surface.

653. Sharpen Planer Blades

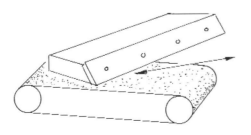

The blades for a planer or thicknesser must be straight along their sharpened edges; one way of sharpening is shown. Plane a piece of wood to the sharpening angle and attach the blade to it, either level or protruding slightly.

Move this about on a belt sander with a fine abrasive. Keep it moving across and lengthwise above the sander pressure plate and maintain pressure on the blade.

654. Close Edges

If when using a planer to prepare edges for joining, the fence is not absolutely square to the saw table, when 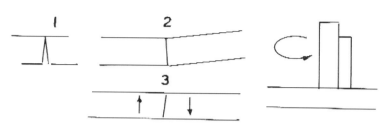 you bring the planed edges together, you either have a gap (1) when you keep the boards level, or one slopes in relation to the other (2). If it is important to keep the face side upwards, plane the edge of one board with the face side towards the fence and the other board with it facing the other way, then any error in squareness will cancel out (3).

655. Disc Right

 The abrasive on a rotating sanding disc cuts upwards on one half and downwards on the other half. In a disc sander this means it presses the job on to the table on one side and will lift it, if you let it, on the other side. Most jobs can be sanded where the pressure is downward, but to remind you not to stray on to the upward side without being prepared it is helpful to draw a line on the table opposite the centre of the disc.

656. Cool Blades

Coping and scroll saw blades cannot be expected to last very long from wear in use, but they can be weakened by heat. Try to not overheat a blade by using it too long, particularly on hard wood. A pause occasionally for a short time could ensure a longer life.

657. No Raggedness

If you use a fret or scroll saw to cut shapes from many types of softwood they are likely to splinter on the underside of the cut. To minimise or prevent this happening, stick masking tape on the underside of the wood. It can be peeled off later without marking the wood.

658. Power Sanding Round Rods

If you want to get the ends of pieces cut from dowel rod smooth and accurate, the jig shown can be used with a belt sander secured on edge or a disc sander. For a one-off job make it with a single hole, but for several sizes of rod you could prepare it with several holes.

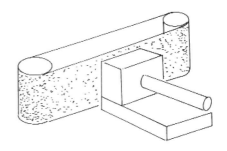

659. Drain Pipe Rollers

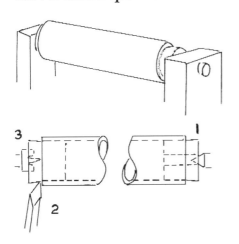

When passing wood through a planer or circular saw, it is helpful to have a roller support for long pieces. A roller could be turned from wood, but there is the problem of length and providing it with an axle. A piece of plastic down or drain pipe, as used on houses, can make the main part of a roller, and could be any reasonable length.

The tube has turned wood plugs at the ends, drilled for a metal rod axle. Mark all round the tube ends, by wrapping strips of paper round and pencilling against that. Saw as accurately as possible. Turn wood plugs on the lathe. Drill one on the lathe for the axle. Leave the other for the fork centre to drive. Drive the plugs in the tube (1). They could be secured with epoxy adhesive. Mount the assembly in the lathe and use the side of a skew chisel to true the ends of the tube (2). Remove from the lathe and drill where the drive centre was (3) and fit the axle.

660. Improved Grip

The control handles on many power tools are shiny plastics, which look good but do not provide a very good grip. To prevent your hand slipping and give more positive control, drill for two short pieces of small-diameter dowel rod and fix them in with epoxy adhesive.

661. Fold Flat Roller Trestle

A roller is needed to take the out-feed from a circular saw or planer. If your space is limited, this one will fold flat for minimum storage space. It can be altered in height with the rope to suit more than one machine. The roller suggested is in three parts, which are easier to turn and drill centrally. The two parts are similar, except one is able to fit inside the other (the inner one is shown). Use an iron rod as axle. Make the crosspieces deep enough to keep the legs rigid. Take the rope through central holes. Knot the ends, but leave enough extra at one end for adjusting to different heights.

662. Stay Put

If you have a power tool mounted on a box stand that can be wheeled out when needed. It is important for accurate work and safety that the stand does not move when the tool is in use. The brake shown can provide friction on the floor to serve as a lock.

Make it of wood about 18mm thick, with a piece at the top to form a handle. Drill for a stout pivot screw or bolt and use this hole as the centre for the curved end. However, rather than cutting a true curve, make the radius a little more towards the heel, then the lock will tighten against the floor as the lever is pulled back against a stop.

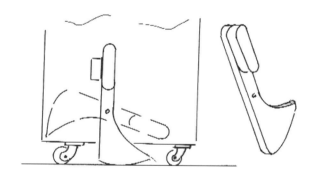

663. Big in Small

If you are equipping a small workshop, think of how you will deal with long stock. Mount the circular saw at a height that will allow long wood to pass through an open window or door, maybe in one and out the other. Similar considerations apply to a drill press. A planer or thicknesser is more likely to be used with shorter lengths. If you are building the workshop, have the sill of a window at bench level, so large assemblies can extend.

664. Steady

If you have a machine on a cabinet or bench on wheels, you have to make sure it does not move when you are using it; the arrangement shown will keep it rigid and steady. Use fairly stout wood: 75mm by 50mm would be suitable. Hinge the parts together so in the lowered position the bottom part has enough friction on the floor to stop movement. You may need

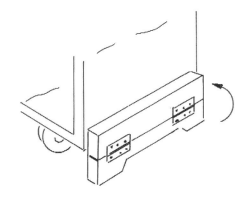

fittings at both ends. You can kick a foot up. If the hinges are stiff enough it may stay up, otherwise you can use a hook and eye.

665. Workmate Take Off

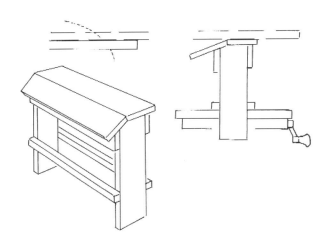

Long pieces of wood coming off the circular saw, planer or band saw need support if you are to keep control. There might be a roller on a stand, but this is an alternative that can be put out of the way when not needed. The sloping front catches sagging wood and leads it to the top. The whole item is gripped by a Workmate, or similar folding bench, and the height is controlled by crosspieces. Your band saw is probably higher than the circular saw and the planer might be lower. You can change the take-off support to suit with different crosspieces.

666. Clean Lubrication

The groove for the mitre fence guide on a router table, circular saw or band saw can be lubricated by rubbing with a candle. This will not mark wood and should last longer than grease.

667. Less Noise

Padding reduces noise, but if it is too soft it could affect performance of a machine. If a power tool is to be mounted on a metal or wood stand or bench, a cork pad is firm enough and will reduce noise. Suitable material is sold as cork floor tiles and one or more can be included when the machine is being fixed down.

668. Smoother

Surfaces of circular and band saws, and similar machine tables, tend to rust and get dirty, so wood does not always pass smoothly over them. You can keep them clean, without risk of marking wood, by treating with spray furniture polish. This deposits a thin layer of wax, which protects and lubricates.

669. Key Handles

Allen keys are needed for many adjustments on power tools and a lost key of the right size can cause delays. They are more easily found, and you get more leverage, if you push them into holes in short lengths of dowel rod. You could turn special handles. In any case, painting them bright colours makes them even easier to find.

670. Magnet Help

Car sundries firms sell self-adhesive magnets, intended to be fixed to car dashboards. They can be useful on machines to hold spanners, callipers or other steel tools.

671. Mitre Saw Lengths

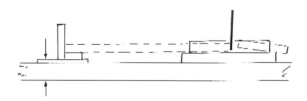

There is no provision on a normal mitre or chop saw for limiting lengths when you need to cut several pieces of the same size. A separate stop can be made, as shown, and cramped to the bench at a suitable distance. Use plywood as the base and mount on it a stop piece and a support block the same height as the table of the saw.

672. Pointed Fret Cuts

When cutting patterns with a scroll or fret saw, you should not turn a cut on a point, whether external or internal, if you want that point to look sharp. If the point is outward go up one side and into the waste. Cut around so you can make another cut towards the point. If it is an internal cut, such as a shaped hand hole, cut into one corner, then back out and cut to the 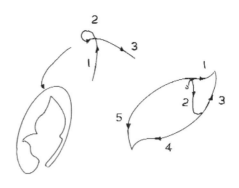 other side and go into the corner again. The waste will drop out and you can cut the sides towards the other corner to make a hand hole with perfect points.

673. Only Enough Countersink

You may use a power drill for making holes, but using the machine for countersinking is not always the best way. It is easy to overdo it, so a screw head goes below the surface and you cannot put it right. You get better control and can see progress if you use a rose countersink bit in a carpenter's brace.

674. Is It an Overlay?

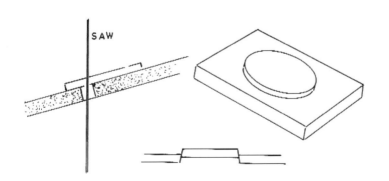

If you have a power fretsaw or scroll saw, its table can be tilted and this can be used to produce an overlay effect. When the saw has made a cut, it leaves a narrow space. If you tilt the cut slightly around a shape, once you have removed the saw blade, the shape can be pushed up to look like a piece mounted on solid wood. A little glue will hold it in place. Experiment with saw and angle to get the amount of projection you want.

675. Frictionless Sawing

If you wish to cut green wood on a circular saw, it will probably try to cling to the metal table. Instead of putting a lubricant on it, lay on an old glossy magazine cover. The wood will move easily on it and if the paper touches the saw blade no harm will be done.

9. The Router

The modern electric router has developed largely because of tipped cutters that can do considerable work without sharpening. It has become a versatile tool. With the right cutters it can perform some functions of other power tools. There are many ways of adding to it to improve work and these are the subjects of a large number of tips. Do not expect too much from your router, look after it and do not overload the motor.

676. Easy Rods

The rods for the fence on a router make a close fit in their holes. When the router is used without the fence, dust gets into the holes and could interfere with the fit. To clean out and lubricate the holes, use a piece of dowel rod rubbed with candle wax, which is clean and acts as a lubricant.

677. Another Fence

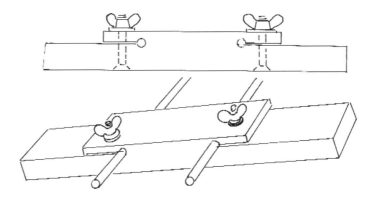

There are occasions when a second fence would be useful, as when keeping a cutter central on an edge when mortising. This wood fence is best made of close-grained hardwood, such as beech. Drill it to match the guide rods and saw into the holes to provide spring as the wing nuts are tightened. Bolts 6mm or 8mm with washers and wing nuts are suitable.

678. Ready-fit Fence

For most routing you do not have to fit the fence so close that the opening in it is needed. In that case, you get better control with a continuous fence edge, usually made by screwing on a strip of wood. You can reduce the screwing to one screw, as shown. The addition could be longer than the metal fence, if you wish. Rout a suitable rabbet on the edge of a wider piece and cut it off. Make the inside piece and its screw so the face piece is held up level.

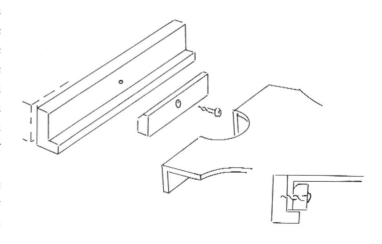

679. Dual Pads

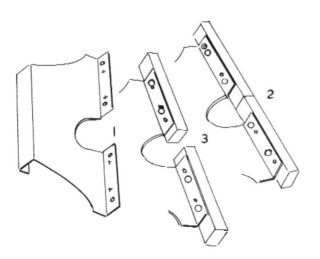

Most router fences are drilled for you to screw on what pads you wish. The usual pads are a pair to leave the opening or a long one to close it. If you drill more holes, you can use a pair of pads to serve both purposes.

Mark and drill holes (1) inside the others at a distance equal to half the width of the gap. If you put screws in the inner holes and screw wood there (2) to fill the gap, it can be arranged so when you move to the outer holes (3) there is a sufficient gap between the pads.

680. More or Less

A router cutter shank should extend far enough into a collet to obtain a sure grip and not damage the collet. If you want to get maximum extension, it is important that enough is left in the collet. On the other hand, the cutter should not be forced close to the collet, since there is a small fillet where the shank

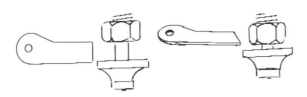

meets the cutting part that prevents the collet from fully tightening. Most standard cutters have shanks about the same length and about two-thirds of this should be inside.

The gauge shown can test maximum and minimum extension. Stiff plastic is a good material; a discarded credit card is suitable. Cut it to show the maximum extension advisable. Its thickness will check how tight the cutter could be inserted.

681. Tight Cutter

There is a small radius around a router cutter and its shank. The cutter should not be pushed so far into the collet that this small curve is trapped. An old credit card is the thickness that the minimum gap should be. If the collet and shank are clean, the cutter should come out easily. If not, the thin end of a small screwdriver can be inserted and twisted to release it.

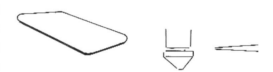

682. Router Depth Gauge

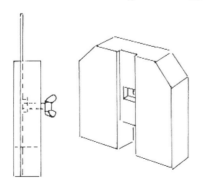

This tool is intended mainly for checking the extension of a router cutter, but it could be used as an ordinary depth gauge. It uses a 150mm (6 in) steel rule. If the recess is made 25mm deep and the overall height is 100mm, depths can be read directly from the rule. Make the main part of solid wood, thick enough to stand on edge - 18mm should be satisfactory. The front can be 6mm plywood. Cut a groove the rule can slide in and a recess at the bottom. The rule could be locked in place with a woodscrew driven through the back, but it is better to use a wing screw engaging with a nut let into the groove. Glue and screw the wood parts together.

683. Combi Height

A combination square makes a good height gauge for setting a router cutter. The blade can be slid back as far as usually required and still locked by the screw.

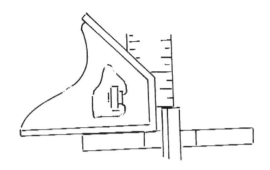

684. Marking Gauge Help

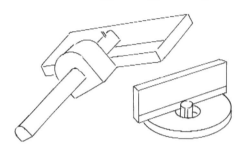

There are several ways of measuring the projection of a router cutter, but a simple and accurate way uses a marking gauge and a straight piece of scrap wood. Set the gauge to the projection you need and scratch a line. Put this across the base of the router and set the cutter to it. For a more permanent device you could scratch several lines at projections you regularly use and mark these sizes against the lines, for future use.

685. Cutter Projection

The gauge shown is marked with several standard amounts of projection for router cutters. The wood is thick enough not to wobble on the router base. Mark the lines deeply with

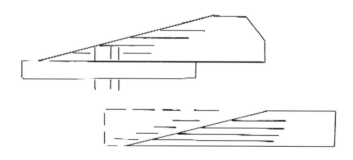

a marking gauge before cutting the slope. Running a pencil along each line will help visibility. Write the height against each line.

686. Plunge Gauge

If the waste wood from a mortise is to be removed with a straight router cutter, it usually has to be done in stages, particularly with hardwood. This gauge is to

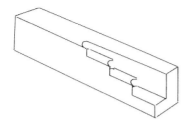

check the amount of projection of the straight cutter in two or three equal steps. Use the cutter near the edge of a piece of wood and first go the intended full depth, then do the same at the other depths.

687. Inverted Stand

When setting a router or changing a cutter, it is helpful to invert a router. Most

routers have flat tops, but the small area means they are liable to fall over. With this stand, the router can still rest on its top, but the notches fit round the handles and prevent it falling. Tenon the sides into the bottom, which should be large enough to stand steadily. Make the notches an easy fit on the handles.

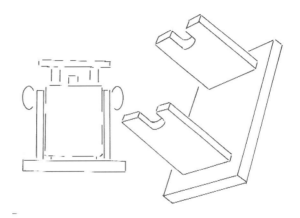

688. Most Rigid Router

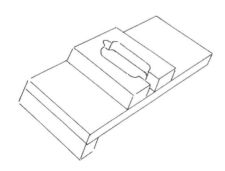

The flat tops of many routers, if there is one, are not very big and support is advisable when it is inverted for adjustment. The support shown rests against the edge of the bench like a bench hook and should be a close fit on the top of the router. A slot at one side will clear the cable and admit a band saw to cut the shape.

689. Ready Rack

You may store all your router cutters and other equipment, but when you are tackling a routing job, you want the things you need within reach, but some of them are small and may disappear in the clutter on the bench. This rack is intended to have the spanner and the cutters you need at hand. If you expect to change collets or fit anything else, it is easy to add more hooks or nails.

Use the spanner as a guide to size. Make the base large enough to remain steady. Drill at an angle for cutter shanks. Cup hooks will hold the spanner and some other items.

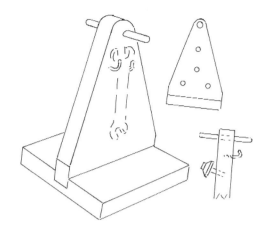

690. Invert Safely

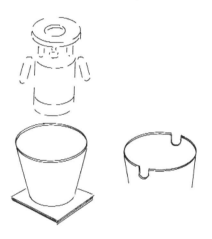

When preparing a router for use, it is often necessary to turn it over so the base is upwards. Not all routers have flat tops, and even if yours has, it is not a very big area and the router might fall over. One way of holding the router inverted is shown, using a plastic flower pot. Drill the base of the pot for screws into a wood base, to provide steadiness. For some routers, the pot can be used without further attention, but in some cases you may have to cut notches to clear the handles.

691. In Use Router Stand

It is unwise to put a router down on its extending cutter. This stand is intended to put on the bench when the router is in hand use. It is made of three thickness of 12mm

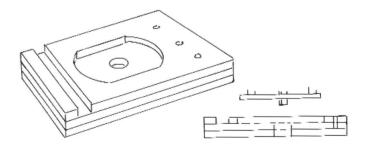

plywood. Cut the recess an easy fit on the router base plate in the top piece. Drill through the other two a hole bigger than any cutter you are expecting to use. Put some holes for the cutters you will be using at one side. Have a slot big enough for the spanner at the other side.

692. Complete Stand

The stand shown will hold a router, with or without a cutter projecting. Its cable can be coiled at the back, the spanner fitted across the notch and spare cutters kept in the front. It might be used as a place to put the router during a job, a semi-permanent stand between needs or the regular home for the tool.

Make the base stout enough to stand steadily. Drill it to clear the largest cutter you expect to use. Make the notch to fit your spanner. Make the back about the height of your router.

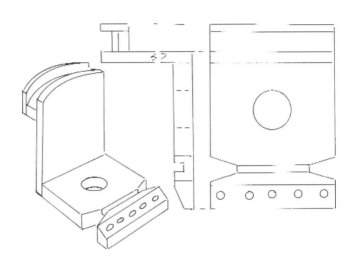

693. Tighten

The thumbscrews that hold the fence bars to the base of a router become

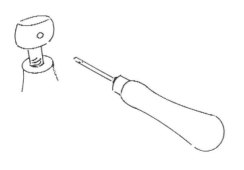

difficult to get at and tighten when the plunge bars are used to give a cutter a long extension. If not really tight they tend to vibrate loose, altering the setting. One way of getting a bit more torque in these circumstances is to drill through the wing head so a bradawl, or something similar, can be pushed through to use as a lever.

694. Safer Tommy Bar

Some basic routers are provided with a short length of steel rod to insert in a hole in the collet holder to prevent rotation when using a spanner. To prevent its loss it could be given a handle. The handle may be any shape, but it is shown as a wood disc, drilled to take the rod and with a hole for hanging or a string.

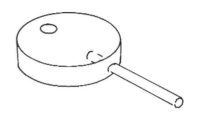

695. Double Wing Spanner

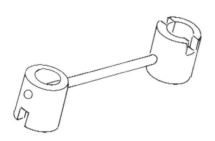

At some settings of a router, wing screws — especially those for the fence rods, are difficult to get at and anything used to turn them may not line up with the heads. This double-ended tubular wing nut spanner has grooves at right-angles to each other, so any angle screw head should be possible to fit. Use metal tubes that go easily over the screw heads. Cut slots for an easy fit. Make the tubes as short as possible, for easy access. Join with a metal rod, which might jamb in or, preferably, is soldered.

696. Smaller Radius

There are several devices to allow a router to cut circles, bought or shop-made, but if the centre has to be only a short distance outside the router base, many of them cannot be used.

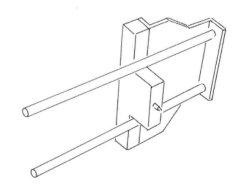

You can locate a centre as close as needed by using the router fence inverted, as shown. Screw a block of wood to the metal fence, with the extended piece level with the setting of the router base you need. Drive a nail into this, cut it off and file a point to make a centre. This allows you to cut a circle any size up to the limits of the fence bars.

697. Fenced Curves

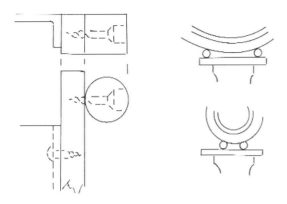

If you want to cut a groove or other shape parallel with a curved edge, the fence has to be altered to provide two bearing points that can follow the curve. Most fences are not wide enough to allow these points to be arranged far enough apart, except for small curves.

Make an auxiliary fence surface extending wider than the ordinary fence. Make a pair of round pads, thick enough to give clearance when against the curved edge. Drill for counterbored screws, as shown. Fix them near the end of the bar for large curves and move them in for smaller ones.

698. Open Ended

If a curved router cut has to be made parallel to a shaped edge, it is usual to thicken the ends of the fence to provide bearing surfaces against the edge. However, it can be problematic when an end of the cut is to be open and the outer guide goes off the wood when you need a little more cut. This can be managed by only having one block, so the router base is tilted in relation to the guide.

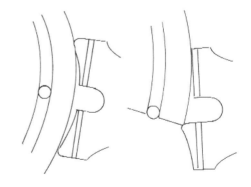

699. Simple Circulate

You can take the fence off its bars and use the extension shown to provide a centre for cutting circles. The extension could be any length you wish, but a moderate length will take care of many jobs. Arrange the assembly so it extends to the same level as the router base. Cut a block to suit and drill it to match the bars. Make cuts across the holes so screws can make the wood pinch and hold the bars. The extension below can be plywood, thickened for the centre with a small block. You could drill a hole through to take an awl or make a permanent point below with a nail driven in, cut off and filed to a point.

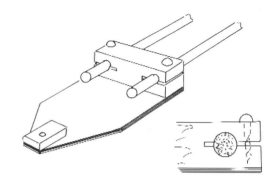

700. Cutter Box

This is a box for storing or carrying router cutters. The example shows two rows

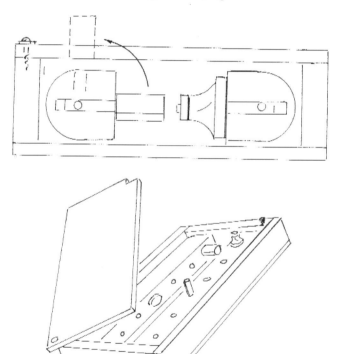

of six cutters, but it could be altered to suit your needs. Use square-section wood for the holders. Mark centres for screws at the ends. Round the reverse sides to allow the strips to pivot.

Make the box to suit the holding strips. It could have a hinged lid, but it is shown pivoted on a screw at one corner and closing on to a screw at the opposite corner.

701. Easy Mover

If you fit an auxiliary base to a router, whatever the material, remember to take off any sharpness around the edges. Sand a chamfer on the edges of the part that will be in contact with the workpiece. This will stop it catching, so it runs smoothly.

702. Always There

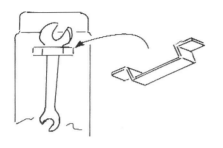

Without the spanner, you cannot use a router, so you must be careful not to lose it. The best place to keep it is on the router. On most routers there is sufficient rear surface for a spanner to hang.

A strip metal bracket can be attached with epoxy adhesive. Make sure the meeting surfaces are clean metal-to-metal, with no grease or paint.

703. No Rust Risk

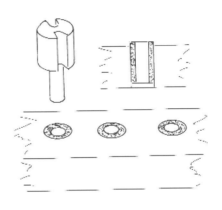

It is unwise for long-term storage of router cutters to just push them into holes in a piece of wood, as all wood, however well-seasoned, contains moisture, which will rust the steel. You will see metal or plastic liners in bought sets, but it may be difficult to find suitable tubes to cut yourself, and then it is difficult to make a neat job of the cut ends if you do not have a metalworking lathe. A good alternative is rubber tubing, which can be glued into holes and its flexible nature grips the cutter shanks, but allows them to pull out easily.

704. Cleaning Collets

If your router is to maintain accurate cutting for a long time, cutters and collets should be kept clean. It is easy to see if a cutter is clean, but the inside of a collet is difficult to check. A brass brush is useful, but this could be followed by this method. Use a piece of dowel rod slightly smaller than the bore of the collet. Soak it in WD40 or something similar and work it through the collet a few times. Besides removing dirt and grit, it leaves a deposit that protects the metal.

705. Cushioned Cutter

A router cutter can be stopped from being forced too far into the collet, and provided with some cushioning, by putting a water tap rubber washer over the shank. A standard washer will stretch over a 6mm shank and can be drilled for larger sizes.

706. Candle Grease

Router cutter shanks should be tight fits in the collets, but if you find it difficult to push a clean cutter in, do not use oil since it is messy and may mark the wood. A clean lubricant is candle grease. Rub the shank on a piece of candle.

707. Help from the Kitchen

Parts of a router get dirty, and this is particularly so on the base since it picks up resin as well as dirt from the wood being worked. The answer may be under the kitchen sink. Most kitchen cleaners, such as 'Flash', will remove most grime and grease without affecting the surface. Smear on and leave a short while before wiping off with a damp cloth. Spray furniture polish on the cleaned surface will lubricate and protect from further contamination.

10. Hand Routing

An electric router is best treated as a powered hand tool. It is most versatile when used by hand. It produces best results if it is allowed to cut near its top speed. If it labours on a cut, it would be better to do it in two stages. The bearings of a small router will become worn if you overload it by attempting work more suitable for a router taking cutters with a larger spindle diameter.

708. Cut Direction

As you look down on the top of a router, the cutter is being driven in a clockwise direction. Cuts should be made so the wood being worked meets the cutter opposite to the direction of rotation. This may seem obvious on external cuts, but be careful on internal ones (1). If a groove is cut with two passes of a cutter, to get the best edges, follow the rule by changing directions (2). If a groove can be cut with a single pass of a cutter, follow the rule for the upper side of it (3). In some wood the other edge may be ragged.

If you use a cutter in the opposite direction, it will try to run like a wheel on the edge of the wood, if you do not restrain it. In normal circumstances, the only justification for reversed cuts is when you are working an edge starting at a corner, and there is a risk of the cutter

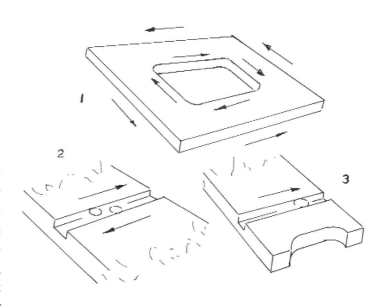

damaging the corner if you do not locate it right. Then you can start a very short distance along the edge and make a short reverse cut there, after the rest of the edge is finished.

709. Clean Corners

You should use a router cutter from left to right for most cuts, but the wood may break out at the far side of a cut. This can happen when moulding or chamfering around four edges. The problem can be reduced if you work in sequence as shown. The start of normal cuts should 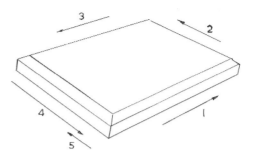 reduce any raggedness from the ends of previous cuts. At the fourth side, cut almost all the way across, and then make a controlled reverse cut towards it (4 and 5). Care is needed, as the cutter will try to run away in that direction.

710. Safer Shelving

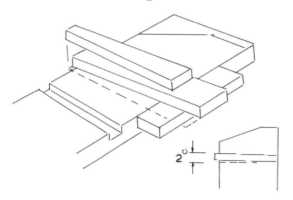 In some places, such as a workshop or kitchen, a variety of things are put on shelves and some of them are liable to roll off even if the shelf is level. In use some shelves start to sag slightly, to make the condition worse. It is better if the shelves are slightly higher at the front than the back – about 2° is enough and this is not noticeable.

To cut grooves at an angle in supports for shelves with a router, you probably have a T-square guide at 90°. You can use this with a packing cut at the new angle to put alongside it. Go to the opposite side of the T-square for the opposite support, or change to the other edge.

711. Easier Wider Grooves

Most router bases have one or, more often, two flat edges. This gives two different distances from a cutter. Check what they are. If you have to make a wide groove with a straight cutter, you may be able to avoid one alteration of the guide strip setting. Make the first pass cutting the near side of a groove with the flat side of the base against the guide strip (1). Make another pass with a rounded

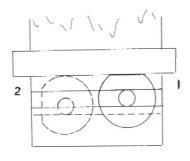

edge against the guide strip (2) and this will remove at least some of the waste in the centre of the groove. Reset the guide strip to cut the far side of the groove. If it is a very wide groove, you might save another setting by reversing the starting technique: cutting the far edge guided by the rounded edge, then bringing it back to remove more waste by making another pass using the flat edge.

712. Routed Halving

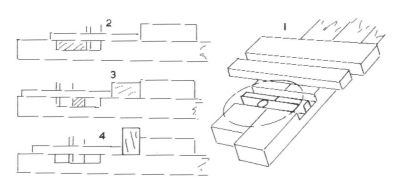

If you have an assembly with many identical halving joints, they can be cut quickly with a straight router cutter. Have a guide piece to cramp across a batch of two or more parts (1). For the first pass, set this so the cutter does the near side of a groove (2). Do not move this guide for other passes. Instead, use a packing to let the cutter do the far side of the groove (3). Arrange the thickness of that packing so when it is stood on edge another pass of the cutter removes the waste from the middle of the groove (4).

713. Groove Gauge

When cutting a groove across a board, the distance the guide strip is cramped from the groove will vary according to the diameter

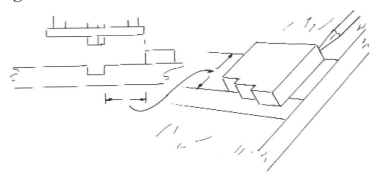

of the straight cutter being used. To avoid having to measure each time, make a gauge as shown, with the distances of the notches from the edge to suit grooving with your most-used cutters.

714. Flush Fence Strip

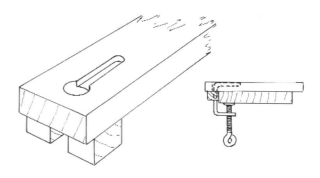

When using a router to groove across a board, there has to be a guide strip cramped on. With normal cramps, part of one or both will normally project above the strip and interfere with use of the router. A strip made as shown has a cramp top flush with the surface. The cramp is a type sold by fretwork firms, intended mainly for holding a sawing board for hand fretting.

Cut a guide strip to suit your anticipated needs. Drill a hole near one end, through which the cramp can be passed, and rout a groove from it an easy fit on the cramp top. Put two blocks underneath beside the hole to hold the strip square to the edge.

715. Non-slip Square

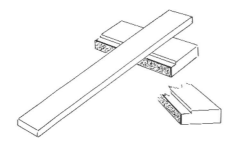

A square or guide bar for controlling the router base when making grooves or other cuts across a board is worth making as a permanent tool. Make the stock short enough to miss the cutter as it runs through and let the blade extend behind it to guide the router as it approaches the work. A shallow rabbet helps the tool fit closely to an edge. It is disconcerting if the stock slides just as you are positioning and tightening the cramps. This risk can be reduced if you glue fine abrasive paper to the face of the stock.

716. Better Grooving

A router with a straight cutter is frequently used for cutting grooves across boards and this is usually down with a single guide piece cramped on. Any wobbling will cause an error in the groove. If you regularly use the same router

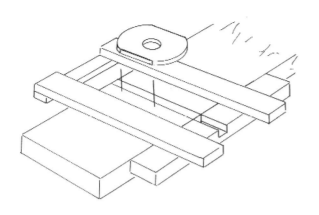

for this work, it is worthwhile making a double guide as shown. Space the guide strips so they allow the router base to slide across freely, but without any risk of sideways movement. Make the assembly long enough to span the widest board you expect to work on and it will be just as useful on narrower pieces.

717. Close Fit

If you can cut a groove for a housing joint with a single pass of a router cutter

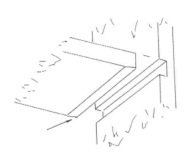

and it is marginally narrower than the thickness of the board that is to go in it, there is no need to plane the wood or make another pass to widen the groove. It is better to chamfer the end of the board slightly on the underside, where it will not show. When cramped, this will be tighter than if you tried to exactly match the parts.

718. Double-end the T

The T-square to guide a router when making grooves across a board is often improvised as needed. The one shown is made double-ended and with grooves of commonly used size. It should be long enough to be larger than the widest board you expect to cut. Cut grooves of the standard widths

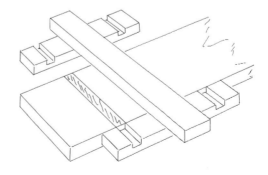

across the two stocks. These can be lined up with the marked grooves on the job using the T-square whichever way round is better for the purpose.

719. Housing Layout

When laying out a series of housing joints, as in the side of a bookcase, it is helpful to also mark the positions of the guide strip for the router. Make a strip of wood, measured from the centre of your router base to the edge, and use this as a gauge to mark this additional line in each position.

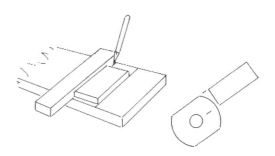

720. Narrow End

The gap in the fence of a router table is wide enough to clear the largest cutter likely to be used. This may be wider than a piece of wood you wish to mould across the end, as in some feet. Holding tightly against the mitre fence may not

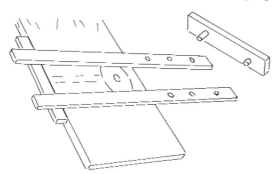

be sufficient control to prevent spoiling.

One way to feed the work smoothly and make a good cut is to put a strip across the end to more than span the gap, held temporarily with panel pins or nails.

721. Clean Grooves

If a groove across the grain is made with a cutter the full size of the groove, the edge of the groove in the direction of rotation of the cutter may finish rough. For a groove with both edges smooth, it is better to use a smaller-diameter

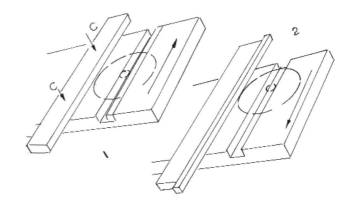

cutter and make the first cut so the wanted edge is against the direction of rotation (1), then move the cramped guide piece or use a packing, so you can cut in the other direction on the second side (2).

722. Multiple Grooves

If you want to make a series of grooves, you can keep marking out to a minimum if you prepare the T-square guide. The example shown has diagonal grooves, but the same method can be used for square grooves.

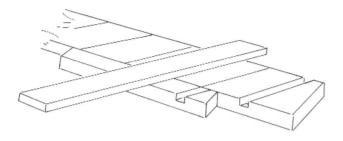

Mark out and cut the first groove fully, including across the stock of the T-square. All you need do is mark out one line of the other grooves and line up the groove in the stock with this. If you make the blade long enough the other way, this allows you to change sides at an end and work the other side as a pair.

723. Cleaner T

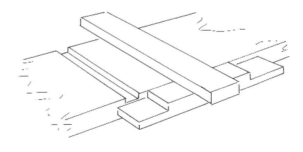

If you use the same T-square guide for cutting grooves across boards with several size straight cutters, the stock becomes ragged from the different cuts. The top of the stock does not need to be level with the surface of the job throughout its length. It could be cut away, as shown, to keep it out of the way when grooving, to avoid damage and prolong its life.

724. Groove without Wobble

The usual way to cut a groove across a board with a router and straight cutter is to run the base of the router against a guide strip that is cramped on. If you have a short guide strip, the router base may wander and affect the groove at the start and finish of the cut. A narrow guide strip does not allow much clearance when cramping and your hand could touch a cramp as you move the router across, causing an imperfection in the groove. A longer and wider strip keeps the router in line before it starts in the groove and cramp heads can be kept away from your hand.

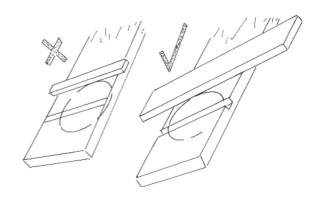

725. Right or Left

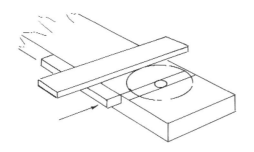

One of the simplest T-squares for router control when cutting grooves, is made as shown. Cut the stock to the width between the edge of the cutter and the rim of the router base. If it projects this much on both sides of the blade it is possible to use either side, which is helpful if you are cutting a series of grooves in bookcase sides or something similar. Make the blade wide enough for a cramp head to be well out of the way of your work and extend it far enough to control the router as it approaches the cut.

726. Cleaner Grooves

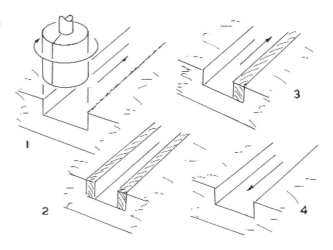

If you use a straight cutter of the same size as the groove you want to cut across the grain, the edge of the groove on the side cut against the rotation of the cutter will be smooth. In many woods the edge on the other side of the groove could be rough and ragged (1). This may not matter for some jobs, but if it is important that both edges finish smooth, it is better to use a cutter of smaller size, with several passes.

Remove the bulk of the waste with a cut along the middle of the groove (2). Make another cut along the edge of the groove that would be against the direction of rotation, in any case (3). Make a final cut in the other direction (4) to get a second smooth edge.

727. Secure Guide

The usual T-square guide used when routing grooves across a board can be improved if you arrange a securing block at the far side in addition to one or more cramps.

Plough a slot along the centre of the T-square that will allow adjustment to any size you expect to need. This should clear a 6mm or 8mm bolt through a block notched to slide in it. Use a washer and wing nut to secure the block where needed.

728. See The Limit

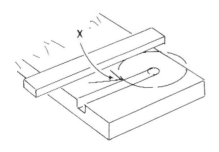

When using a router against a guide piece to cut a stopped groove, you cannot easily see when the limit has been reached. One way of checking exactly is to mark where the edge of the router base comes when the cutter is there. Additionally a sloping line, which shows first, allows you to see when you are approaching the stop (X).

729. Wide Grooving

When routing a wide groove across a board, you can use a packing piece against the T-square guide to make the second cut, but this is liable to move. It can be improved with a stop piece at one end. To get clean edges on the groove, the cuts against each side of it should be made against the direction of rotation. The stop piece allows the strip to be used at either side of the board.

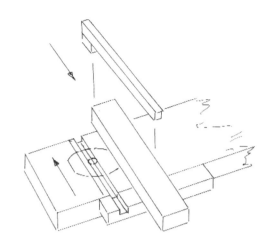

730. Bar Cramp Grip

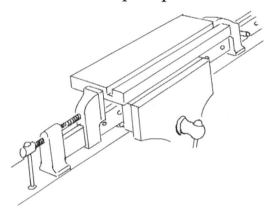

A cramp with a flat bar, such as a sash cramp, can be held in a vice with packings and used to hold routing work by the ends to any length within its capacity. For most work it can be arranged so the working area is completely clear for the router movement. Pack both sides of the bar so the heads and screw are not restricted.

731. Mutual Support

A frequent use of a router is to cut grooves for plywood panels in frame parts. The narrow edges do not give much support to stop the router base wobbling and it is usual to put a piece of scrap

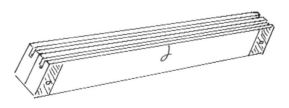

wood alongside to increase the width. A simple alternative is to attach opposite frame pieces together. Allow extra length and screw or nail through the waste parts, arranging face sides outwards and upwards, so the finished parts will match.

732. Simple Guide Strip

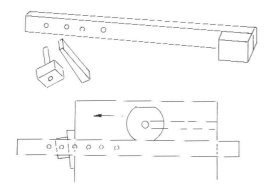

For long cuts with a router away from an edge a straight guide strip can be cramped on, but if you make these cuts often, the wedged guide strip shown provides a quick fix.

Use a straight piece of wood longer than the widest wood you expect to have to cut. Put a stop block under one end and drill a series of holes to take a dowel along the centre. Make a block with an extended dowel and a suitable wedge. You can put this across the job, with the stop block one side and the wedge and the dowelled block bearing against the other side.

733. Safer Shelf

If a shelf for the kitchen or workshop may have to hold things liable to slide or roll off and you do not want to put a strip along the front, a shallow groove parallel with the front edge will discourage many things from falling off. Even a large item can run into it and stop. The groove does not interfere with putting things on or removing them from the shelf.

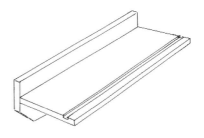

734. Better Ends

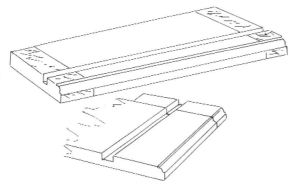

The doubtful part of a hand-held router cut is at the beginning or end of a cut, whether in the body of the wood or on an edge. For a cut with the grain it is advisable to do the router work before the wood is cut to length, so that any flaws will be cut off. When cutting across the grain, a scrap piece of wood cramped to the far side will prevent breakout or flaws due to wobble.

735. Tenon to Fit Mortise

When you cut a mortise with a straight router cutter you do not have control over the final width. Because of this, it is advisable where possible to cut mortises first and then fit the size of tenons to them.

736. Grooving Support

A frequent use of a router is making grooves in the edge of fairly narrow strips of wood. There is not much bearing surface on the wood and the router base could 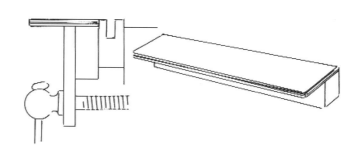 wobble if no further support is provided. One way of providing extra support is shown. Make the top piece wider than half the router base and the upright part deeper than the widest wood you expect to work. The router should slide easily on plywood, but a refinement would be to glue on Formica or something similar, for even more smoothness.

737. Cleaner Grooves

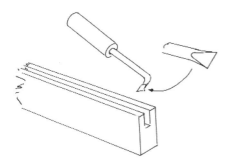

When cutting a narrow groove, as for a plywood panel, in some woods with a straight router cutter, much of the waste stays in the groove. You should be able to avoid poking this out by running the cutter back to the start, to clear the edges of the groove as well as lift away the waste.

738. Router Reverse

When a router makes a grooved cut, one side of the cut is against the direction of rotation and is smooth. In many woods the other side may not be. This is particularly apparent in a V cut. The second side can be improved by taking the cutter back along the cut slowly.

739. The Right Groove

If you accumulate straight router cutters, their sizes are not always very obvious. This is complicated by some being metric and some being imperial measure. For instance, 8mm and $^5/_{16}$in look alike, but they are not. A problem comes when you have to make grooves for plywood or other panel, and want it to fit.

Then it is helpful to have a board with specimen grooves into which you can try

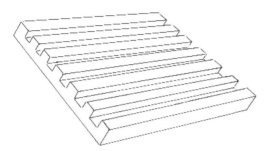

a panel. The one shown has grooves long enough for testing. The cutters can be stored in the same order as the grooves. To get clean grooves, have the wood a little longer when you cut the grooves, so any discrepancies at the groove ends is cut off.

740. Cut Level Halving

When two pieces of wood of the same thickness are to cross with a halving joint, it is important that they finish level (1). The convenient way to cut the joint with a router is to cramp the two pieces together under a guide strip and

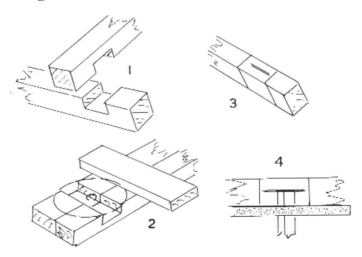

make the cut with several passes of a straight cutter (2), but you have to get the depth right.

One way of setting the router cutter depth correctly does not involve the use of a rule. Set a gauge to about half the thickness and gauge from both sides to leave two lines (3) close together. Set the router to the mid-point between the lines (4) and this will make the cut across the two pieces the right depth.

741. Stronger Halving

In a normal halving joint, half of the joint is cut from each piece. The total strength of the joint is increased if the solid wood in the joint is about the same volume in each part. You leave a little more depth 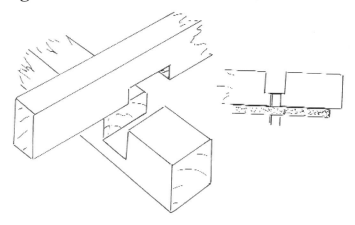 in the solid part of the lighter piece than in the thicker part, as shown.

You can avoid measurements, if you estimate and gauge the thinner portion of the larger piece. If you set the depth of the router cutter to this, that will be the depth of cut in the lighter piece.

742. Mortise in Stages

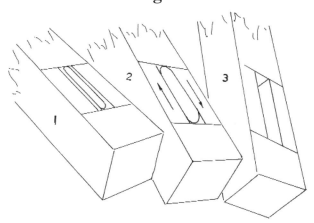

If a mortise is cut with a full-width cutter, the side that meets the cutter against rotation will be smooth. In some woods the other side could be quite ragged, due to fibres of grain tearing out. This may not matter, but if it does, it is better to use a narrower cutter and first remove the waste in the middle (1), then cut back to the lines in turn, cutting each against the cutter rotation (2). When the ends are trimmed, it should have clean edges all round (3).

This method could also be of value if it is a large mortise and your router is low-powered, or you do not have a full-size cutter.

743. Tenon Grooves

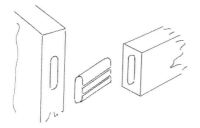

An inserted tenon is used in a similar way to a dowel and, similarly, it has to allow for surplus air and glue to escape when it is driven in. It helps to make one or two shallow lengthwise saw cuts as escape channels.

744. Clean Mortises

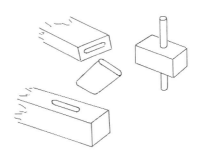

If you make mortise and tenon joints with inserted tenons, it is important that the mortises cut with the router are deep enough and without ridges that will impede the tenon during assembly. A simple gauge for checking is shown. It is a piece of dowel rod of the same diameter as the thickness of the tenon, pushed through a block of wood and projecting the right amount. If this can be moved about in a mortise, the tenon will go in.

745. Start and Finish

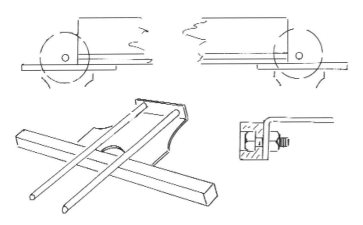

When making cuts using the fence, inaccuracies usually come at the start and finish of the cut. The normal fence is comparatively narrow and it does not have much bearing against the wood, when bringing the cutter into action or leading it out of the cut. Extending the fence both ways can reduce the problem. It could be screwed through the metal fence, but the load at its tips could be considerable and it is better to use thicker wood and use nuts and bolts sunk in it.

746. Another Fence

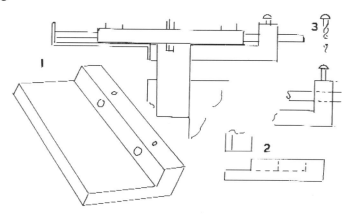

When grooving or mortising with a straight router cutter, accuracy depends on holding the fence tight against the wood at all times, otherwise the cut wanders. Accuracy can be assured if there is another fence travelling on the opposite side of the wood. If the fence rods are allowed to extend on the far side, a shop-made wooden fence can be fitted.

It is shown made from solid wood, but it could be built-up for solid wood (1). Make a series of cuts with a straight cutter (2) to remove the waste. Drill for the rods. Lock with wood screws. Drive the screws into the holes, to cut threads, then withdraw them and cut the ends flat (3) for a good bearing against the rods. In use, set the tool with the main fence, then bring the other up to the other side.

747. Fence for Curves

If you have to make router cuts parallel to a curved edge, you can add blocks to the normal fence. However if you expect to do this often, it is worthwhile making a special fence to suit a range of external and internal curves. The shape need not be exactly as shown, providing there are curved bearing parts near the ends and hollows for clearance near the middle. Make the block to grip the rods so the shaped piece below clears the router base the same amount as the standard fence. Keep the edges of the shaped part square across the wood. Any wood might be used, but if you expect much use, choose a close-grained hardwood.

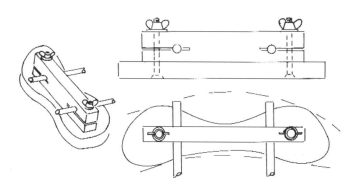

748. No Wobble

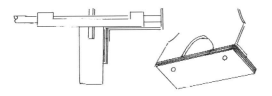

When grooving the edge of a piece of wood, you can increase the bearing area for the base of the router with scrap wood, so it does not wobble. Another way, particularly if the wood is wide, is to increase the depth of the fence face. Use plywood of a suitable depth. It could be longer than the metal fence. Attach it securely, preferably with bolts, and check for squareness.

749. Curved Groove

If you want to cut a groove or other router cut parallel with a large radius curved edge, the fence can be adapted as shown. Make a block with a curved extension and either screw it to one side of the fence or hold it there with tape, as shown. This block and the other side of the fence will guide the tool. If it is a smaller radius curve, you may need two blocks.

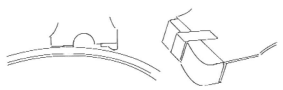

750. Press-on Fences Pad

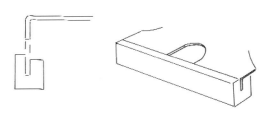

If you need a false face on the fence for extended use it is advisable to screw or bolt it on, but for occasional use a piece of wood can be made to press on, as shown. Reduce the height on the inner side of the groove.

751. Safer End Cuts

The standard fence on a router does not have a very long bearing against the edge of the wood and this leads to difficulty at the start and end of an edge cut, when the router may wobble and spoil the cut. This may

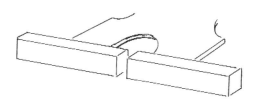

also be caused by the size of gap at the centre of the fence. To counteract this and make spoiled end cuts less likely, add wood extended faces to the fence, with only a small gap. If the job requires the cutter to go partly in the gap, let it cut itself into the wood, so there is a minimum loss of bearing surface.

752. Curved Rabbets

A curved rabbet has to be cut in two stages, either from a solid piece or a section of wood locked to another piece to take the centre. The radius could be anything, but it is shown fairly small, using a block of wood on the fence rods.

Use a straight cutter of sufficient diameter to more than cut the width of the rabbet and cut to the depth of the rabbet. Move to the inside of the rabbet and cut right through. This could be done from the same side, but if you want the best finish on the other side, turn the wood over.

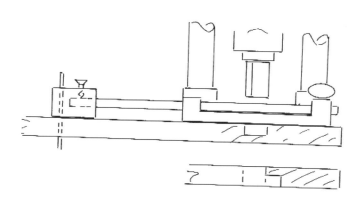

753. Around The Curve

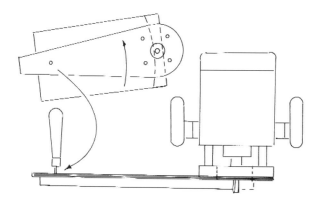

There are several ways of providing a radius control when cutting curves with a router, but for moderate curves the arrangement shown is suitable. This is a thin plywood extended base on the router, using the screws already there, and with a hole to clear the cutter. For a one-off job there is no need to do any special shaping. For a centre, push an awl or a nail through at the required distance from the cutter.

754. Curved Routing

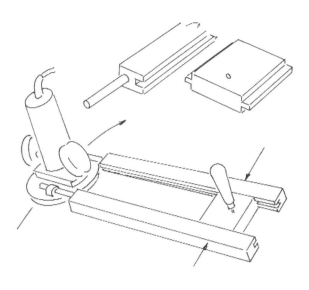

One of the ways of allowing a router to make a curved cut is shown. Any radius is possible. The compass attaches to the router through the fence rod holes. The adjustable centre slides in grooves and can be locked with a cramp, as shown by the arrows. Groove two matching strips of the length you want. The connection to the router could be dowel rods or, preferably, steel rods. Fit them and test the distance between the strips before making the sliding piece. The centre could be an awl or nail.

755. Cross-grain Rabbets

A router rabbet cutter makes a good rabbet along the grain, but when used on end grain it may leave ragged ends to the cut, particularly on softwood. This can be reduced if a cut is made almost to the end, then making a careful slow reverse cut there. Another slow pass at the start will clean up there.

756. Different Rabbets

Router rabbet cutters work on a limited range of sizes and are the best cutters to use within these limits, but if you need to make rabbets of other sizes, you can do it with straight cutters. Use a large straight cutter. It does not have to be the size of the rabbet; a larger one will make a cleaner cut. Set it to the depth of rabbet you need. Set the width with the router fence, probably overlapping the cutter. For a very large rabbet there may have to be two settings and two passes.

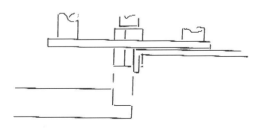

757. Level Rabbets

If you rabbet the parts of a frame and then join them, it is unlikely the rabbets will finish exactly level all round. The alternative in many cases is to do the rabbeting after the parts have been joined. The rabbets will be parallel with the surface, but you will have to cut away the rounded corners. Most frames are not wide enough to give a good steady bearing for the router base, so use a piece of scrap wood against each side in turn.

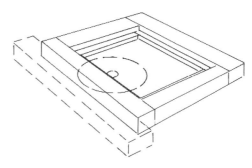

758. Tidy Dovetail Halving

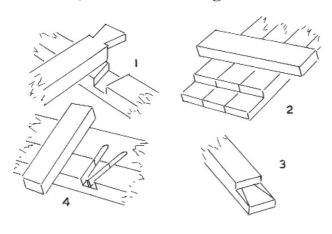

The dovetail halving joint has a good resistance to pulling apart (1). It can be made almost completely with a router. Cut the ends in batches, using a cramped-on guide strip (2). Saw the dovetail shape (3). Cut the sides of the groove in the other part with a straight cutter and a guide strip (4), running into a waste piece. Cut out the rest of the groove at the same setting for a level finish.

759. No Wobble

When using a bearing-guided router cutter, only half of the router base is in contact with the wood and there is a risk that it might not remain flat during a cut. One way of increasing the bearing surface and giving a better cut, is to add an auxiliary extended base, as shown. It can be attached with the screws intended for fitting the router to the plate in a table.

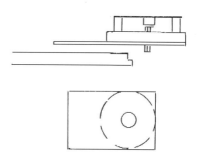

The auxiliary base can be any thin material stiff enough to keep its shape. Thin plywood, Perspex, steel or aluminium alloy are possibilities. Make it to extend at least as much as half the base and cut a hole to clear the cutter.

760. Wider Rabbeting

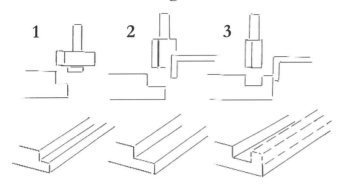

A rabbet cutting router bit is limited in the width it will cut (1), although many depths are possible. For other widths you can use a large straight cutter, controlled in width by the fence (2). If you want an even wider rabbet, you can cut a groove and then remove the waste at another setting of the same cutter or use a rabbet cutter (3).

761. Sash Fillister Rabbet

A rabbet cutter makes a rabbet directly on the edge. If it is important that the rabbet is exactly parallel to the other edge, a bearing-guided cutter will not do it. Before the coming of 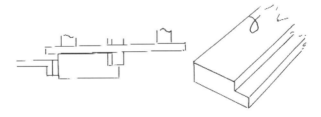 electric routers, a rabbet like that made with a router cutter, was made with a side rabbet plane. If it was important that the plane should be guided by the opposite edge, a fence could be extended on a sash fillister plane. To use a router to have this effect, use a straight cutter guided by the router fence set to run on the opposite side.

762. Moulding Accurately

Moulding for frames cannot normally be held and worked on in the final size. It is wasteful to work it on the edge of a wide board and cut it off. If there is much moulding to be made, the jig shown can be held in the vice and you can use wood cut to the final size. The top and front surfaces are level with the job and provide bearing for the router, to ensure accuracy.

Leave off the front strip, at first, or make it removable. Put all the pieces to be moulded in the jig in turn and cut the rabbets. Fit the front strip and cut all the moulded edges. At one time, when mouldings were cut with hand planes, the jig was called a 'sticking board'.

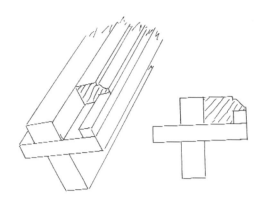

763. Tighter Fit

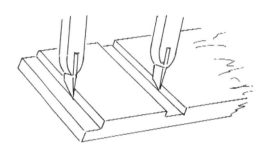

When wood is machined across the grain, all of its fibres may not break away and leave the wood as expected. This is so when some woods are cut across the grain with a router to form rabbets or grooves. An enclosed angle may be blocked by particles of wood clinging there. To ensure maximum tightness of a joint, it is worthwhile cutting into an angle with a knife and pushing or blowing away the dust.

764. Routing Limits

When routing a mortise or a stopped chamfer, it is not easy to see the limits and therefore you need guidance to keep within the limits. This can be done with masking tape, as shown. Measure the distance of the edge of the router base from the edge of the cutter and mark this on the wood with masking tape, so you know when the base reaches it, the cut is the right length. The tape peels off without leaving marks to be removed.

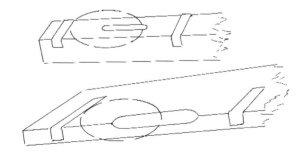

765. Reed Limits

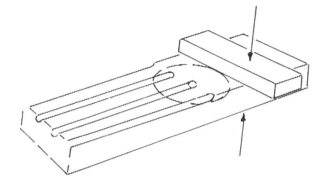

If a surface is to be decorated with router-cut reeds, it is important that they and matching work should finish exactly level. To ensure this, cramp a stop piece squarely across in the position the edge of the router base should be when a reed is complete.

766. Coved Handles

Rod handles with finger grips suit many doors, drawers and lids. Do not try to make them from narrow pieces. Make several in line on the edge or a wide board, then cut them off and make more on what is left.

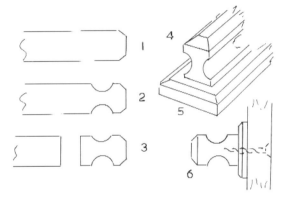

The example shown has chamfered front edges, but they could be rounded. Do this first (1). Using a cove router cutter, make grooves each side (2). Cut off (3). Cut the handles to length and chamfer the ends (4). Sand away any sharpness on edges and corners. The handle could go directly on the main surface, but you could make a thin backing (5). Drive two screws into each handle from the back (6).

767. Routing Ends

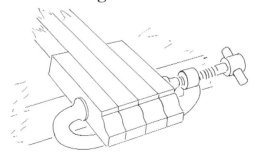

When pieces have to be moulded, as when making feet, they can be grouped and cut together. However if the outer pieces are not protected, the grain will break out and spoil appearance. This can be avoided by cramping on scrap pieces, which will not matter if damaged. For hand routing the parts can be assembled as shown, but for work on a router table, the whole assembly can be inverted.

768. Curved Sanding

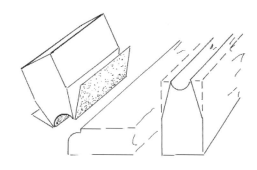

In many woods it is advisable to follow moulding with a router by sanding. Doing this with hand-held abrasive paper will not give even results. If an edge is rounded over, you can use the sanding block shown. The curve should be the same or slightly bigger than the moulding. To allow for getting close in if there is a shoulder, taper to thin edges.

769. Cutter/Scraper

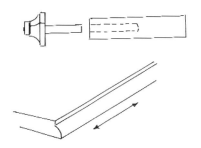

Work on an edge may not finish smoothly with the pass of a router, particularly if the grain is uneven or flawed in some way. The cutter used to make the moulding can be pushed in a hole in a piece of dowel rod and used as a hand scraper before, or in place of, sanding.

770. Base Support

To cut accurately on an edge, a router base should have as much support as possible to reduce any tendency to wobble and spoil the cut. An example is a rabbet, with the wood flat. Where possible, have a board of the same thickness opposite, to give more support to the base,

If the rabbet is to be cut edgewise with the wood in the vice, cramp a thick square-edged piece behind it, or arrange a flat piece at the correct level on the bench top.

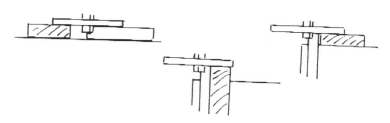

11. Routing with a Table

An electric router is primarily a hand power tool, which is very versatile. There are some operations better controlled when the router is mounted in a table. The table fence ensures straightness and accuracy, but for much shaped work the router is usually more effective if hand-held.

771. Set with a Bearing

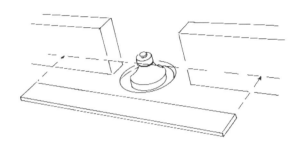

A bearing on a router cutter that serves as a guide for hand routing edges is not needed when using a table, but there is no need to remove it. It can serve as a guide to accurately set the fence with the cutter. Put a straightedge across the two parts of the fence and adjust it so the straightedge just touches the bearing and the tool will make a full cut.

772. Guide Line

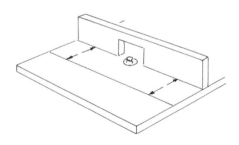

If you have a router table without a mitre fence slot to form a guide, mark a permanent line on the table that can be used for setting the fence square in line with the cutter.

773. Fence In

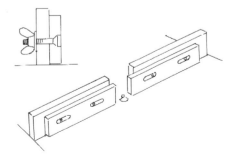

Router table fences have gaps wide enough to clear the largest cutters, but when you are using smaller cutters it would be better to have a narrower gap in order to give better control of the wood being fed across it. The auxiliary fence pieces shown can be regulated to adjust the gap as close as you wish to the cutter.

Use a close-grained hardwood and sink the slots slightly so that the bolt heads are below the surface. Metal-thread screws 6mm or 8mm with wing nuts and washers should be suitable.

774. Close Push

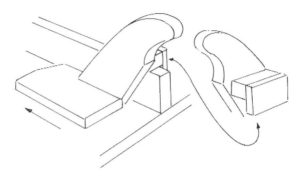

An alternative push stick for use on a router table is shown. It can be used with any wood, but is particularly useful for narrower pieces. Make the base with an angled front to hold in narrow stock. Make the handle high enough for a comfortable grip above the fence. Put a built-up clip behind it to loosely ride on the fence.

775. Guarded Push

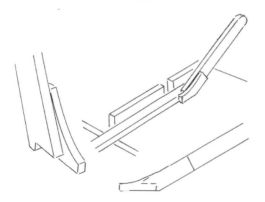

When fairly narrow wood is fed past the cutter in a router table it has to be held in and down. Besides a side push stick, it is worthwhile putting a side piece on the end push stick to help in keeping the wood close to the fence, as shown.

776. Square Push

When work has to be done on the end of a narrow piece on a router table, it may be difficult to feed it squarely. The mitre guide can be used, but most are not very wide and are some way from the cutter. The push stick shown acts as a large set-square against the fence as well as giving a good push close to the cutter.

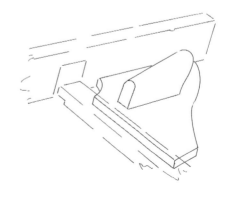

777. Tighter Push

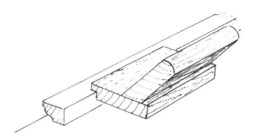

If a narrow piece of wood is fed past the cutter in a table router, it tends to ride up and therefore results in a poor and inaccurate cut. The side push stick shown has a rabbet to go over the edge of the wood, so the workpiece is pushed down as well as sideways and should be kept as close as possible.

778. Better Push

The mitre fence supplied with a router table is small in relation to the job it has to do. It is rarely needed for anything except pushing wood square to the fence. The fence shown is made of wood and much larger than the original. Make it square to

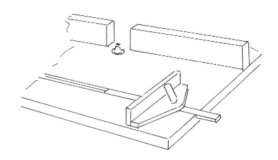

the guide strip and use a dowel handle. It could be any size in order to suit your machine.

779. Stop Breakout

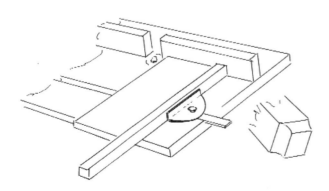

When a cutter runs through across the grain, it will usually leave a ragged edge. When working with a hand-held router, you might avoid this with a short reverse cut. On the other hand, with a router table, that is awkward to accomplish and might not give a good edge, so it is usual to run through.

You can minimise raggedness at the breakout if you push with a thicker piece, preferably hardwood, even if the job is softwood. If you use a square piece, it can be turned to expose a square edge after each pass, then you cut off the end to start again if necessary.

780. Square Push

An alternative to the mitre fence for feeding a narrow piece of wood past the cutter in a router table is a fairly thick block cut squarely. It serves as a push stick and holds the workpiece square to the cutter. It may be the only method if the workpiece is short.

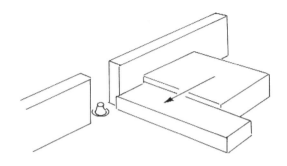

781. Consumable Push

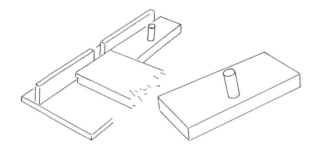

When making some cuts on a router table, it is necessary to run through to give a clean end to the cut. This will cut into and damage a push stick. The simple tool shown can be used a few times, then thrown away if damaged. Have a block of wood straight and square at the working corner. Use an off-centre piece of dowel rod as a handle.

782. Safe Hold-down

When you feed wood across a router cutter in a table, besides pushing, you have to hold it down and close to the fence, if you are to get the best results. The pressure pad shown will do this.

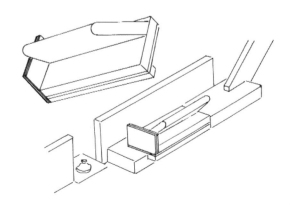

The base can be about 150mm by 75mm. Facing it

with hardboard gives a smooth surface contact. Slope the handgrip from close to the working edge to keep pressure where it is needed. A piece of plywood at the forward end will keep your hand away from the cutter.

783. Best Moulding

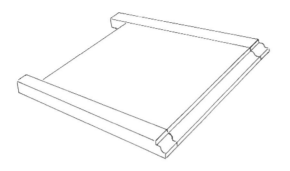

If a piece of wood is to have moulded edges all round, as on a table top, the sharpest corners are obtained by using scrap wood held close, so the router cutter runs through it. Start with scrap wood at both edges. For the other edges it is only important to have one at the end of a cut.

784. Picture Framing

Picture frame moulding cannot be made with a router with a narrow piece of wood. Instead, you can do the shaping on the edge of a board and cut it off. Arrange the section so there will be a piece of square edge at the right depth for the bearing of the moulding cutter to run on. Cut the rabbet (1). Turn the wood over and cut the moulding (2). Cut the piece off (3) and start on the next one. With some designs

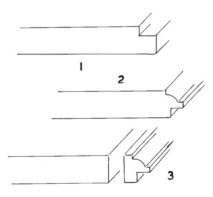

and thickness of wood, it may be better to cut the moulding before the rabbet, but the square edge must be at the right position to suit the second cutter.

785. Hard Cuts

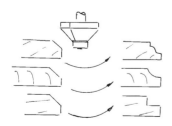

A router produces the best surface if it is not forced and the cuts are light. When an edge cut, such as a moulding or rabbet, has to be made in very hard or twisted-grain wood, it helps to get good results if a cut is first made with a chamfer cutter to remove some of the surplus wood.

786. Oversize Rabbets

You can use a router rabbet cutter to make rabbets of a moderate size, usually with one pass, but a larger rabbet has to be cut in stages.

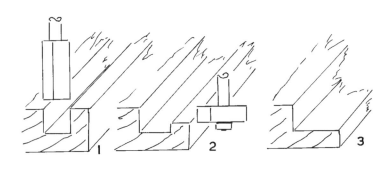

The limit of the rabbet, in width and depth, can be cut with a straight cutter (1). The waste could be removed with another pass of the same cutter, but you may prefer a rabbet cutter. If it will not remove all in one pass, cut what it will (2) and level it with another pass (3).

787. Thinned Edges

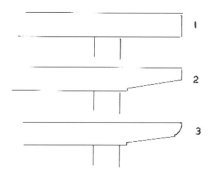

If you use thick wood for a table top and feel that the edges give it a heavy look (1), you can lighten the appearance without having to plane the top thinner, by using a panel-raising router cutter on the underside (2). You might consider making it look even lighter by working a moulding underneath (3).

788. Secure Lipping

If wood lipping is to be put around thick MDF, which may be veneered, it is stronger to fit it with a tongue and groove than to just glue a flat piece on. Plough a groove about one-third its thickness in the MDF. Make the lipping on the edge of a wide board slightly thicker than the MDF. The tongue

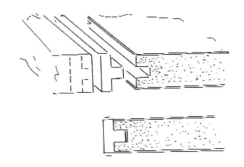

should not quite reach the bottom of the groove. Cut off the lipping and make more, as required. Trim the lipping level after gluing on.

789. Height in Router Table

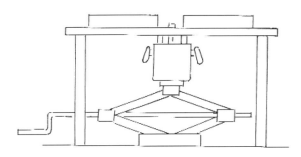

One problem with a router table is adjusting the amount of projection above the table of the router cutter, and this has to be done by moving the body of the router up and down. In most router tables, access under the table is restricted and much of what you do has to be by feel.

If you are making a router table, consider making its legs long enough for including a car jack under the router. With an existing router table, you might be able to pack up the existing legs sufficiently. The ordinary car jack has considerable movement and could adapt if you change routers.

790. Up and Down

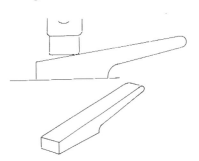

The wedge-shaped block shown will provide a means of raising and lowering a router inverted in a table and hold it in place while you lock it. If necessary it can be used over a packing piece.

791. Fine Lifting

With many router tables, it can be difficult to make fine height adjustments and something is needed to support the router as you do this. A plain wedge piece of wood can be used, but the parallel action of folding wedges is better. The pair

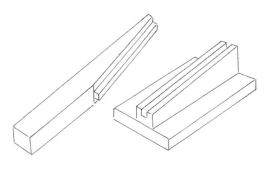

of wedges shown are kept in line with a sliding tongue and groove. A base under the lower wedge keeps it steady and a projection on the top one forms a handle. A lower wedge about 150mm long and a slope of 1 in 6 allows a rise and fall of about 23mm.

792. Systematic Picture Framing

If you have a router, and the usual cutters, making a picture or photograph frame from bare wood is easy, if you follow a routine. Make the moulding from a piece of wood long enough and wide enough to give the router base a good bearing and room for cramps or holdfasts.

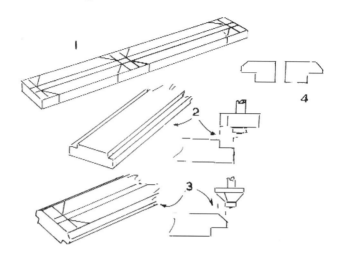

Mark out the size and mitres of the frame on opposite sides of the wood surface (1). Turn it over and cut the rabbets (2). Turn to the front and either chamfer or mould the edges (3). Cut off the frame parts (4). The mitres are already marked and you can cut the four sides.

793. Space-save Doors

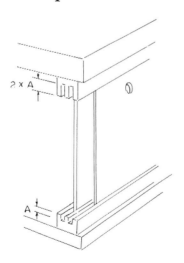

Hinged doors need space to swing. If space is restricted, it may be better to have sliding doors, but normal sliding doors still cover about half the cupboard. You can make sliding plywood doors that use an idea borrowed from furniture with sliding glass doors. Make grooved guides for top and bottom, but make the grooves in the top guide twice as deep as those in the bottom. You can slide the doors in the normal way, but when you want more access, you can lift them to clear the bottom guide and take them out.

794. Drawer Bottom

It is usual today to let a drawer bottom into grooves in the sides. If the drawer slides on the sides, the bearing surface is not very wide and wear could soon occur. The traditional way uses a slip inside the drawer side (1). This more than doubles the bearing area. Use a router to make the slips, working on the edge of

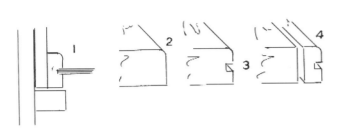

a wide board. Round over the edge (2), then cut a groove for the bottom (3). Cut the piece off (4) and use the new edge to make another slip.

795. Routed Drawer Pulls

Handles for drawers can be made on the edges of a wide board, for convenience in holding, and then cut off. Use a rounding-over cutter (1). Turn the wood the other way up and use a cove cutter (2). Cut off the handles (3) and attach them with screws (4). The piece left from the centre can be used for more handles.

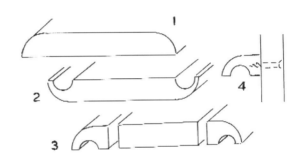

796. Quarter-round Moulding

You can make your own quarter-round moulding with a rounding-over router

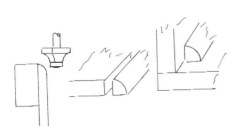

cutter. Choose a wide piece of wood of a thickness to suit the rounding-over cutter. Hold it level with a thicker block in the vice. Round over one or both edges. Cut the quarter-round piece off and do it again on the remainder until you have enough moulding.

797. Better Moulding

When you make a moulded edge all round a tabletop or similar piece of furniture, one cut will be with the grain, while another will be against the grain, and two will be across the grain. If the moulding section has a narrow shoulder, this may finish rough or ragged in the last three directions, especially in some softwood.

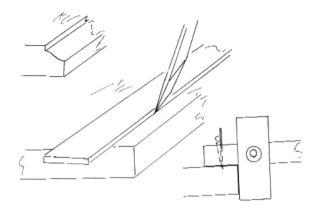

To avoid this, it is a good idea to cut through the surface fibres of the wood before using the router. Do it with a knife against a straightedge or with a cutting gauge. Cut a short length of moulding on a piece of scrap wood, to check the distance of cut from the edge.

798. Repro Chamfers

If you make a stopped chamfer with a cutter in a router, the ends of the chamfer

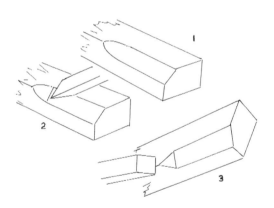

will be rounded (1). This is acceptable and attractive in modern furniture. In older furniture the chamfers were cut with a chisel and the ends of the chamfers were angular. If you are making reproduction furniture, the ends of routered chamfers should be altered. Make a nick across the rounded end (2), then chisel away the rounded part (3).

799. Handleless

There does not always have to be a knob or handle on a door, and in some places its projection could be a nuisance. An alternative to a handle is a hollow finger grip, as shown, made with a router cove cutter. The same idea can be used with anything that has to be lifted, such as a kitchen chopping board.

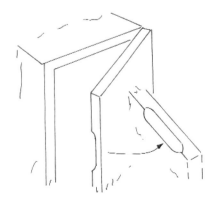

12. The Lathe

A woodturning lathe is more of a tool than many other machines. Success depends on the user's skill more than any other machine tool, most of which do an excellent job for which they are intended, but within limitations that the user cannot alter. A lathe can be quite basic and produce good results. Too many elaborations are to be avoided. Skill in using tools, which are kept sharp, is the most important consideration.

800. Centering Simply

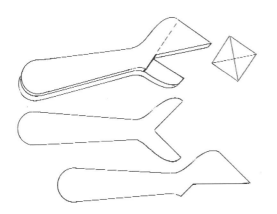

Much work between centres is with wood of square section, on which you have to mark the centres at the ends. The tool shown provides a quick and accurate way of doing this. Of course, it can also be used to find the centres of round objects. For most spindle turning, jaws 50mm long will have adequate reach. The two parts could be made of solid wood, but plywood is convenient. The lower piece could be 9mm and the top piece 6mm. Make the lower piece first and use it as a template for the top piece. Have the 90° opening in line with the handle and make the other piece to accurately bisect it. Glue the parts together and round the handle to a comfortable grip.

801. Hermaphrodite!

If you need to find the centre of a dowel rod, or any small round thing that is not already centred, the tool for the job is a hermaphrodite calliper. That long word can be loosely said to mean 'Not one thing or the other'. It has one calliper leg and one divider leg. Use it as shown, set to somewhere near the radius, to scratch four small arcs from about equal positions around the rod. Centre-punch a dot in the centre of these marks.

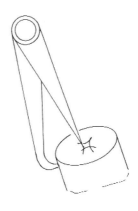

802. Small Centre Square

For spindle work on a lathe a normal centre square is larger than usually needed and tends to be awkward. This smaller tool will draw the diagonals of squares and mark the centres of round objects. A suitable size would be between 75mm and 100mm square.

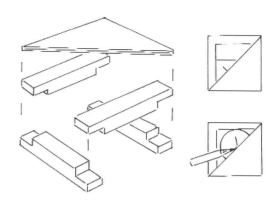

Make a frame with four identical strips halved together. Fit a thin piece of plywood with its 45° edge exactly bisecting the square

803. Cutting Calliper

If you can find an open-ended spanner of the size to match a hole you can drill, it makes a good fixed calliper for checking a dowel end to fit a hole, as in a candlestick, but you can take it a step further.

Grind back the upper jaw a short way, and then grind away the rounded exterior to make a cutting edge, preferably angled to slice towards the tailstock. If you turn near to size, the spanner can be used to give a final trim to the exact size.

804. Another Centre Square

A combination square has one face of its stock at 45° to the blade. If you put something with a square corner against where the blade and stock intersect, the blade bisects the angle and forms a centre square. Cut a small block of wood with a square corner and use a small cramp to hold it to the blade. This will find the centre of circular pieces within its range.

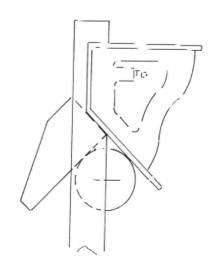

805. Turning Centres

Most centre squares are large to accommodate many sizes, but for most turning between centres wood is fairly small in section and a big centre square is rather clumsy. The shop made centre square shown could have a capacity of 50mm and suit most needs.

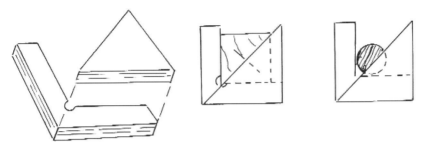

Use 6mm plywood. If the tool is to be used on square stock it is helpful to drill a small hole at the internal corner to provide clearance. Make sure the triangular piece bisects the angle of the other piece and glue it on.

806. Help Allen

Most lathes and other machines have socket-head grub screws of the Allen type. A little angle-ended hexagonal wrench is provided, but in the smaller sizes this is often awkward to use. A tool more like a screwdriver would be easier to use.

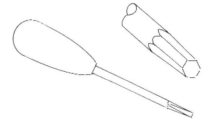

You can make one with a length of steel rod fitted into a handle. File the end hexagonal as accurately as you can by eye. Getting it precisely exact is not so important. A slightly inaccurate end will still turn a screw.

807. Roll Over

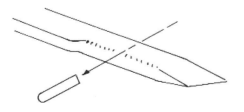

Most skew chisels have square angles on the edges. This does not roll easily on the tool rest and could damage its surface. It is an improvement to grind the edge opposite the lower part of the angular end to a curved section, for a distance more than will be used on the tool rest.

808. Knobs On

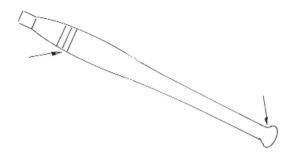

Long turning handles come with the end just tailing off at the same diameter. If you have to replace a handle or prefer to make your own, consider putting a knob on the end. You can then tell by feel when you are at the end. You can also adopt an identification code of lines. Their position could indicate chisel or gouge and the number of lines might increase with width.

809. Sharpening Lathe Tools

Lathe tools are ground on a high speed dry grinding wheel, and stops are fitted to control the position against the tool rest, but there are differences in grinding ordinary chisels and plane irons. The stop for a gouge needs a hollow in the lower part and enough depth to stay against the tool rest when the gouge is rolled on it. A skew chisel needs the stop pieces extended to come below the grinding angle. If the other side is to be ground without altering the stop, both parts should be deep enough to bear against the tool rest.

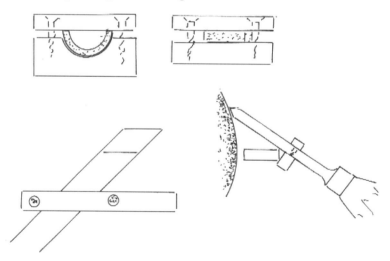

810. Centre Cleaning

On most lathes the headstock and tailstock centres fit into Morse taper sockets. These are often neglected, but they ought to be cleaned occasionally. Turn a taper on a rod at about the same taper as a centre. Use this to push a piece of cloth soaked in penetrating oil or WD40 into a socket. Move it about to remove any grit or dirt. Wipe the tapers of the centres at the same time.

811. Bumper Outer

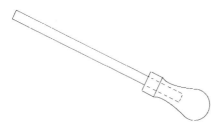

A Morse taper centre in a hollow tailstock needs a hammer effect to knock it out. A piece of dowel rod is not very much use. It is better to use a metal rod of as large a diameter as will go through the hole and rather longer than the bare distance. The bore for a No.1 Morse taper will usually pass a 9mm rod and a No.2 taper a 14mm rod. A plain rod end may be uncomfortable on the hand and you can turn a knob handle to make a worthwhile bumper outer.

812. Scrape Better

Much turning on the faceplate or with bowls and other cross gain work has to be done with a scraper. This can have its cut improved if the sharpened edge is turned over in a similar way to that used for 'ticketing' a cabinet scraper. You can do it with a gouge. Give several hard rubs on the cutting edge, until you can feel that it has been turned over in the direction of cut.

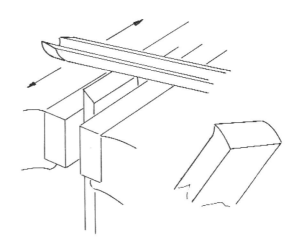

813. Centre Safety

The most important part of a lathe centre is its point and this should be protected. If a centre has a Morse taper and has to be knocked out, you have to

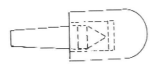

catch it. To prevent damage to it or yourself, turn a block of wood, as shown. Put a piece of leather or plastic at the bottom of the hole. Use this to hold the centre while knocking it out.

814. Turning Extraction

It is difficult to arrange a dust extraction system to remove all that comes away when turning, but this idea should suck away much that you turn away in spindle work. There is a piece of cardboard forming a scoop, either pushed into the extractor hose or wrapped round it, then held with adhesive tape. It can be held on a stand or attached to the lathe bed, so the open part of the scoop is towards the job and moved for long work.

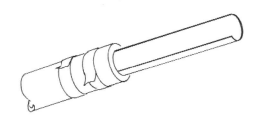

815. Tool Tray

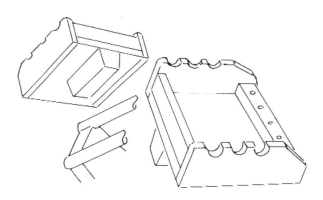

This tool tray can be fitted between the bars or bed of a lathe at its end and can be removed when you need to take the tailstock to the limit of the bed. The important part is a flat piece of wood on a block that will jam in the bed. If the block is short, the tray can extend past the end of the lathe. The rest of the tray can be arranged to suit your needs. It is shown with grooves for turning tools, holes for centres and a safe space for callipers and other small tools.

816. Tidy Turning

Small tools or parts can get lost in the accumulation of shavings and chips that gather below a lathe. This tray can be fitted to the end of the lathe bed and hold tools and other things out of the way, ready to be reached

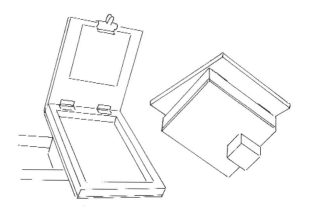

when needed. It is a shallow box with a fold-down plywood lid that will hold sketches and notes.

Put a block underneath, as shown, to press between the sides of the lathe bed. This will cause the tray to extend past the end of the lathe allowing most of the lathe to be used, but it can be lifted off if the tailstock has to be moved to the end.

817. Chuck Protection

If you use a three or four jaw chuck on your lathe, the jaws project as you open them further. These rapidly rotating projecting ends can damage your hands if you take a knock. A broad rubber band stretched over them will make you aware of them and cushion the blow if you do get knocked.

818. Faceplate Safety

Most faceplates are heavy and some chucks heavier and awkward to handle. If one drops while you are unscrewing it, it might damage itself or the lathe bed. To protect both parts, a thin piece of plywood with pieces to fit over or between the bars or bed will 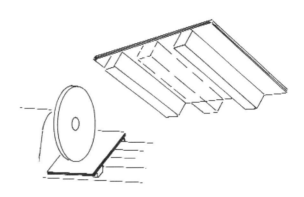 take the load. It might also have other uses at other parts of the bed, possibly as a tray for tools.

819. Rest Smooth

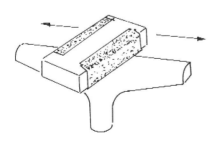

Turning tools are harder than the tool rest. Square-edged chisels can dig in, producing an overall roughened surface. When you need to make a sweeping cut, you will find the tool hesitates in places, interfering with your action. Give the top of the tool rest a polish with abrasive paper or, preferably, emery cloth wrapped on a block of wood. Finish with metal polish for the finest finish.

820. Lever Tightener

On several lathes the screw that locks the tool rest has a lever handle. There may be similar levers elsewhere as well as other machine tools. Getting the screw tight by hand pressure only may be difficult and the tool rest moves just at the 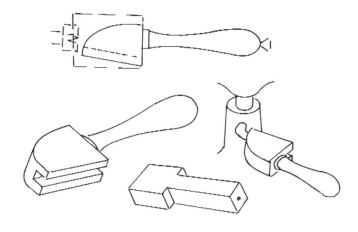 wrong moment. The wrench shown can give you extra leverage and a tighter screw.

Use close-grained hardwood, such as beech. Size depends on the lever. Use wood large enough for the working end and saw the part to be turned to a square section. Mount in the lathe and turn the handle. Cut one side of the rectangular part to a slight angle and make a groove in it to fit over the lever. Shape the other side to reduce its bulk.

821. Tighter Screws

 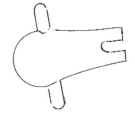

The tool rest is held in its base with a screw with a wing head on many lathes. This does not provide much leverage and it is sometimes difficult to get it tight enough. The extension handle could be turned from an oddment of close-grained hardwood. Put dowel rod through as a handle and cut the slot a push fit on the screw head.

822. Octagonal Grip

At one time chisel manufacturers offered a choice of handles. The best had an octagonal grip (1). It was usually made of boxwood. You might have difficulty getting boxwood, but you could turn your own handles from another hardwood.

This needs care, as you could find the octagon out of true with the round parts. Start with perfectly square wood. Some prepared square wood shrinks to a diamond section in store. Draw diagonals on both ends to find the middle (2). Measure half a diagonal on a surface from one edge (3) and make a thumb gauge to this size (4). Use it with a pencil to mark lines on all sides. Centre-punch at the crossings of the diagonals on both ends. Plane off the corners to the lines and check that you have eight equal sides (5). Your first turning cuts will show if you have the octagon concentric with the round parts.

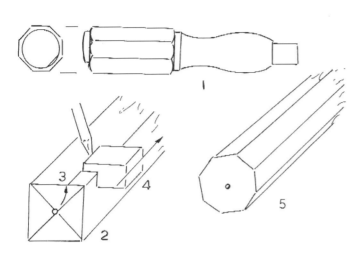

823. Lathe Lock

Many lathes are not provided with a means of locking the head to prevent rotation and this may be needed if carving or other work is to be done on the turned wood in the lathe. This device is intended for use on a lathe with a two-bar bed.

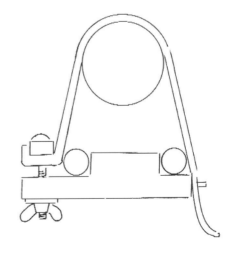

Locking is with a piece of leather trouser belt, with its buckle holes. The block below can be wood about 50mm square. The rear notch should fit around the bar. Extend the front notch to take the tensioning arrangement. Drive a screw that will fit the belt holes at the rear. Cut off its head to make a peg. At the front there is a short crossbar tensioned with a bolt, washer and wing nut. Allow enough belt for the biggest job you expect to lock and glue it to the crossbar. In use, hook a suitable hole on the peg and tighten the belt with the wing nut.

824. Foot Stop

If you need to move around a turned part for carving or other work, for example to mark lengthwise positions, you need a temporary stopping arrangement that can be used without trouble or delay as you need to move the job round.

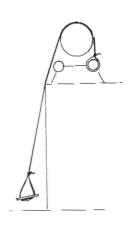

A foot stop is shown. To get plenty of friction to grip the job, webbing should be used in contact with the wood, but rope could be used to fasten to a bed rail and join the foot pedal.

825. Skew Angles

There have been discussions about the angles of skew chisels, but it is the angle of the edge to the direction of cut that matters. The angle it is ground affects how the tool is held, not how it cuts. The common angle (1) suits most people, but some turners like a square push (2) and others prefer to hold the tool squarely with an acute angle (3). The tool cuts the wood the same way.

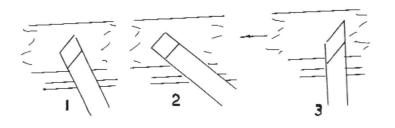

13. Lathe Work Between Centres

Most owners of lathes find the greatest variety of work is done with the wood supported between headstock and tailstock centres. Many older lathes were not designed for anything else and much traditional turning was of this type. It is possible to do first-class work on the simplest lathe, possibly shop made. Not so long ago turners earned a living with pole lathes. They could not be much simpler. Improve your skills with the basic functions. You do not need elaboration.

826. Turning Sequence

When turning a long piece between centres, particularly if the central part is to be comparatively slender, the whole piece could vibrate and bend if you cut central details first. When you have roughed the wood to a cylinder, it is better to concentrate on end work first and progress towards the centre, retaining stiffness there as long as possible.

827. Better Lathe Steady

Support for long slender turning is often just a bit of notched scrap wood lodged between the lathe bed rails. This may work, however, a better alternative that also lodges between the bed rails is shown, but it is pivoted and can be adjusted with a wedge. The pivot can be a long nail or a piece of steel rod.

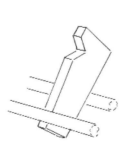
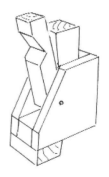

828. Need a Long Rest?

Much earlier turning was between centres, making table legs, pillars, pedestals and other long work. A long rest was often improvised to avoid having to frequently move the usual tool rest. We still have the problem when turning something almost as long as the lathe. Besides allowing quicker work, a long rest helps you make a better job of long sweeping curves.

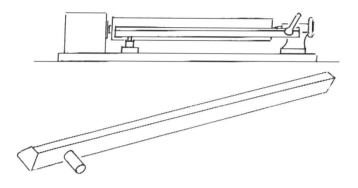

The long rest shown fits in the normal tool rest support near the headstock end, and the other end is held by a cramp to the tailstock. Bevel the top of a square strip and round the edge your tools will slide on. Turn and fit a peg near the left-hand end. Allow enough length for cramping to the tailstock.

829. Better Beading

The turning chisel sold as a beading tool is usually made with a square section. In use, it is held square to the lathe centerline and rolled to form the bead, but the angular section cannot roll with a semi-circular action, and it is difficult to make the bead shape even. It would be better made from round rod.

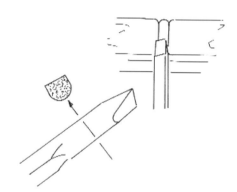

To make a square-section beading tool easier to use accurately, grind the underside rounded a little further back than you expect to have on the tool rest; fully semi-circular if possible or at least take off the squareness.

830. Smoother Spindles

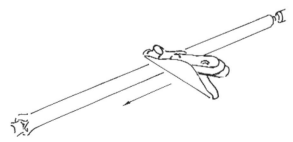

When turning a long spindle, either parallel or with a slight taper, there is the problem of keeping the surface smooth as well as dealing with whipping, if it is slender.

If you turn close to size in the usual way, you can finish it smoothly and accurately by changing to a block plane.

308

Set the lathe at a low speed and plane along the wood with the plane held at an angle, as shown. It will work like a skew chisel, but the sole will help it even out any slight inaccuracies and whipping will not be a problem.

831. Wooden Catch

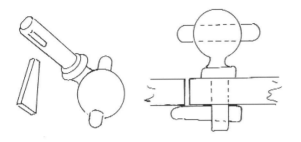

A catch for a cupboard door will be appropriate for a period-type piece of furniture and is an interesting turning job. Make the main part with a cylindrical part going through the door. The knob could be as you wish, but allow for a dowel going through it to provide leverage. Arrange the direction of the wedge through the other end the same as the dowel, then the dowel indicates when the door is fastened.

832. Knob Fix

A turned knob may have a dowel end to go right through a door. It may be satisfactory just glued in, or it can be wedged. If you want

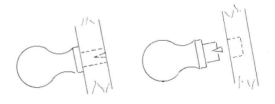

to wedge it, but do not want the end to show inside, you can use a stub tenon as shown. Make the wedge shorter and with a more obtuse angle. Put it in a saw cut and estimate how much you can expect it to push in. Arrange the wedge across the grain of the door, so there is no risk of splitting. It is better to squeeze the glued knob tight, with a vice or cramp, than to hit it.

833. Hollow It

If a turned part has to make a tight fit against a flat surface, it is always wise to slightly hollow it, although a square cut seems appropriate. This may be a spindle turning with a dowel end, as in a candlestick or lamp standard, or something, such as a knob, to be screwed in place.

834. Hidden Screw Head

A turned knob, intended to be screwed from the other side of the door, can have the screw head buried if you do not want it to show.

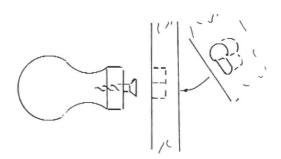

Drive the screw into the knob so its head and a short length of its neck are still projecting. Mark on the door where the knob is to be and go a short distance along the grain and drill a hole that will pass the head of the screw. Go a little deeper than the screw projects. Use a drill the same diameter as the screw neck to make a slot back to where the knob is to be. Insert the screw head and knock it along the slot to its final position. Knock it back again and remove it. Tighten the screw a half turn, then apply glue and knock the knob back into position.

835. Turning Marking

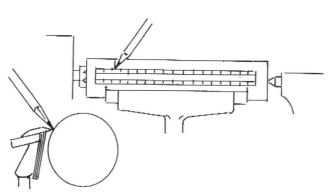

When a piece of wood has been roughed to a cylindrical form, the next step is usually marking on the rotating wood the positions of main features. This is often done with a hand held rule on the slide rest, with a pencil against it. Quite often there is movement and errors.

For easier marking and more accuracy, this device can be used on any lathe. A strip of thin wood attached to a piece of plywood is shaped to fit over the angle of the tool rest. Over this is glued a wooden rule or a section of it. This projects slightly so the tool rest can be adjusted to bring it close to the work and a pencil used at the appropriate graduations to mark the rotating cylinder.

836. All The Same

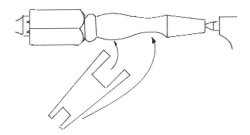

When turning sets of legs or other items that should match, it is possible to get shapes similar, and lengthwise dimensions right, and yet the effect is spoiled when the diameters of curved parts are obviously different. You can check with callipers, but you may need to alter them during use, with the possibility of errors. An alternative is to make a jig of vital measurements from the first leg. It can be one piece of scrap wood with notches cut at opposite ends to suit largest and smallest diameters.

837. Two-step

When turning several parts between centres which have to finish the same diameter, it is useful to make a two-step calliper gauge from plywood. The inner opening is a guide to the diameter to turn the wood (A) with a gouge. The outer opening is the size to finish the wood (B) with a skew chisel.

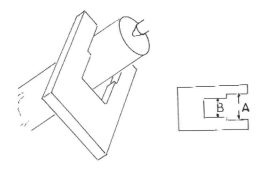

838. Check Strip

We often drill a hole in a piece of scrap wood for testing something such as a chair rail end. Most of us only use a few sizes of holes, so a gauge for these sizes

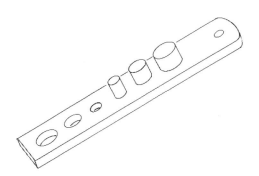

would be better than having to drill test pieces every time. The strip shown has three holes, but it could be more. There are also specimen pegs turned to the same sizes, for setting callipers.

Put the holes near the end and include an extension to use as a handle. A small hole lets you hang up the gauge.

839. Equal Spacing

If you need to divide the cylindrical part of a turning into a number of equally spaced parts, as for attaching feet or brackets, do it before taking the job off the lathe. Put the tool rest against the cylinder and draw a line on the job along it. Wrap a strip of paper around the cylinder and use a nail or spike to pierce

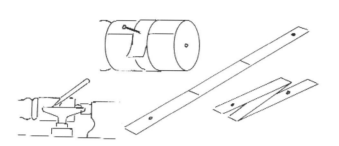

through the overlap. Open the paper and divide the distance between the holes into the number of divisions needed. An easy way to do this without measuring is to fold the paper the required

number of times and mark on the folds. If you measure first, folding will check your accuracy. Put the paper back on the cylinder and mark the divisions. Draw them along the edge of the tool rest before taking the wood off the lathe.

840. Matching Legs

If you intend turning a matching set of four or more legs, you will be more successful if you first spend some time making one or more templates, either from the first master leg, or a drawing. Just marking lines round after turning cylindrically may help in spacing, but profiles and diameters may be wrong.

If there will be square parts, mark all these before mounting in the lathe, then turn the cylindrical parts between, using callipers to check these are all the same. Make one or more card or thin wood templates for the round parts. Cut shallow nicks on a straight edge so a pencil does not slip when marking locations of key parts. Cut profiles of the outlines on the other edge. This is important for sweeping curves, which can vary between legs, with-out you noticing until the furniture is being assembled.

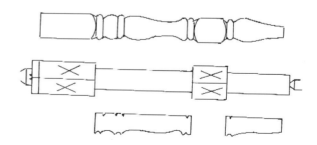

841. Remote Dowels

If you want to make a dowel on a piece of work between centres at the tailstock end of the lathe, it is easy enough to test it in a hole of the size it is to fit. On the other hand if it is at the headstock end of the job, it has to be tested in a different way.

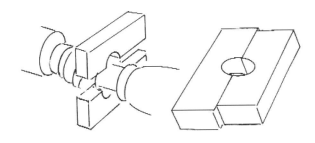

You can check with callipers, but a more accurate way uses a hole the size it is to fit. Cramp two pieces of scrap wood together and drill a hole through their meeting edges. Try this over the dowel, as shown.

842. Drive Centre

If you make a small lathe with an electric drill as its power unit you need a drive centre to fit in the chuck. Bought centres have Morse taper shanks, which are unsuitable for a chuck.

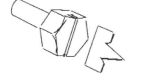 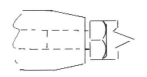 A centre can be made from a bolt, as shown. Cut it to a suitable length and make a saw cut centrally across its head. Cut a piece of sheet steel to the shape shown. Make it as symmetrical as possible, but it can be trued after fitting. Solder it into the slot. Try pulling it round by hand in the chuck and file the point, if necessary, to get it central.

843. Same Way Round

In theory, if you take a spindle turning off a spur centre and replace it the other way round it should still rotate concentrically, but you 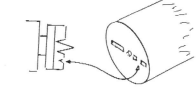 often experience a slight wobble of the working surface as you continue cutting. This idea is a way of identifying the original way round, so you put the wood on the centre the same way. File a nick in one of the side blades of the spur centre. This will show a gap on the wood, so you can replace the same way round.

844. Centre Lubrication

If you do not have a rotating centre and use a plain centre in the tailstock, you can reduce the amount of lubrication needed by drilling a small hole and pressing candle grease or wax into it. A Slocombe drill, as used by metal turners, will make this hole along with one to match the centre angle in one operation.

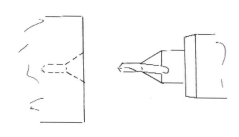

845. Accurate Bores

When you have turned a handle and fitted a ferrule, you have to drill for the tang of the tool and care is needed if the tool is to be secure. If it is a tapered tang, it is usually satisfactory to drill in three steps with slightly undersize drill bits and go a little deeper than the length of the tang.

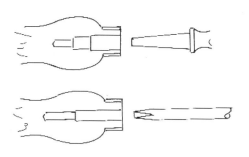

If it is a parallel tang, particularly if it is a tool that will have a twisting action, it is advisable to file flat tapers on the end. Drill only slightly undersize for most of the depth, then make a hole further undersized for the tapered end to enter. In both cases you can give greater security by using epoxy adhesive.

846. Chuck Stop

When drilling from the tailstock there may be a tendency for the chuck tapered stem to slip and let the chuck turn as the hole gets deeper, particularly in some hard or twisted-grain

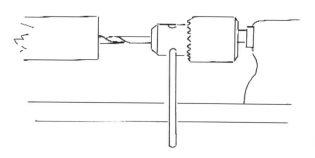

wood. If it is a keyed chuck, you can stop this by pushing a rod into a hole and letting it bear against the lathe bed. This could be a metal rod, but a piece of dowel rod or even scrap wood might serve.

847. Depth Check

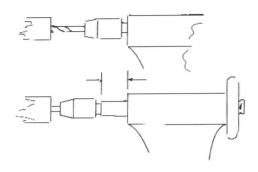

When drilling from the tailstock, as when turning a tool handle and making a hole for the tang, there is an easy way to measure the depth drilled. Start drilling with the end of the spindle level with the surface of the tailstock. If you measure the amount of the spindle that has projected, that will be the amount the drill has penetrated.

848. Lathe/Drill

If you need to drill accurately in the end of something too long to fit under a drill press and you do not trust a hand-held drill, the lathe can be used as a horizontal drilling machine.

Make a box-section support with a piece to go between the sides of the lathe bed. Fit a drill in a chuck in the headstock. Remove the tailstock. Pack the support to bring the job to the right height. Keep the workpiece, which can be any length, straight and feed it by hand.

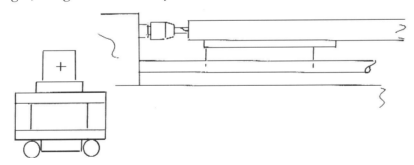

849. Tighten That Ferrule

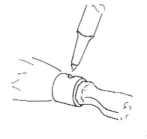

Wood may shrink with age. A ferrule that was tight may loosen. If you turn slightly too small, the ferrule may not be as tight as you wish. In both cases, rest the ferrule on an iron block, or something similar, and make a dent with a centre punch.

850. Finishing Ferrules

Oddments of brass, copper, and aluminium tubing can be cut to make ferrules for tool handles. However even if you file them carefully, it is unlikely you will get the ends perfectly concentric. The inner end is not so important, but you can true the exposed end as follows.

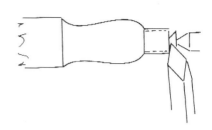

Mount the ferrule on the handle while it is still possible to support the handle with the tail centre. Use the side of a skew chisel close up on the tool rest. Alter the angle of tilt until the chisel cuts the metal with light cuts. Follow with a file to remove any burr and polish the metal while it is rotating with emery cloth.

851. Better Ferrules

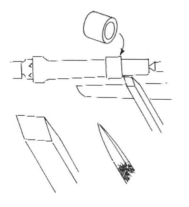

The outer end of a ferrule cut from tubing can be trued in this way after fitting to a handle, but that leaves the inner end as you sawed and filed it. If you want to have both ends true, you need a mandrel. Turn a piece with a slight taper on which a ferrule will fit tightly. Hold the edge of a skew chisel against the tube at its tailstock end. Experiment with the tool angle until you make it scrape the metal. Complete truing with a file. A better tool is made from an old triangular file, with its teeth ground off and taken to a point. This has a more acute cutting angle and removes metal more easily. When one end is true, reverse the ferrule on the mandrel. If you try to true the second end in the first position, the thrust of cutting will push the ferrule off the mandrel.

852. Saw Centering

You can find the centre of the ends of a square piece of wood for mounting between centres by using a band saw. Hold the wood on a V-block and move it up to the saw so the saw enters at a corner. Do the same the other way and at the other end. A

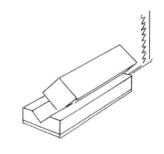

saw cut will also take the spur centre. Do not make the cuts without the V-block as the saw might snatch dangerously.

853. Breakthough

If a spindle turning breaks in use, such as a chair leg, it is almost certainly at the

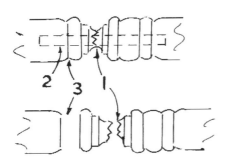

smallest diameter (1). To reinforce a repair, there has to be a dowel through (2), but attempting to drill in the damaged ends will only result in more damage. Instead, use a fine saw and cut through a hollow, probably beside a bead (3). Glue the damaged parts and let the glue set, then drill both ways for the stoutest hardwood dowel that can be used.

854. Better Through

When turning between centres, it is better with some woods to prepare the wood by planing off the corners. For that you need a trough to support the wood while planing. This is usually made in a single length and sometimes it is not as long as the wood to be planed.

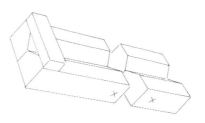

If the trough is cut in two, the parts can be moved to allow for greater lengths. Mark the meeting pieces in case there is a slight difference if they are reversed. It is usual to let the stop piece in, but it works better if it is put on top.

855. Repetition Help

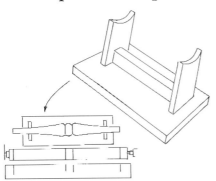

If you wish to turn a number of identical pieces, such as chair rails, it is helpful to have a specimen in front of you, as near as possible to the one you are turning. This is in addition to the usual marked stick as a guide to getting lengths right.

The stand shown is at about centre

height, with a moderately hollowed top to take a variety of specimens. It need not be very long, as large jobs can overhang.

856. Foxtail It

When turning parts to fit holes, you do not always get the turning as accurate as you wish. In the days before reliable glues, most stub tenons were given mechanical strength by spreading the ends, whether round or square, using foxtail wedges in saw cuts, as shown.

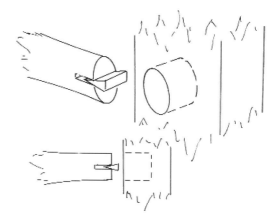

You may not want to do this with all joints, but if there are any that you think might be too slack, cut fairly steep-angled short wedges and position them in saw cuts so they spread the ends in the direction of the grain. Cramp tightly to force the wedges into the cuts.

857. Better Cable Holes

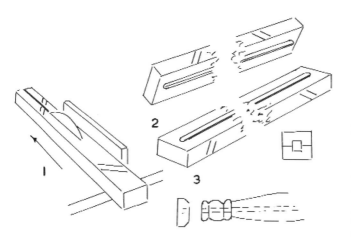

It is difficult to drill cable holes in lamp standards, as the hole may not run true and finish too rough to push a cable through. There is a limit to the length that can be drilled and may mean the complication of joints in a tall lamp standard.

It is possible to make a clean straight hole of any length by using a router with a straight cutter. Put identifying marks on the square wood to be used and cut it down the middle. Use the router cutter to make grooves in the meeting surfaces to within a short distance of each end, centrally and to form a square hole when brought together (2). Glue the pieces together and turn the design you want, leaving enough scrap wood at the ends so the solid pieces can be removed and the hole exposed (3).

858. Sanding Drum

This is a sanding drum to make and use on the lathe. Make it to take two grades of abrasive paper, either cut from a sheet or bought in rolls. A diameter of about 100mm will take a strip cut from a standard sheet.

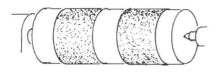

Turn a parallel drum of sufficient length. Make sure the spur centre and tailstock centre are deeply fitted, as they will be taking the load in use as well as while turning. Glue on the abrasive strips and secure them with rubber bands until the glue sets. Mark on the drum the direction of attachment, so it is always put back the same way and there is no risk of vibration.

859. Hold The Split

The common way to turn a pair of flat mouldings is to start with two pieces of wood glued together with paper between, but separation while turning can be a nuisance or even dangerous. Putting the spur centre across the paper line (A) may take care of that end, but the tail centre could have a splitting action.

It is better to allow enough waste at each end for the glue to be reinforced with screws (B), and then tool work can be kept away from those parts (C). After turning, the ends can be cut off and the parts separated along the paper line (D).

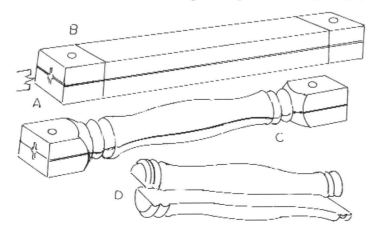

860. Better Burning

When burning in decorative lines in spindle turning, the iron wire has to be tensioned and plenty of pressure applied to cause enough friction to char the wood.

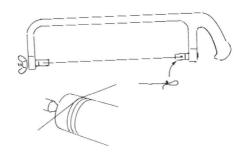

One way of holding the wire without having to use your hands on it is to take the blade out of a hacksaw frame and loop the wire to the pins at the end. Start with the screw slack, then tension the wire. The frame is not affected and can be put back to its normal use easily.

861. Reverse Sanding

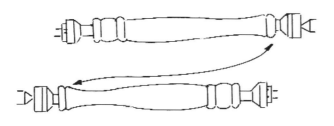

An item turned between centres may be sanded while it rotates, but for the finest finish it should also be sanded the other way to remove the tiny bits of wood fibre bent over instead of removed.

Most lathes cannot be reversed to permit this, but if the work can be moved end-for-end the normal rotation will have the same effect. If this is to be done, you have to allow for it during preparation. Deeply centre punch both ends and try mounting and running the wood both ways, before starting turning. Allow similar amounts of waste at the ends, to be cut off later.

14. Lathework on Faceplate

Work on wood of larger diameter than length has become possible with improvements in lathe design. Not very long ago, there was very little of this work done and it was impossible on most lathes. Care is needed; it can be dangerous to mount wood that is irregularly shaped and turn the lathe sat too high a speed. Use tools at the correct angles. A wrong approach angle can be more serious on a large diameter than when spindle turning.

862. Speed

When turning wood it is the surface speed of the wood presented to the cutter that matters. Therefore the larger the diameter and hence the circumference, the slower the speed of rotation needed to achieve the same surface speed as a fast-rotating piece of small diameter. If you double the diameter, you should halve the speed of rotation to get the same surface speed. Fortunately, in using a lathe, speeds are not that critical and we use a slower speed for a bowl than a tool handle. There is no need to be more precise.

The type of wood has to be considered, but this is more the concern of experience. Close-grained wood finishes better at higher speeds that open-grained wood. It is not just choice of hard and soft woods.

Spindle turning in most woods can be done best at high speeds. For faceplate turning of large size, start with a slow speed, before trying something higher.

863. Tape Away

If you use double-sided tape for temporary assemblies of various types, the joint may seem too good when you try to break it apart. If you cut off a corner and mark where it is, you can insert a knife blade there to start separation.

864. Permanent Pad

Not much work is done with wood mounted directly on the faceplate and we make a pad from plywood or other material for each situation. A permanent plywood pad on the faceplate will save time and it can be removed when something different is required.

Most faceplates have two or more sets of four screw holes. Use one set of these to attach a piece of 12mm plywood and turn it to match the faceplate. Drill through the other holes, ready for attaching the next workpiece.

865. Paper Off

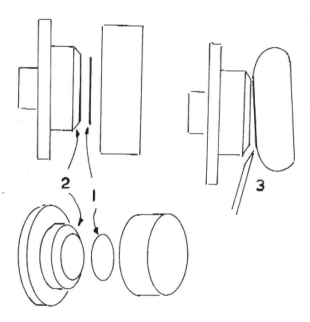

One way of holding a block to be turned into a bowl or similar pattern is to glue it to a block fastened to the faceplate, with paper in the joint. The joint is then split with a chisel, but it is not always easy to find the edge of the paper and wood may be split or damaged. This risk can be minimised if the paper (1) is glued to the block with a turned chamfer, then it is easier to accurately position the chisel when prising off. (3).

866. Faceplate Lever

The action of turning tightens a faceplate on the thread of the headstock spindle nose and some leverage may be required to remove it. The lever shown engages with three holes in the faceplate and can be used on either side of it.

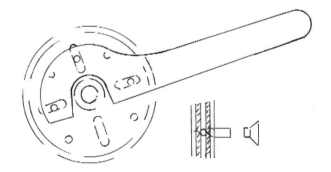

Designs vary but you should be able to find three holes or slots that the lever can connect with. Use 12mm, or thicker, plywood. Cut away to pass over the spindle. Make the pegs with three stout screws and cut the heads off to leave ample length to fit in the faceplate.

867. Faceplate Screws

Faceplates are drilled for screws of a certain gauge. If you use screws of a smaller gauge, there will be a risk of movement during turning. When you have found which screws fit best, keep some of different lengths in your lathe kit, instead of using anything available.

868. Anti-lock Faceplate

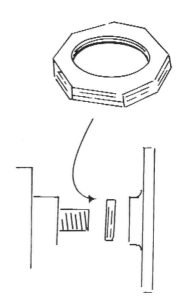

A faceplate can be very difficult to unscrew after it has been in use some time or you have been turning large diameter work. It will release much easier if it has a semi-stiff washer behind it. A suitable material is plywood. Drill a hole to fit on the mandrel nose and trim away the outside, to leave an area sufficient to pad the faceplate. This cutting need not be very accurate.

869. Turner's Depth Gauge

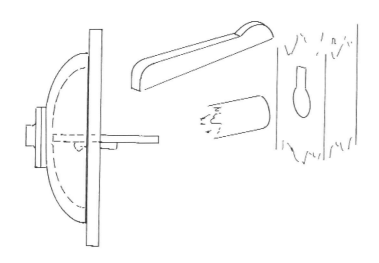

Ordinary depth gauges are not wide enough for bowl turning. To test the internal depth of a bowl or other hollowed work, you can make a gauge with a stock of any length. Wood about 18mm square and a length of 9mm dowel rod should be suitable.

Drill centrally and squarely for the rod and cut a slot in it for a wedge. If you make a captive wedge, as shown, it cannot fall out in use.

870. Centre Protection

If you do much faceplate turning, the socket for the centre will be open and could accumulate debris that might affect the fit when you want to use the centre. You could turn a plug to keep it clean or even use a bottle cork. If not, remember to clean out the socket before inserting a centre.

871. Two-way Depth Gauge

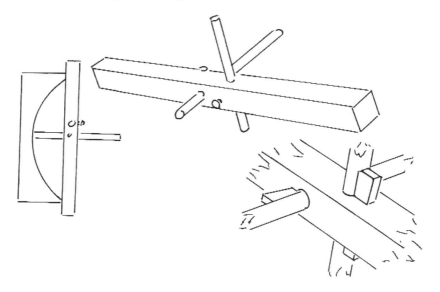

When turning, you may sometimes find it helpful to test two depths without having to alter a single gauge. The simple gauge has two pieces of dowel rod through holes in a square strip. They are held with wood screws. When making the gauge, drive the screws fully into the holes to cut threads in the wood, then withdraw them and file off the points, so they will lock the dowels without marking them much. Alternatively, you could cut slots for wedges.

872. Drill Depth Gauge

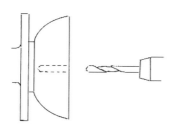

When turning a bowl and reversing it to deal with the inside, you need to know the depth you will go. Instead of testing with a depth gauge as you progress, you can mark the maximum depth with a hole drilled from the tailstock.

873. Big Drill

When making a bowl, drilling from the tailstock to the depth you want is good practice, but it may be worthwhile enlarging the hole as much as possible. If you have a hole you can get a gouge into, you can turn away some of the waste wood easier from the middle outwards as well as from the rim towards the centre.

874. Wide Depths

If you do not have a suitable depth gauge for a large bowl or other turning, put a straight piece of wood across and use a combination square.

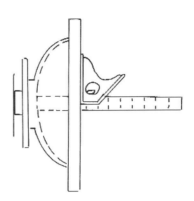

875. Rule Depth Gauge

If you use a steel rule in a depth gauge, you get an instant reading of the depth. For bowl turning the depth gauge shown can be made without affecting the rule for its normal use.

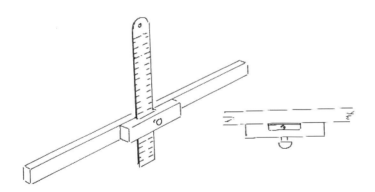

Make the crossbar as long as you need. Attach to its centre a piece cut out wide enough to admit the rule, but deeper than its thickness. Locate a screw at its centre. Drill and drive this fully to cut its thread, then withdraw it and file its end flat to bear against the surface of the rule and spread the pressure.

876. Quick Depth Gauge

If no other depth gauge is available, drive a long nail through a strip of wood so that it projects the amount you want.

877. Dual Scraper

Because of the direction of rotation and the usual location of the tool rest when finishing the interior of a bowl with a scraper tool, cutting is nearly all done with the left half of the cutting edge. If you shape the end of the tool so the right half is straight, you have a scraper to use outside and inside a bowl.

878. Multi Tool Rest

When turning the inside of a bowl or other hollowed work, it is helpful if the scraper or other tool is supported as close as possible to the work. Standard metal tool rests are a compromise and do not always get very close. This three-sided wood rest will get into most places with its three different curves, or can be easily altered to suit. It is not intended to be long lasting, but the top can be planed and the whole thing replaced easily.

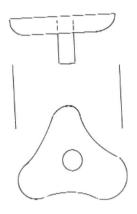

Use a close-grained hardwood. Turn the stem to suit the tool rest holder. Start by marking out a triangle and superimpose on it the shapes you expect to need. Round the lower edges to give clearance.

879. Big Drill

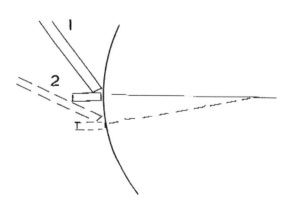

When making a bowl, drilling from the tailstock to the depth you want is good practice, but it may be worthwhile enlarging the hole as much as possible. If you have a hole you can get a gouge into, you can turn away some of the waste wood easier from the middle outwards as well as from the rim towards the centre.

880. Bowl Wall Calliper

As you turn the inside of a bowl you need to be able to check on the wall thickness as you progress. There are specially shaped callipers, but this shop made tool will do the job.

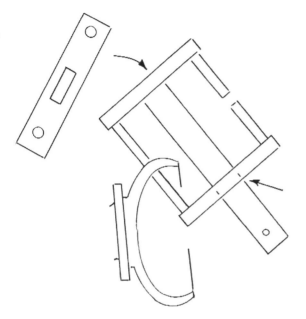

Make two similar ends with holes for dowels and a slot for the handle strip, which is glued in one end, but should have a sliding fit in the other (arrowed). Glue in four pieces of dowel rod, all extending the same amount. In use, close one pair of dowel ends on the bowl. The gap at the other side is the thickness. You can try many places without removing the calliper.

881. Bowl Support

If the blank you cut for turning a bowl is not exactly round when mounted, it is wise to bring up the tailstock centre as extra support if you are turning over the bed. Use a low speed at first until you have turned the outside true and the disc runs smoothly. You could leave the centre in position while turning the outside and turn out some of the inside waste around it.

882. Centre a Blank

Bowl blanks on sale are marked and cut from a template and you have to find the centre for mounting in the lathe. Put the blank on a piece of paper. Draw round it and cut this out. Fold it in half and then into quarters. Snip off the point and open the paper out. The snipped hole is the centre.

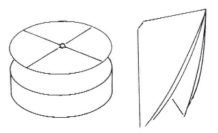

883. Mini Faceplate

Most screw centres have holes drilled for screws in their rims in addition to the normal central screw. If you want to turn disc type work that would be small and awkward to mount on a faceplate, you can mount work up to 100mm or more on the screw centre with steadying screws through these holes. An advantage is that you can work on more of the back without needing to reverse the workpiece.

15. Finishing

We tend to think of finishing only as the application of polish, paint or varnish, but that is only a final stage. The surface has to be prepared well if the final finish is to be of the best quality. Sawing, planing, and maybe scraping, should lead up to sanding. Abrasives have been improved in recent years and advantage should be taken of all available types and grades.

884. Abrasive Store

If you have many grades of sheet abrasive paper, a good way to store them, sorted and ready to use, is in a multi-compartment file, obtainable from a stationer or an office supplier.

885. Hand Sanding Economy

A full sheet of abrasive paper can be divided so four surfaces can be used, without cutting into pieces. Mark the back of a sheet into four. Cut on one line to the centre (1). Fold down one side of the cut (2). Fold across that (3) and turn over the remaining piece on to it (4). When the outside surfaces are worn, you can refold until all surfaces have been used.

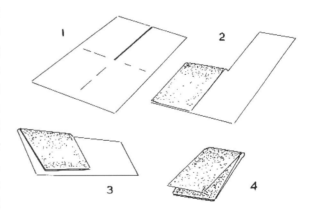

886. Multi Sanding

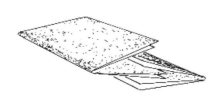

When hand sanding you can have several surfaces to use, if you fold the abrasive paper as shown. You can use two different grades interweaved with each other. Each piece offers four faces to use before you discard it.

887. Multi Sanding Block

A sanding block made as shown should be suitable for hand sanding wood of most shapes. The broad flat side will deal with normal flat surfaces and external curves. The rounded edge takes abrasive paper into hollows and the sloping edge goes close into square angles, as well as more acute angles.

For most purposes make the block to suit a quarter sheet of paper, but you might prefer half sheet size. The drawing shows plain wood, but you could cover the surfaces with sheet cork or rubber.

888. Accurate Cutting

If you cut sanding sheets for a flat sander, it is a help if you make a template the size of the sheet, with a handle that could just be a strip or a shaped handle or knob. Cut sanding side down on a flat surface.

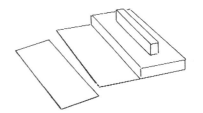

889. Exact Sanding Sheets

Sheets of abrasive paper of suitable size for hand sanding can be estimated and ripped against a steel rule, but when you have to fit a piece in an orbital sander, or something similar, the tear needs to be more exact. The sheet tearer shown uses a 12 inch worn-out hacksaw blade as the cutter.

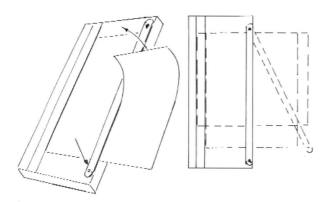

Mark a board with two lines at half-width of a sheet horizontally and vertically from the edge, as shown. Mount an old hacksaw blade, with its teeth outwards at this edge, pivoting on a screw at one end. To tear a sheet, put it under the blade up to the relevant line, then hold down the other end of the blade and pull the sheet upwards. Turn the paper and do the same at the other line.

890. Accurate Tears

For hand sanding, abrasive paper can be torn by eye, but if an orbital or other sander is to be used, more accuracy is required. This method uses a try square with a blade longer than the width of a sheet.

Mark on the stock of the square half widths of a standard sheet of abrasive paper horizontally and vertically, measured from the outer edge of the blade. Hold a

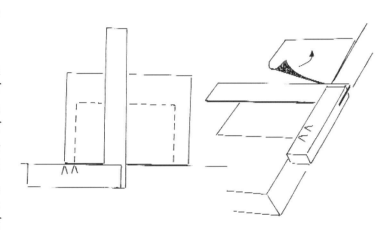

sheet level with the edge of the bench and put the square on it with the half-length mark level with the end of the sheet. Hold the blade down and rip the sheet up and away, then do the same the other way, if you need quarter sheets.

891. Hand/Belt Sanding

A sanding belt that has served its purpose on a machine may still have some useful life for hand sanding. You might cut it into pieces, but a holder to use it

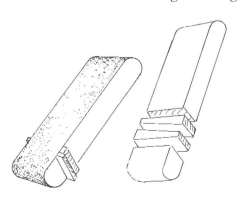

as it is can be made, and can be used on flat or hollow work. A wood block has to tension the belt and this is done with folding wedges. Of course, you may find this so successful that you put a new belt on a block.

Shape a block to any thickness you wish. It does not have to be the same as the supports in a machine. Make a pair of identical wedges with widths the same as the thickness of the block and much longer than the width of the block. Cut a space to admit the wedges. After a trial assembly, you can trim the lengths of the wedges, but let them project a little to allow for later adjustment.

892. Surform Sanding

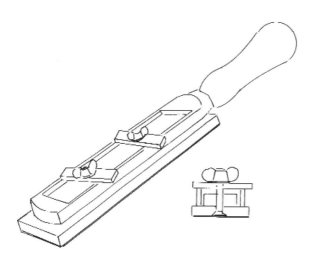

A Surform blade makes a coarse cut and will remove wood rapidly, but sanding has to follow for a smooth finish. You can use the same holder for sanding by removing the blade and fitting a sanding block.

Make a block to fit easily in the Surform frame, but a little thinner than the depth of the opening. Fit another piece below to overlap the frame, as shown. Put two countersunk screws through, long enough to take turn buttons, washers and wing nuts. Position their holes so when the turn buttons are in line, they will pass through the opening.

You could glue abrasive paper direct to the wood, but it would be better to use cork sheet (floor tiles) to cushion between the wood and the abrasive paper. If it is a file-type Surform frame, make the thickness below the frame so the abrasive sheet will be below the level of the handle, then the whole tool can be pushed over a large area.

893. Into The Angle

Using a power sander or hand sanding on a flat block will leave the extreme corner of an inside angle still needing treatment. Abrasive paper folded over the straight end of a putty knife will get close in effectively. Change folds to use all the paper.

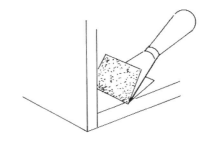

894. More Sanding

If you use a disc or orbital sander and think the sanding disc has worn out, examine it. Almost certainly you will find that there is no more cut in the abrasive around the circumference, but nearer the centre there is still life in it.

You could wrap the whole disc round a block or cut out the usable area for hand sanding. You will get maximum use out of a rather expensive piece of abrasive paper.

895. Less Mess

If a chair, table or other piece of furniture on legs is to be varnished, standing it on paper to keep the floor or bench clean results in it sticking to the paper. It is better to drive a screw into each leg to lift it above the paper, and leave it there until the varnish is dry.

896. No-wobble Support

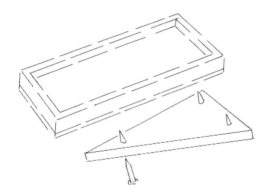

It is common practice to support a job being painted or varnished on the points of nails driven through scrap wood, usually four nails. This may be necessary in some cases, but there is always the risk of the job wobbling. You can avoid any risk of this happening if you use three nails. Three supports cannot wobble, hence the camera tripod to use on any surface.

897. Pin Support

It is fairly common practice to support a job that has had a finish applied all over on the points of nails, but for smaller items it is simpler and less trouble to use drawing pins (push pins). Use any number of pins, but three do not permit the job to wobble.

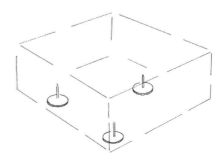

898. Steady Finishing

When a piece you have made has to be finished all over, you may drive nails through scrap wood to support it, which may be unsteady. If you expect to do this job frequently, it is worthwhile making the pair of supports shown. They are two-way and have folding feet to give ample stability. One has a single nail one way and the other has wide and close spaced nails, to offer a variety of arrangements. The wood could be 40mm square, with the feet extending about the same amount each way.

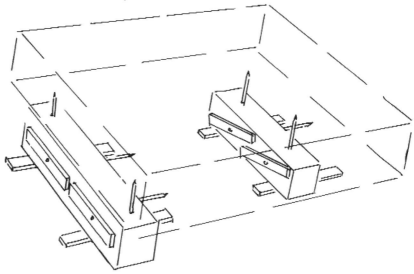

899. Painting Sequence

Paint is a fairly tolerant material to apply, but there are certain rules if you want the best results. Undercoat soaks in and dries evenly, but it is advisable to follow the same order of working as a top coat.

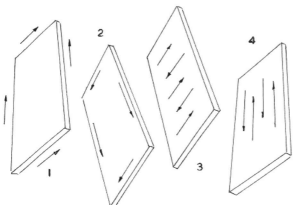

If it is thin material, paint the edges first (1), then go round the surface smoothing the paint that has come on to the surface (2). Cover the whole surface adequately, but not to excess in any convenient direction (3). Finally, brush lengthwise with reasonably light overlapping strokes (4). An exception might be if the wood is to be used vertically with the long direction horizontal. In which case it might be better to brush the short way.

900. Paint Level

Before you seal a paint can for later use, after using only part of the contents, use a wax pencil to mark the paint level on the outside of the can. You will not then have to open to check what is left later.

901. Ready Brush

Oil and water do not mix. If you have used a brush with an oil-based paint and wish to keep it overnight ready for use next day, immersing the bristles in water will stop the paint in them hardening. Wipe off the water and the brush is ready for use again.

902. Cleaner Brushes

A paintbrush should have a much longer life than many of us give it. Cleaning needs to be thorough, rather than just dropping it in white spirit and hoping for the best.

Work out surplus paint or varnish on scrap wood or newspaper. Squeeze out even more with a paper towel or a rag. Soak the brush in white spirit, or other solvent, if that is what the paint or varnish maker recommends. At least cover the bristles. Work it at intervals in the liquid. When you work it out on paper or squeeze with paper towel or rag, very little colour should appear. If it does, put the brush back in the white spirit for a while longer. Now move to washing-up liquid or general-purpose household cleaner. Immerse the brush in this neat at first, then top up with hot water and let the brush soak. Finally, wash all this away with clean water and squeeze out before leaving to dry.

903. Catch the Drips

When you use paint or varnish straight from the can and wipe the brush on the edge, you soon get runs down the outside, with the inevitable mess. This can holder can be made from scrap wood. It will catch the drips and will be more convenient to use than holding a can in your hand.

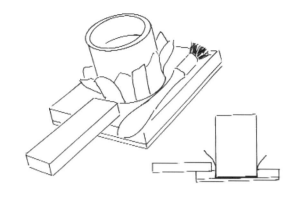

The can fits in a hole and rests on a plywood bottom. Allow for pushing newspaper or plastic sheeting into the hole, which could be cut with a jigsaw. If you cut it with a band saw, cut in from one edge and cover the slit with the handle. The holder should stand up to many uses before you scrap it.

904. Two-can Stand

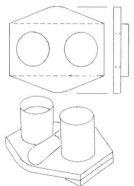

A 1-litre can of paint is heavy. It may be preferable to tip what you want to use into a smaller can. A cleaned food can, of the common 75mm diameter, would be suitable. The stand shown is intended to hold two of these cans with a space between for a brush. The second can could hold white spirit for cleaning or mopping up dropped paint or varnish. The extended sides of the stand act as handles.

Plywood 12mm thick is suitable. Make the holes in the top part push fits on the cans. Take sharpness off all round.

905. Non-drip

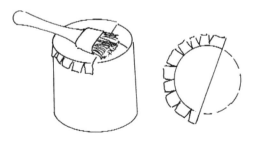

Wiping a brush on the lip of a can of paint soon results in runs down the outside and drips where you do not want them. The improvised part-top shown gives a central wiping edge and keeps the outside of the can clean. The top is made from the opened-out body of a cleaned food can. The usual small food can will make a top for a 1-litre paint can. Stand a paint can on the flattened tinplate overhanging the straight edge a little more than halfway. Draw round the shape and cut away about 15mm outside it. Cut nicks to allow tabs to be turned down. Precision is not important.

As you have cut more than half a circle, the tightened tabs resist the tinplate lifting off as you wipe a brush on it, but it is easily removed when required. You should be able to use it several times.

906. Brush Cleaning

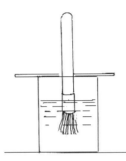

This is an old tip, but a good one. We tend to put a used brush in a can of white spirit and leave it there. It stands on its bristles, which bend and the solid matter from the paint drops to the bottom and cakes on the bristles.

It is better to have a hole in the handle, so it can be hung on a stiff wire, then the bristles are immersed and do not bend and solid matter falls clear, so the brush keeps its shape and cleans better.

907. Varnish Flow

Most varnishes do not flow properly if they are cold or even slightly cool. It is always wise to stand a can of varnish in warm water long enough for the heat to penetrate, before use.

908. Large-mouth Funnel

If you wish to pour a thick liquid, such as paint or varnish, from one container to another, as when saving a small amount of paint by decanting it into a smaller can, you need a funnel with a larger mouth than an ordinary funnel. One can be made from an empty plastic bottle with a large neck. Cut it off at a suitable level.

909. Better Varnishing

Varnish is more sensitive to preparation than paint. Most varnishes can be used straight from the can without mixing. If a varnish appears to need mixing, stir it gently with a flat piece of wood. Do not stir violently or shake the can. This would cause small air bubbles that would spoil the finish. In cold conditions, warm the varnish moderately, and the wood, if possible.

910. Varnish Sequence

Getting the best result from varnish needs more care than painting. Do not brush any more than necessary. Avoid brushing out, as you would with paint. Too much brushing causes bubbles, which spoil the finish. Do not use the

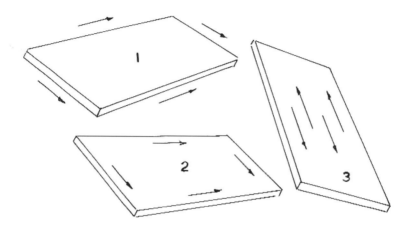

varnish when it is very cold. Warm it to at least room temperature and do the same with the wood, if possible. Keep brushes for varnish. They should not have been contaminated with paint, even if thoroughly cleaned.

Varnish provides its own undercoat, so you will be applying at least two coats of the same varnish. Follow the same sequence with all of them, even the first coat, which will soak in. If there are edges to deal with, do them first (1). Go round smoothing any varnish run on to the surface (2), then apply enough varnish smoothly along the wood (3) with overlapping strokes. Try to avoid having to work out excess varnish. So far as possible, resist touching-up strokes.

911. Clean Hands

Disposable latex examination gloves are available fairly cheaply in boxes of 100. They are ideal for paint or varnish work, where you cannot avoid getting the liquid on your hands. You can feel what you are doing through them, then they peel off to leave your hands clean.

912. Free Filling

Candle wax makes a good filler of nail holes or cracks. Rub a candle over the area, and then sand the surface. Particles of wood dust will mix with the wax and help the colour of the filling match with the surrounding wood. Unlike prepared fillers, candle wax will stay flexible and move with expansion and contraction of the wood.

913. Matching

A clear finish on top of stain will often affect the final colour more than you expect. If this is important it is advisable to be patient and try the intended finishing process on scrap wood of the same sort, right up to the fully dried stage, before using stain on the actual furniture. Some stains need shaking before use. If so, make sure you do this the same amount when testing and finally applying.

914. Dust Off

One way of getting a surface as free of dust as possible before applying a finish is to hold pieces of masking tape sticky side out and wipe them over the wood.

915. Sock It

A good item for applying wax polish is an old sock. Any material will work, but cotton is particularly good. Another advantage is that you can put a hand inside like a glove.

916. No Dent

To get rid of a dent on the surface of wood, try covering it with a damp cloth, and then work the tip of a domestic iron over it to steam it back level.

917. No Oak Stain

Iron and steel in contact with oak will cause the wood to stain a dark brown in the vicinity. All other metals, including stainless steel, do not affect the wood. Zinc plating (galvanising) gives limited prevention, but the effect may not last long. Where non-staining is important, brass or stainless screws and nails should be used. Brass hinges usually have steel pins, but these should not touch the wood, so should be safe. If there is no alternative to fitting a steel component to oak, insulate it from the wood with stiff plastic and use the appropriate screws.

918. Beer Polish?

A traditional farmhouse method of cleaning and polishing oak furniture may be worth trying. Boil beer with a little sugar and beeswax. Apply warm with a soft brush and leave to dry, and then rub well with a soft cloth or chamois leather.

16. Sharpening

If you have only one edge tool, you need the means of sharpening it. This is usually a honing stone, and either a grinder or a very coarse honing stone to use in place of it, although some alternatives are mentioned in these tips. Time spent sharpening is always worthwhile. You will do better work more safely if you have sharp tools.

919. Grinder Safety

A high-speed dry grinding wheel is quite brittle. It may never break, but if it does while rotating, dangerous pieces can fly in all directions, particularly in line with its spin. Stand to one side when starting a wheel and avoid standing in front, except when necessary to watch sharpening closely.

920. See Better

All parts in the operating area of a grinding wheel are dark and the tool edge may not be very prominent, so it is difficult to see what you are doing. Try putting a piece of white paper or card on the bench below the tool rest.

921. Ready Stop

If you wish to grind a plane iron and arrange a stop against the grinder tool rest, a cap iron can be used. Change sides and turn it square across.

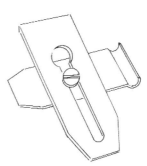

922. Square Edge

A plane iron should have its cutting edge square across; otherwise you will have difficulty in setting it. In preparation for grinding the edge, check with a try square and put a piece of masking or electrician's tape across close to the edge, to give you a guide to the squareness of the new edge.

923. Grinding Gauge

If you put stops on a tool being ground, these have to go on at the same distance from the edge each setting. A gauge will help you set the tool to the same angle each time. A simple one is shown. If you use different angles, make another setting on the other side.

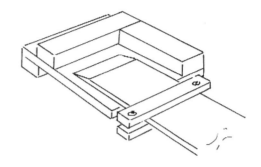

924. Maintaining The Angle

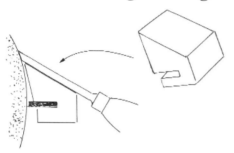

When you sharpen a tool on a high-speed dry grinding wheel, you have to remove and cool the steel to prevent it losing its temper. It is not easy to replace it always at the same angle. One way of doing this is to make a block, as shown, to fit on the usual flat tool rest. Cut it away to clear the wheel and make the slot a push fit on the metal tool rest.

925. Mark It

If you sharpen tools on a high-speed dry grinding wheel, you have to withdraw the tool occasionally to cool it and prevent loss of its temper. This brings the problem of replacing it so the same bevel is presented to the wheel. If you have the usual horizontal tool rest, it helps to mark where the tool has to

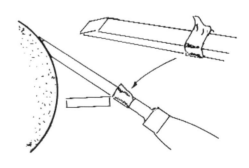

come against its edge. A quick way of marking this on chisels or gouges is to wrap on a small piece of masking or electrician's tape.

926. Inverted Scraper

Most of us sharpen turning scrapers on a grinding wheel in a similar way to

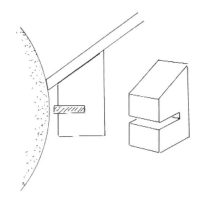

other turning tools, but it could be better to turn them over so they slope down on the wheel. This leaves any burr on the cutting edge where it is needed.

You can maintain a suitable angle on a wood block, as shown. Its angle and position will depend on the diameter of the grinding wheel. Experiment with a tool. Make the slot a press fit on the tool rest.

927. Same Angle

Most high-speed dry grinders have a tool rest level with the centre of the wheel, and we grind tools at an angle to it. An alternative is shown. Chisels and plane irons can be ground to the same angles and there is a point on the circumference of the wheel where a tool held horizontally will be ground at this angle.

The auxiliary tool rest shown is a block of wood that will support a tool to grind at the correct angle. Draw a section on paper or experiment on the grinder.

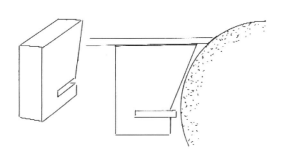

928. Cross Sharpening

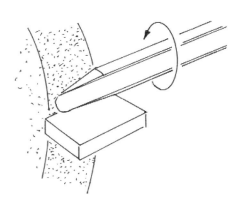

You can grind a turning gouge by rolling it on the grinder tool rest, but do not use the tool straight from this process. The grinding marks will be across the cutting edge, which will not cut satisfactorily as it is. Use an oil or waterstone to hone these marks from the outer edge and clear them from the inside with a slip stone.

929. Grinding Gauge

The recommended grinding angle for a plane iron is 35°. This also suits most chisels, although paring chisels might have slightly more acute angles. This gauge allows you to check when grinding. In its simplest form it could be cardboard. You could use an outdated credit card. Soft metal sheet would be best: aluminium, brass or copper.

Mark the angle and drill a small hole at its point before cutting. You could also scratch the angle as a further guide and a hole at a corner allows hanging up or tying to your grinder.

930. Same Sharpening Angle

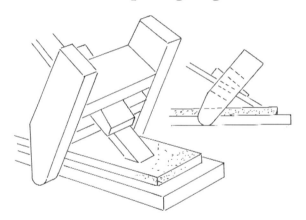

This jig will hold a chisel or plane iron at a constant angle to a sharpening stone as you move it along. The angle can be set by adjusting the amount that projects before tightening the wedge. Cut the wood for a side and experiment with this and your stone and its case to get the positions for the crosspieces to give the angle you want. Make the assembly wide enough to take your widest plane iron and clear the width of the case, with an allowance for sideways movement.

931. Stone Ends

When you make a case for a sharpening stone, cut the recess long enough to take two pieces of hardwood. Cut them as deep as the stone, with their end grain upwards. They protect the ends of the stone and when a tool runs over it keeps level, does not falter, and the edge you are making will not be harmed.

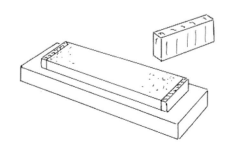

932. Economy Sharpening

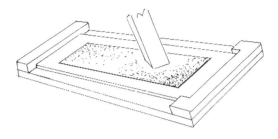

Edge tools can be honed on abrasive paper glued to glass. For perfect flatness use plate glass, but window glass is flat enough for all practical purposes. You could use different grades on opposite sites of the glass. Support the glass on wood blocks at the ends, as shown, to keep the glass in place. If the block is notched around the glass, it stops it moving sideways, but it can still be lifted out.

933. Sharper Quicker

It is common to use a light lubricating oil on an oilstone, but in time this can clog the pores of the stone and make it slower sharpening, particularly if the stone is not wiped after sharpening. A stone at this stage should be soaked in stove paraffin oil and scrubbed with a wire brush, then dried. Paraffin can be used alone as a lubricant when sharpening, or it could be used mixed with light machine oil.

934. Steady Sharpening

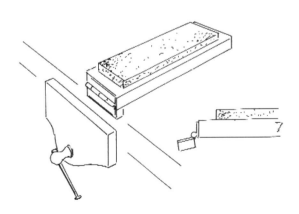

It is helpful to have a sharpening stone held steady when using it. This is a method of holding it on the bench with the vice, using a built-in attachment. This is a small strip of wood, narrower than the end of the sharpening stone box, held to it with a hinge, so it can be kept folded up and lowered when needed to grip in the vice.

935. Another Sharpening

There is an alternative to an oil or waterstone for sharpening chisels and plane irons. Get some valve grinding paste from a car sundries store and smear it on a piece of glass. Rub the tool on that. The paste is available in two degrees of coarseness.

936. Non-slip Stone

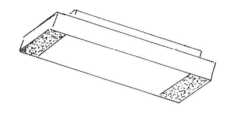

If your sharpening stone tends to slide about in use, glue strips of coarse abrasive paper under the ends.

937. Stone Stand

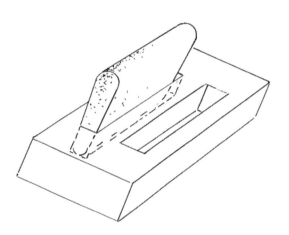

A slip stone for sharpening inside gouges has two curved edges and can be used for removing burr from gouges sharpened on the outside when held in the hand, but sharpening inside has to be done with this stone, using pressure for some time. For such work it is better to have the stone on the bench and the tool rubbed on it. To support the stone, make a grooved block of wood, as shown, with one groove to support the stone with its larger curve upwards and the other with the smaller curve up. This can be put on the bench or gripped in the vice.

938. Another Sharpening Stone

A farmer's supply store stocks two types of sharpening stones for scythes. Although scythes are not much used, the stones are still available. The traditional stone is round in section, but there is a flat stone, elliptical in outline. The material is similar to a Carborundun oilstone, but a scythe stone should be much cheaper. You can sharpen all your edge tools on it. Either use it in your hand like a file or rub the tool on it. Choose whether to lubricate with water or oil. They do not mix.

939. Blade Grip

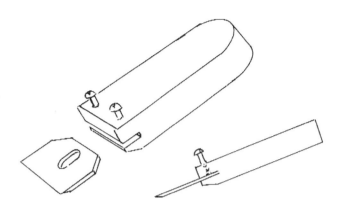

A spoke shave cutter works like a plane blade and needs to have as good an edge, but it is awkward to hold when grinding or honing. The holder shown will give a better grip and help you put on a better edge.

This is a piece of wood almost as wide as the blade and it could be 15 to 18mm thick. Cut a slot to fit over the blade. Bevel the lower part of the end to keep it clear of the sharpening stone. Drive two screws fully to cut threads, then withdraw them and file the ends flat to give a better bearing on the blade, before driving them again. Take sharpness off the edges of the wood for comfort.

940. Plane Sharp

If you have difficulty in holding a spokeshave blade when sharpening it, you have a convenient holder in your plane. You can grip the small blade between the cap iron and the blade of a plane, so it projects a convenient amount for sharpening.

941. Flatten Sharpening Stones

A stone used for sharpening a variety of tools tends to wear unevenly, making it difficult to get a good edge on such things as plane irons, which need a flat surface. A good way of flattening is to use a piece of glass, coated with valve-grinding compound, bought from a car sundries shop. If there are two grades, choose the coarser. Rubbing well on this will remove high spots. Get rid of any compound left on the stone with paraffin or white spirit.

942. V Burr

A V carving tool is difficult to sharpen satisfactorily. Having got the outer bevel correct, there is the problem of removing the burr from the inside of the cutting edge. A knife-edge slip stone wears and breaks along its edge, so does not get into the corner. An alternative is to plane a piece of scrap wood to an angle very slightly less than the tool and use very fine abrasive paper around it, 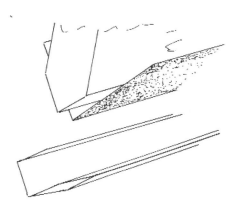 lubricated with a few drops of oil. It only needs a few strokes to remove the usual burr.

943. Is It Sharp?

After sharpening, slice the edge across the edge of a soft piece of scrap wood, to remove any particles of steel clinging to it. Hold it edge-up under a bright light and move it about. If no light is reflected it is sharp; if light is reflected, it is still blunt on the reflecting part. A nick on the edge will show a bright spot.

944. Sharpen Your Plane Correctly

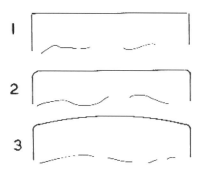

The cutting edge of a plane iron should have the correct profile if it is to do its intended job properly. A block plane iron should be sharpened with a straight edge right up to the sides. The cutter for a rabbet plane, or any other plane intended to cut right to its edges, should also be sharpened in this way (1). If you sharpen a plane intended for working on large surfaces in this way, you would not be able to avoid making ridges. The main cutting edge should be straight, but round the corners to stop them digging in and making ridges (2). A jack plane is intended for removing a lot of wood, so is usually set rather coarse and does its job better with a slightly rounded cutting edge, still with corners rounded to avoid ridges (3).

945. Quicker Edge

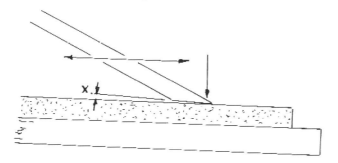

The cutting iron in modern steel planes is thinner than those in traditional planes and is intended to be ground at a single angle. The coarse grinding marks have to be honed away by sharpening on an oil, water or diamond stone. It is only the actual cutting edge that matters, so if you lift the bevel a small amount off the stone surface (X), put plenty of pressure on the actual edge and rub hard. You can soon achieve a good cutting edge, even if the surface further back is still rough from grinding.

946. Plane Angles

The plane iron in most modern steel planes is set at 45° to the sole and the recommended sharpening angle is 35°, leaving the bevel at 10° to the sole and the surface of the wood it is cutting. There can be some tolerance in the working angles. For the finest finish on softwoods you could reduce the standard angle slightly, but

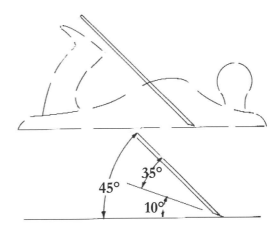

making the cutting angle too acute would mean it might blunt rather quickly. If you will be planing really hard wood, particularly any with twisted grain or large knots, it might be better to give it a greater resistance to blunting by making the cutting angle a few degrees more obtuse.

947. Restored Phillips

Phillips screwdriver points get hard use and wear, particularly if allowed to slip when power driving. The tips and edges of the four fins get rounded. Grinding lightly on the four faces will reduce roundness there, and then grinding squarely across the end will match that to the new fin angles.

948. Strop It

When open razors were in general use, the razor was stropped on a length of leather before every shave. This kept the cutting edge true and any slight irregularities were straightened out. You can keep chisels in the sharpest condition longer by doing a similar thing.

Glue a piece of old leather belt to a piece of wood and keep it soaked with light lubricating oil. Draw both sides of a chisel along this a few times occasionally and a sharp edge will be kept in condition longer.

949. Press Hard

Turning over the edge of a cabinet scraper with a round steel burnisher requires plenty of pressure; yet burnishers are supplied with only one handle. You can press harder and more comfortably if you put another handle on the outer end.

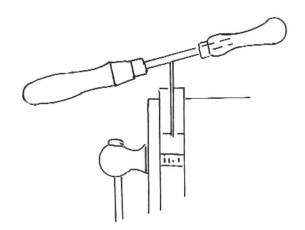

950. Scraper Sharpening

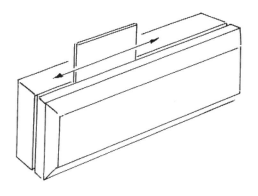

If you have an oilstone in a box with a lid, you have a ready made tool for getting the edge of a cabinet scraper square. Put the scraper between the box and lid and rub it backwards and forwards with plenty of pressure.

951. Which Oil?

At one time craftsmen had their own choice of oil or a mixture of them for use on oilstones. Some even made a secret of it. You could buy special sharpening oils. Today, any thin lubricating oil can be used, even car oil thinned with paraffin oil. If an oil is suitable for a sewing machine, it is suitable for an oilstone. If an oilstone gets clogged or dirty, soak it in paraffin oil and let it dry.

952. Keep It Flat

A sharpening stone starts with a flat surface, but it wears at the same time as it wears away steel (not diamond stone). It may not be much each time, but the surface will gradually become uneven. This usually means it becomes hollow in the length and width. There are ways of flattening, but they are laborious. It is better to try to keep it flat. So far as possible, use the whole length with a wide cutter, but move it from side to side. Sharpen narrower cutters by moving them about near the end. Rub knife blades with a circular motion near the ends and rub burrs off any tool there. It is rubbing narrower tools at the middle of the stone that does most damage.

953. No Sharp

This is a non-tip. Some kitchen appliances have as an extra, something described as a knife sharpener, where you draw the blade across two hard steel discs. Do not attempt to use them for workshop knives or other edge tools. They may take off steel and do something to the edge, but it is not what we regard as sharp.

954. Round Stone

If you use a sandstone grinding wheel lubricated with water, do not leave enough water in the trough to immerse the stone. There is a risk that this part will soften and the stone will wear out of shape.

955. Sharpen Away

If you have a diamond nail file and are away from your workshop facilities, you have the means of touching up the edge of a knife or chisel. The nail file has the same surface as a fine diamond sharpening stone.

956. Better Slip

When using a slip stone to sharpen inside a gouge or remove a burr, there is a temptation to hold the tool as well as the stone in the hands. You will always get better control and more effective sharpening if you hold the tool against the edge of the bench or somewhere else solid.

957. No Wire Edge

The old-time carpenter always sliced the cutting edge of a chisel or plane iron across the edge of a scrap piece of softwood after sharpening it. This ensured that the remains of a wire edge were removed. This is still good practice.

958. Sharpness Gone

If you cut a piece of glass, the exposed edge is extremely sharp. If you need to soften the edge to make it safe, use an oilstone like a file, with plenty of thin oil or paraffin on it.

17. Household

Many things made in wood are for use in the house or garden. Furniture makes up the bulk of this and all kinds of woodworking processes and construction can be related to household applications, so most of the tips in this book are relevant and should be considered. However, there are some tips specially related to house and garden woodwork and they are included in this section.

959. Better Plugging

Most walls to be plugged are brick, which has been plastered. There is no strength in the plaster and it may crumble or crack when a screw is driven. This is particularly so if the screw has a parallel neck and it goes through something thin. It is a good idea to punch the plug with a nail punch, so that it is a little way below the surface, and so that the screw gets maximum strength in the brick, and threads are clear of the plaster.

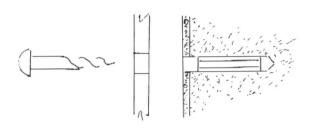

960. Multi Plug

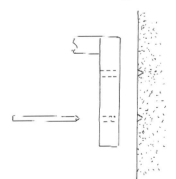

If you have to mark the positions of several plugs in a wall to match the screw holes in the item to be hung, there is little tolerance and the holes in the wall should be positioned exactly. Make a punch from steel rod that is an easy fit in the screw holes. File or grind a point on it. It does not have to be hardened to make dents in plaster or brick.

961. Matches to the Rescue

If a pilot hole is drilled too large, or a screw will not grip, a piece of matchstick pushed in the hole is the solution. The softwood has been treated to make it suitable for matchmaking and this makes it better for this purpose than a sliver of any oddment of wood on the bench.

962. Target

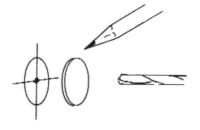

It is not always easy to see the marked position of an intended hole to be drilled in a wall. To be certain of accuracy use a centre punch on the spot, indicated by two crossing lines, and use a coin and pencil to mark a concentric circle around it.

963. Drilling Tiles

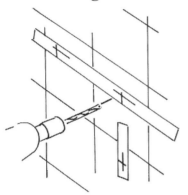

The surface of tiles used on bathroom and kitchen walls has a hard brittle glaze, which may chip or craze when drilled. This risk can be reduced if the places to be drilled are covered with masking tape. This also provides a good surface for marking out accurately and can be peeled off without leaving marks. Use a masonry drill and start slowly.

964. Laminate Panels

When you lay wood laminate flooring, you will almost certainly have off cuts that seem too valuable to throw away. Consider using them as cupboard door panelling. A section of flooring can make an attractive alternative to plywood in a framed door.

965. Safe and Quiet

If you transport tools in a plastic or metal toolbox, they move about noisily and could damage each other. A piece of carpet or drawer liner in the bottom will improve things.

966. Pot Stands

If you make many projects, you will probably accumulate off cuts from the sides

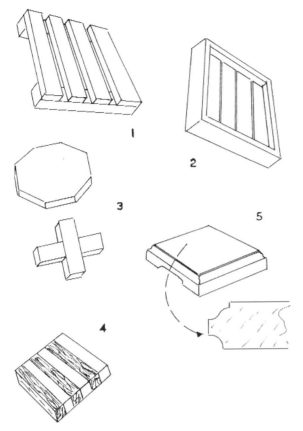

and ends of boards and many of them seem too good to throw away. Stands for hot pots in the kitchen and plant pots and vases elsewhere in the house can be made from some of them. Sizes depend on available stock, but anywhere between 100mm and 200mm square should suit most needs. Waterproof glue will hold the parts, but panel pins will locate parts while the glue dries.

Strips spaced a little way apart will make a basic stand (1). Round exposed edges and corners. You can keep the contents in place by framing all round (2). An end off cut can be cut square and made into an octagon, it could have a chamfer or moulding worked around the edges. It can be supported on two strips halved together (3). The strips could be level with the edges or extended with the ends finished to match the edges of the top.

If you have strips of wood in contrasting colours, they could be glued to make a butcher-block board (4).

A square piece may have a routed moulding around it. There could be finger hollows on opposite sides (5).

967. Real Butcher Block

There are designs for table tops and similar pieces of furniture with tops described as 'butcher block', having a great many random lengths of wood glued together to make up the width. These may be attractive, but are not true butcher block.

A butcher uses a fairly massive block with pieces of wood glued together with the end grain upwards. A smaller version makes one of the best kitchen chopping or cutting blocks. The butcher's block was traditionally beech. You can use that or the lighter colour of sycamore is attractive. Do not use softwood. This may be an opportunity to use up off cuts.

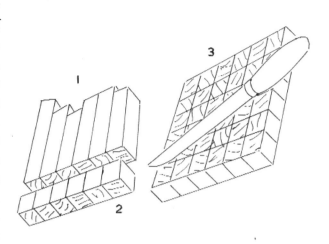

Glue pieces together to make up the width you want (1). Level the surfaces and cut pieces off (2). Do not make the board too thin, particularly if you expect heavy chopping, 25mm should suit a home kitchen. Glue the strips together and level the surfaces (3). The cook could use the board as it is, but it is helpful to treat it with cooking oil. Allow some to soak in and refresh it occasionally during use.

968. Over-door Airer

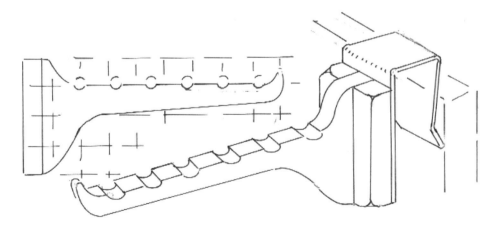

This is a takedown notched rod that can be hooked over the top of a door for hanging clothing after ironing, or similar jobs. This could be made any size, but a suggested size is shown with 25mm squares.

Make the notches by drilling before cutting the shape. The hook is sheet metal, preferably brass, bent to spring over the top of the door. Screw it to the wood. It could be lined with cloth to prevent marking and improve the grip. It should not affect the closing of most doors.

969. Ring Can Opener

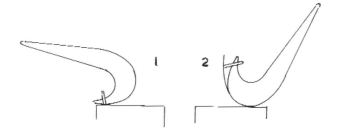

Ring-opening food and drink containers are convenient, but sometimes they are difficult to open with just finger pressure. This opener should be made from hardwood, with the grain lengthwise. A thickness of 12mm and an overall length of 150mm to 200mm would be suitable. Round the edges well. You may have to start opening with the long point, then hook into the ring (1) and lever the tool back (2).

970. Bottle Top Grip

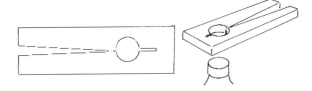

Some plastic and glass bottles of domestic fluids have caps that seize and are difficult to release. This is a grip with a pliers-type action that should shift the stopper or cap. Drill a hole to fit the cap. Saw into it in a long V. Make a short cut at the other side of the hole. This provides the spring. Squeezing the end should grip the cap ready to be turned.

971. Tie Rack

The rack shown could be fixed to the inside of a wardrobe door and used for ties or belts. Use dowels 12mm or less, with the outer one longer than the other. Mark out the projecting piece first. A depth about 150mm should suit most needs. Round the ends of the dowels and all edges.

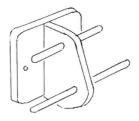

972. No Warp

If you need to ensure a board will not warp, without adding framing, as in a kitchen chopping board or a drawing board, you can add stiffening battens without screws or nails, if you use a router dovetail cutter. Battens cut to the dovetail angle drive into tapered slots. They need not be glued, so adjustment can be made if the wood shrinks or swells.

Mark grooves with a slight taper. Cut through with a straight cutter (1), making a groove wide enough to admit the dovetail cutter. Use a guide strip to cut the sides of the taper with a dovetail cutter (2). Make tapered strips too long at first, then they can be cut to length after driving in (3). It will probably be satisfactory to use simple tapered battens, but they could have a squared section (4) or be cut flush (5).

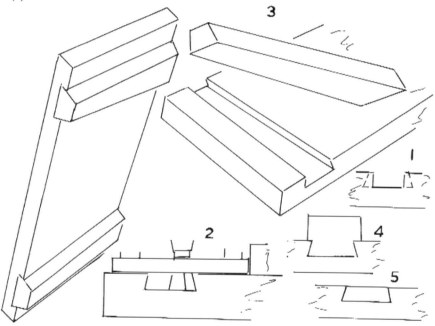

973. Clothes Airer

This clothes drier and airer pulls up to the ceiling and is controlled by a rope to a cleat on the wall. Sizes depend on space available. For most conditions there could be four rails about 25mm by 18mm section on crosspiece 450mm long. There is a double pulley near the wall and the other two are single. Pulleys are obtainable with screws to go into floor joists; use synthetic rope about 8mm diameter. Tie its ends to the cross-pieces and allow enough length for the end loop to go on the cleat when the airier is at a suitable height for loading. Knot the parts together to go on the cleat at the raised height.

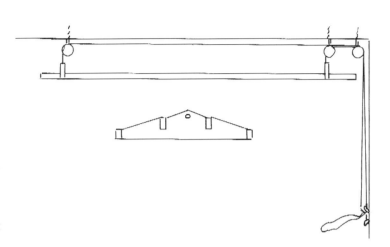

974. Accurate Weatherboarding

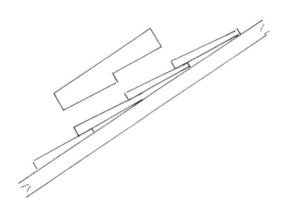

Weatherboarding does not look right unless it is kept exactly parallel. This gauge allows you to check as each board is fixed.

The first board fits flat. The others slope. Starting at the bottom fit the first three boards. The second and third give you the pattern to follow. Make the gauge to this, with the amount of overlap you intend to use.

975. Kitchen Tidy

This is a box to stand on a shelf or worktop and contains a bottle of washing-up liquid in the centre, a washing-up brush at one side and a cloth at the other side. It could be adapted and added to for other items. The controlling size is the central bottle or container. Nailed construction should be adequate. Round all exposed edges and corners. Cloth glued to the bottom would prevent scratching. Paint to match the kitchen.

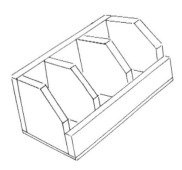

976. Uneven Level

If you are planning a deck or other structure to extend over uneven ground, you have to make several advance checks to determine its layout and position, if the resulting job is to finish true. One way of testing is shown.

A short pointed post is driven into the ground and this has a thin lath extending

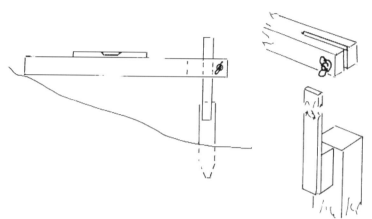

as far as needed above it. The levelling piece has a long slot to fit over it and allow adjustment inwards and upwards. This can be closed to grip the lath with a bolt and wing nut when you have it where you need it.

977. Cabinet Hold

If you wish to fix a cabinet to a wall, it is never easy to get it exactly where you need it and hold it there while screwing to the wall, and just about impossible if

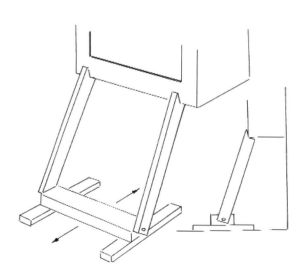

you are alone. The support shown will allow adjustment and hold the cabinet where you put it. For cabinets at different heights you may have to cut or replace the legs.

Give the feet a wide enough size to be steady. Cut the notches at the top wider than a right angle to allow adjustment. Pivot the legs on screws.

978. Close Corners

It is unwise to assume that the corner of every room is exactly square. It may look accurate, but you should not make a shelf or cabinet with a square corner and assume it will fit. It will fit and look better if is at exactly the correct angle. You could try an adjustable bevel in the corner, but it might not finish correct if you extend such short lengths.

In dealing with an angle it is always best to work on lines longer than you will need. Measure along the walls (X and Y) and measure between these points (Z), using sizes greater than the shelf or cabinet (1). Repeat these on the wood (2) and mark out the finished shape.

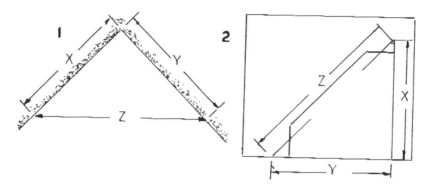

979. Utility Stand

The turned stand shown will hold a ball of string and a roll of Sellotape as well as scissors or a knife. It would be useful in a kitchen or utility room and a similar one, without the Sellotape, could have a place in the garden shed. Make the stem an easy fit in a ball of string, but thick enough for a hole to take the scissors or knife. Make a standard roll of Sellotape an easy fit on the base, which should be large enough for stability.

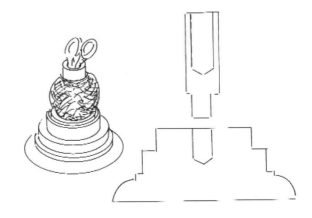

980. Tall Rolls

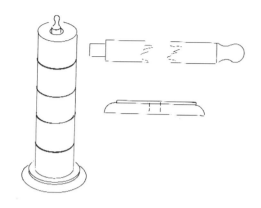

The standing spare toilet roll holder usually only holds two rolls, while the usual family purchase is a packet of more than that. Most lathes have beds long enough to turn dining table legs. If you make a toilet roll holder of that length, it will hold at least five rolls and take up no more space.

Turn the upright with a knob at the top and a dowel end to fit in the base, which should be made large enough for stability.

981. Finger Grip

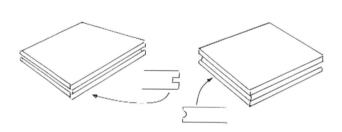

If you make a kitchen chopping board from thick wood or by b u t c h e r - b l o c k construction, plough a groove all round the edge, or preferably, use a small cove cutter, which w i l l g i v e a m o r e comfortable hold.

982. Drips

When making anything exposed to the weather, try to avoid level surfaces where rainwater could lie. This could enter the wood and cause rot. End grain is vulnerable, even if well painted. Slope all you can, for a good run-off. Slope a roof adequately and give it enough overhang, so water does not run down the wall. Any exposed rails or other woodwork that is horizontal should be given

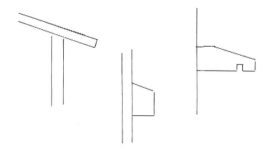

sloping top surfaces. A windowsill should have a mainly sloping top and it is usual to plough a groove underneath to stop water creeping back there.

983. Hinge Security

If your outside shed or workshop has hinges screwed on, it can be burgled by unscrewing the hinges. Bolts in every hole would prevent this, but you can make a hinge just as secure by putting just one round-headed bolt in each part.

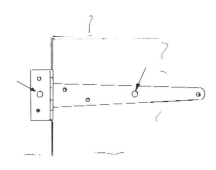

984. Protect Fencing

If the top of a fence post is flat (1), rainwater will settle and soak in and cause it to rot. It is better to cut the top at an angle (2), so water can run off. The post may look better if it is sloped both ways (3). Protection would be better if you add a roof (4). It would be even better if this were to be made from weatherproof metal. You may prefer the look if slopes are cut four ways (5).

Upright fence pieces (palings) should also make water run off. Single slopes, arranged alternate ways (6) are simple and look almost as good as the usual points (7). The rails are best given a slope so water does not settle (8). The alternative for certain shedding of water is a larger piece cut diagonally (9).

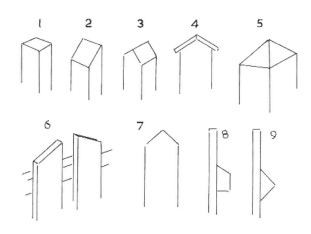

985. Deadly Dust

Sawdust from the workshop may be used for household and garden purposes, but be careful what you do with laburnum sawdust and shavings. They will kill weeds, but they can also kill plants. Yew is also deadly to animals.

986. Rounded Post

If you are rounding the top of a garden post by eye, you can get a reasonable semicircular shape, if you first bevel opposite sides until the bevels are both about the same width as that remaining in the middle (1). Then take off the angles (2)

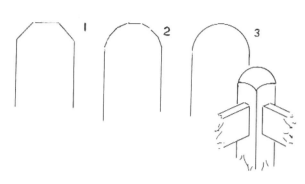

and follow with a rasp or file to complete the shape (3).

987. Greater Support

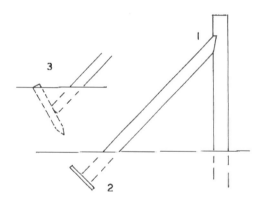

If an end fence post has to withstand strain, as when wire is to be stretched, it can be supported with a strut, which must not move under pressure. Notch the top of the strut into the post (1). If possible, bury a board as a thrust pad for the strut to push against (2). If you are unable to do that, drive a stout stake so the strut can push against it (3).

988. Easier Hinges

Garden and other outdoors gates are often hung on lift-off hinges. If the pin parts are the same length and the same level (1), you have to line-up both parts at the same time and this may be difficult if the gate is heavy. It is better to have a longer bottom pin (2), on which you can start the eyepiece before lining-up the top piece. If you have to use two pin parts of the same length, you can get a similar effect by mounting the upper pin a little lower. You can then start the

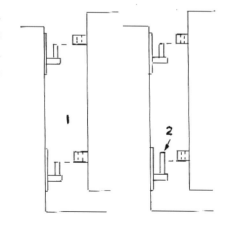

lower hinge before starting the top one, but in the final assembly it will be the bottom hinge that takes most of the vertical weight.

989. Outdoor Strength

For strength in outdoor wood construction it is advisable to provide some mechanical strength, as well as glue, in the form of cut joints or metal fastenings. The best glue is that intended for boat building, which is superior to that described as weatherproof. Plated steel screws are protected from rust, as long as the coating is intact. Be careful not to damage the head with a slipping driver. Brass screws are more weatherproof, but are not as strong, so use a thicker gauge or more of them.

For a suitable finish, get good protection with undercoat well brushed in before applying the topcoat, which should be exterior grade paint. The most durable varnish finish is yacht varnish.

990. Copper Nails

Steel nails will rust in wet conditions, even if they start with zinc or other coating. Copper nails will stand up to any conditions. Boat nails are made in many sizes or your hardware store may have copper plumber's nails.

991. Garden Wood

For garden woodwork we probably have to use whatever wood is available. Treatment with preservative will give softwood a long life. Wood railway sleepers, pressure-treated with preservative, seem to last for ever.

The best untreated wood for long life seems to be English oak. There are many Elizabethan oak-framed houses that are just as good after many centuries. Even until about fifty years ago, it was the chosen wood for field fence posts and rails, but today, if you can find it, its price is very high. Of the available woods, teak and cedar will resist the weather.

992. Shuttering

Making a wooden framework to provide shape for concrete being laid is often regarded as a rough type of woodworking. But there are some important considerations. If top edges are not straight, the concrete will not be flat. If opposite sides have a twist in relation to each other, there will a twist in the concrete surface. If a side strip does not reach the ground everywhere, concrete will creep out. There can be considerable outward pressure from the concrete. A collapsed side during pouring can be disastrous. Use plenty of supporting pegs, driven in securely.

993. Gully Cover

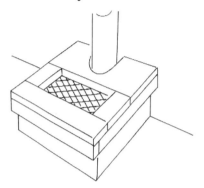

The down pipe from a house gutters usually empties into a gully, which probably has a brick or concrete surround. Leaves and other debris tend to accumulate in this and have to be cleaned out. The cover prevents this, but still allows ventilation.

Wood about 18mm thick could be used. Cut a piece to fit easy around the pipe and use this as a guide to other sizes. The sides could rely on being nailed to the under framing, or be tenoned into the crosspieces. The whole assembly should be an easy fit, so it can be lifted off. Fix small mesh wire netting (chicken wire) to the underside of the opening. Finish with paint.

994. Barrel Tubs

Old wooden casks or barrels make good garden tubs when cut in half. You need to make a true cut to avoid much finishing of the edges. The wood is hard and usually not easy to cut. One tool that should do it is a jigsaw with the coarsest blade you have. For a big barrel allow for at least one spare blade.

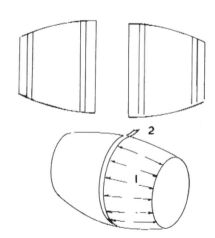

Mark several key positions from the end (1). Fix masking tape around the barrel, with its edge on these marks (2). Drill a hole just big enough to pass the blade on the line of the edge of the tape, then let the saw cut at its own speed. Do not force it. Use a belt sander for levelling the edge.

995. Dibber

The name may be different in some parts of the country, but the tool used to make holes in the ground for such things as bulbs and potatoes often looks like a broken handle of a spade, which often is just that. It involves bending and is not always easy to use. The tool shown can be turned from hardwood, held at a comfortable height and is easy to enter. If necessary, the top could be hit.

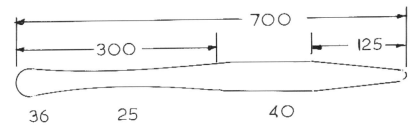

996. Garden Line Winder

The usual garden line winder is short and often improvised. It is close to the ground and getting the line right is not always easy. This basic shape is similar to the dibber, but slimmer. Turn two matching pieces, preferably from hardwood. Plane a flat on one to take a plywood spool. Drill a hole in the other to take the end of the line.

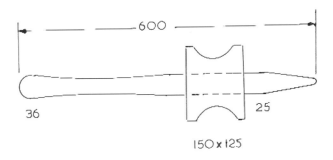

997. Hollow Pillar

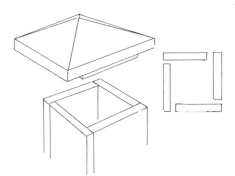

If you need decorative thick posts on a patio or porch there is no need to use expensive solid wood. A post can be built up from boards. Waterproof glue and a few nails will make a strong shape, which will look authentic when sanded all round and painted. Put a solid insert in the bottom. There can be a decorative overhanging top.

998. Outdoor Softwood

Most building quality softwood in Britain comes from the Baltic countries and, as sold, usually contains too much moisture in the form of sap. Even for outdoor use, it is advisable to buy it some time before you use it, to give it time to dry out, otherwise you may find it shrinking, warping or cracking, after you have built something with it. It should have a reasonable outdoor life if treated with preservative or well painted.

999. Conservatory Stands

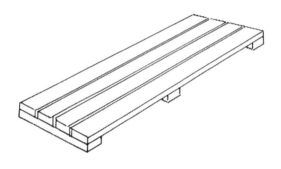

If you have a conservatory or greenhouse, you probably grow things in pots and containers, some of which stand on the floor. A simple job that will use up off cuts and keep the pots away from direct contact with the floor is a set of stands. Several identical ones can be used individually or stood end-to-end neatly. Make each stand long enough for three average pots. A basic shape is shown. Sizes will depend on available wood. Normally, have four slats and do not leave gaps too wide. Round upper edges. Protect the wood with paint. Dark green or brown would be inconspicuous and not detract from flower displays.

1000. Garden Tool Cleaner

Dirt and mud on garden tools will more likely be cleaned off after use if this cleaner is available. There is a flat end for scraping surface dirt and an end to get into gaps and crevices.

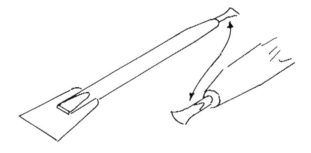

The handle could be a piece of broom handle, a thick piece of dowel rod or be specially turned. The flat end is a piece of sheet steel stiff enough not to bend, fitted into a slot. Make the other end with steel rod, spread to a thin end by hammering on an iron block. Fix both parts in place with epoxy adhesive.

1001. Shed End

If you build your own workshop or garden shed, it is common to make the slope of the roof 45° (1) as an easy angle to use, but a roof looks are improved with a slightly flatter slope. About 35° at the eaves and 110° at the apex looks better (2).

The end of such a roof is usually finished with bargeboards. Plain boards can have their appearance improved by adding pieces at the ends (3). A finial at the apex gives a finishing touch. It could be a flat pointed piece, but a turned part with a square end notched over the bargeboards looks better (4).

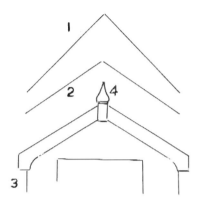

If the body of the shed is treated with preservative, the bargeboards could be painted a contrasting colour.

English and American Woodworking Terms

Most English and American woodworking terms are the same, similar or understood.

Most early craftsmen in America were from the United Kingdom, and many pioneers were sent with a kit of woodworking tools.

These are a selection of terms which may not always be obvious.

English	American
Housing Joint	Dado joint
Circular saw	Table saw
Planer/planing machine	Jointer
Thicknesser	Planer
Plane cap iron	Chip breaker
Length goes first (4 x 2)	Width goes first (2 x 4)
Spanners	Wrenches
Timber	Lumber
Rebate/rabbet	Rabbet
Facemarks	Witness marks
Workshop	Shop
Shop	Store
Cramp/clamp	Clamp
Electricity is 240 volts	Electricity is 120 volts
Joiner	Finish carpenter
Perspex	Plexiglass

Much American building wood is 2 inches thick and collectively know as '2 by'.

Measurement

Metric measure is based on the metre.

Other sizes are proportions of ten and part sizes are quoted in decimals.

The common sizes for woodwork are millimetre (mm), which is one-thousandth of a metre, and centimetre (cm), which is ten millimetres.

Imperial measure originated with lengths of body parts. For woodwork the commonly used basic size is the foot (ft). One foot is divided into twelve inches (in), and three feet make a yard. Part sizes are usualy obtained by dividing and are normally stated in vulgar fractions (Y2, %, ...).

For benchwork conversions it is a help to remember 1 inch is slightly more than 25 millimetres and 1 foot is a little over 300 millimetres.

Other approximate conversions are:

  1 yard (3 feet) is near 91 centimetres
  1 metre is near 39 inches
  4 inches are just over 100 millimetres
  1 kilometre (1000 metres) is about 0·62 miles

It is unwise to mix metric and Imperial measure when working on a project. Wood in Britain is mostly in metric section but may be sold in Imperial lengths. Nails and pins are in metric lengths. Screws may be metric or Imperial.

Books of related interest

A Treatise on Stairbuilding and Handrailing
by W & A Mowat
The classic reprinted text for joiners, architects and fine craftsmen. Originally published in London in 1910.
390 pages. Paperback.

Purpose Made Joinery 2nd Edition
by Edward Foad, MCIOB
Covers windows, doors, frames, wall panelling, counters, fitments, seating, stairs, etc., including examples of modern materials and techniques. The text includes hundreds of exceptionally clear line illustrations.
320 pages. Paperback.

What Wood is That? A Manual of Wood Identification
by Herbert L Edlin
A unique book containing a fold-out wallet with 40 actual veneer samples. Each wood is described in terms of 14 key characteristics to teach the method of identifying these and other woods. Illustrated.
160 pages. Hardback.

World Woods in Colour
by William A Lincoln
This authoritative and hugely popular reference book contains almost 300 colour illustrations showing the natural grain and colour of wood, along with data that includes distribution, properties and uses of more than 300 timbers from world-wide sources.
320 pages. Hardback.

The Art of Segmented Woodturning
by Malcolm Tibbetts
A step-by-step guide to the art of combining various woods into turned objects. A complete guide to the subject.
184 pages. Paperback.

Woodcarving: Book 1 Basic Techniques
by Ian Norbury
17 quick and easy to carve projects for beginners.
86 pages. Paperback.

Sharpening with Waterstones: A Perfect Edge in 60 Seconds
by Ian Kirby
Waterstones sharpen all your woodworking tools better, easier, and quicker than ever before. Master craftsman Ian Kirby teaches you a series of logical steps for putting a perfect edge on planes, knives, chisels, and carving tools.
112 pages. Paperback.

Glossary of Wood – 10,000 terms relating to timber & its use, explained and clarified
by Thomas Corkhill
Terms include tree names, locations, types of timber, workability and use, joints, milling, machine woodworking, seasoning, tools, construction methods, veneering, finishing, and furniture.
670 pages. Hardback.

Building Cabinet Doors & Drawers
by Danny Proulx
A practical book that includes all styles and a thorough discussion of suitable joinery techniques.
112 pages. Paperback.

The Illustrated Guide to Cabinet Doors & Drawers: Design, Detail, and Construction
by David Gettss
This is a must-have reference that covers the construction of all types of cabinet doors and drawers. Includes an extensive gallery of door and drawer styles, cabinet hardware, and what to use and how to install it.
186 pages. Paperback.

Techniques of Spiral Work – A Practical Guide to the Craft of Making Twists by Hand
by Stuart Mortimer
An illustrated book on making a wide variety of traditional and modern twists. It shows how the turned timber is marked out to make decorative twist work.
178 pages. Paperback.

Circular Work In Carpentry And Joinery
by George Collings
A revision of a classic work originally published 1911. New annotated drawings give clear, easily understood explanations of the field of single and double curvature work.
136 pages. Paperback.

Modern Practical Joinery
by George Ellis
The reprint of this classic 1902 text covers a vast scope of joinery practices concerning doors, panelling, windows, stairs, etc. Written by an author of undisputed authority.
502 pages. Paperback.

Book Of Boxes – A Complete Practical Guide to Box Making & Box Design
by Andrew Crawford
Detailed instructions to make boxes using a variety of decoration techniques. Includes 3 simple boxes for beginners and a gallery of designs from well-known makers.
144 pages. Paperback.